Sports Mega-Events: Social Scientific Analyses of a Global Phenomenon

A selection of previous *Sociological Review* Monographs

Theorizing Museums*
ed. Sharon Macdonald and Gordon Fyfe
Consumption Matters*
eds Stephen Edgell, Kevin Hetherington and Alan Warde
Ideas of Difference*
eds Kevin Hetherington and Rolland Munro
The Laws of the Markets*
ed. Michael Callon
Actor Network Theory and After*
eds John Law and John Hassard
Whose Europe? The Turn Towards Democracy*
eds Dennis Smith and Sue Wright
Renewing Class Analysis*
eds Rosemary Cromptom, Fiona Devine, Mike Savage and John Scott
Reading Bourdieu on Society and Culture*
ed. Bridget Fowler
The Consumption of Mass*
ed. Nick Lee and Rolland Munro
The Age of Anxiety: Conspiracy Theory and the Human Sciences*
eds Jane Parish and Martin Parker
Utopia and Organization*
ed: Martin Parker
Emotions and Sociology*
ed. Jack Barbalet
Masculinity and Men's Lifestyle Magazines*
ed. Bethan Benwell
Nature Performed: Environment, Culture and Performance*
eds Bronislaw Szerszynski, Wallace Heim and Claire Waterton
After Habermas: New Perspectives on the Public Sphere*
eds Nick Crossley and John Michael Roberts
Feminism After Bourdieu*
eds Lisa Adkins and Beverley Skeggs
Contemporary Organization Theory*
eds Campbell Jones and Rolland Munro
A New Sociology of Work*
eds Lynne Pettinger, Jane Parry, Rebecca Taylor and Miriam Glucksmann
Against Automobility*
eds Steffen Böhm, Campbell Jones, Cris Land and Matthew Paterson

*Available from Marston Book Services, PO Box 270, Abingdon, Oxon OX14 4YW

The Sociological Review Monographs

Since 1958 *The Sociological Review* has established a tradition of publishing Monographs on issues of general sociological interest. The Monograph is an edited book length collection of research papers which is published and distributed in association with Blackwell Publishing. We are keen to receive innovative collections of work in sociology and related disciplines with a particular emphasis on exploring empirical materials and theoretical frameworks which are currently under-developed. If you wish to discuss ideas for a Monograph then please contact the Monographs Editor, Rolland Munro, at *The Sociological Review*, Keele University, Newcastle-under-Lyme, North Staffordshire, ST5 5BG.

Sports Mega-Events: Social Scientific Analyses of a Global Phenomenon

Edited by John Horne and Wolfram Manzenreiter

Blackwell Publishing/The Sociological Review

BLACKWELL PUBLISHING
350 Main Street, Malden, MA 02148–5020, USA
9600 Garsington Road, Oxford OX4 2DQ, UK
550 Swanston Street, Carlton, Victoria 3053, Australia

First published 2006 by Blackwell Publishing Ltd

Library of Congress Cataloging-in-Publication Data

Sports mega-events : social scientific analyses of a global phenomenon / edited by
John Horne and Wolfram Manzenreiter.
    p. cm. – (Sociological review monographs)
    Includes bibliographical references and index.
    ISBN-13: 978-1-4051-5290-7 (pbk.)
    ISBN-10: 1-4051-5290-7 (pbk.)
    1. Sports tournaments–Social aspects–Case studies.   2. Sports–Sociological
aspects–Case studies.   I. Horne, John, 1955-II. Manzenreiter, Wolfram.

GV712.S66 2006
306.4′83–dc22

                     2006019738

A catalogue record for this title is available from the British Library

Set by SNP Best-set Typesetter Ltd, Hong Kong

Printed and bound in the United Kingdom by Page Brothers, Norwich

For further information on Blackwell Publishing, visit our website:
http://www.blackwellpublishing.com

Contents

Acknowledgements

Earlier versions of five of these papers were first presented at a European Alliance for Asian Studies/Asia-Europe Foundation funded workshop on 'Hosting Major International Sports Events: Comparing Asia and Europe', held at The University of Edinburgh in March 2005. The editors (as co-organizers) would like to thank the sponsors of the EAAS/ASEF workshop and all the participants, some of whose work is reproduced in revised form in this collection, for a stimulating three days. John Horne would also like to acknowledge the financial support of the Government of Canada Faculty Research Program and the Carnegie Trust for the Universities of Scotland for awards that enabled the preliminary research on, and travel to, Canada that underpins material in the introduction and the chapter written with Dave Whitson.

An introduction to the sociology of sports mega-events[1]

John Horne and Wolfram Manzenreiter

Introduction: sport, sociology: sociology of sport

It is surprising that the sociological and social scientific study of sport – ritualized, rationalized, commercial spectacles and bodily practices that create opportunities for expressive performances, disruptions of the everyday world and affirmations of social status and belonging – was still seen as something as a joke by mainstream sociology until recently. A similar comment was made in the introduction to a previous *Sociological Review Monograph* on *Sport, Leisure and Social Relations* published twenty years ago (Horne, Jary and Tomlinson, 1987). Yet, quite clearly, social aspects of sport can be considered from most classical, modern and postmodern sociological theoretical perspectives, even if the 'founding fathers' did not have much explicitly to say about them (Giulianotti, ed., 2004). Ritualized, civic, events and ceremonies (Durkheim); rationalized, bureaucratically organized, science driven behaviour (Weber); commercial, global spectacles (Marx); expressivity and the everyday (Simmel and postmodernism); and male cultural displays and cultural centres (feminism). These are just a few of the issues that have concerned sociological theorists and inform the sociological analysis of sport. It was Pierre Bourdieu, however, alongside Norbert Elias and his colleague Eric Dunning, who has been one of the few leading mainstream sociologists to have taken sport seriously and who recognized the difficulty in doing so: 'the sociology of sport: it is disdained by sociologists, and despised by sportspeople' (Bourdieu, 1990: 156).

This book suggests that just as modern competitive sport and large-scale sport events were developed in line with the logic of capitalist modernity, sports mega-events and global sport culture are central to late modern capitalist societies. As media events, the Summer Olympic Games and the FIFA association football World Cup provide cultural resources for reflecting upon identity and enacting agency. More generally they provide resources for the construction of 'a meaningful social life in relation to a changing societal environment that has the potential to destabilize and threaten these things' (Roche, 2000: 225). Sports 'mega-events' are important elements in the orientation of nations to international or global society. As Munoz suggests in his chapter, mega-events, such as the Olympic games, have also had an important role in the transformation of the modern urban environment, as a conveyor of architectural design traditions. Hence sport, here in its mega-event form, comes to be an increasingly central, rather than peripheral, element of urban modernity (Tomlinson and Young, 2005; Young and Wamsley, 2005; and Vigor *et al.*, 2004 are three other recent collections that discuss the increasing social significance of sports mega-events).

This volume, featuring chapters from leading sports mega-event researchers around the world, has three main objectives. Firstly it aims to demonstrate the social (economic, political and cultural) significance of sports and sports mega-events. Secondly it outlines the sociological and social scientific significance of sports mega-events, by reviewing research and debates about their impact from the disciplines of political science, human geography, international relations, economics as well as sociology. Thirdly it suggests why sociologists and other social scientists should be interested in analysing them and asks what can sociologists and social scientists learn from analysing sports mega-events. This chapter provides an overview of previous studies in the field and thus introduces each of these objectives. First we discuss the scope and growth of sports mega-events in the past 25 years. Next we review debates about the attractions and impacts of sports mega-events. Then we consider the sociological and social scientific significance of sports mega-events. Finally we highlight a research agenda for the study of sports mega-events.

What makes a mega-event 'mega'?

Whilst there have been a number of earlier discussions about 'special', 'hallmark' or 'mega-events' (see for example Law, 1994; Syme *et al.*, 1989; and Witt, 1988) it is Maurice Roche's definition of them that commands our attention today. He states that mega-events are best understood as 'large-scale cultural (including commercial and sporting) events, which have a dramatic character, mass popular appeal and international significance' (Roche, 2000: 1). Two central features of contemporary mega-events are firstly, that they are deemed to have significant consequences for the host city, region or nation in which they occur, and secondly, that they will attract considerable media coverage. By this definition therefore, an unmediated mega-event would be a contradiction in terms, and several of the contributions to this collection focus on this theme.[2]

For Kenneth Roberts (2004: 108) what defines certain sports events as 'mega' is that they are 'discontinuous', out of the ordinary, international and simply big in composition. What Roberts refers to as 'megas' have the ability to transmit promotional messages to billions of people via television and other developments in telecommunications. 'Megas' have attracted an increasingly more international audience and composition. An estimated television audience of 3.9 billion people, for example, watched parts of the 2004 Athens Olympic Games, and the cumulative TV audience estimate was 40 billion. 35,000 hours were dedicated to its media coverage – an increase of 27 per cent over the Summer Olympics held in Sydney in 2000 (see www.olympic.org/uk). The 2002 FIFA World Cup, staged in Japan and South Korea, provided even more – 41,000 – hours of programming in 213 countries and produced an estimated cumulative audience of 28.8 billion viewers (Madrigal *et al.*, 2005: 182). Research on sports mega-events that have taken place, or are planned, in Africa, Asia, Australia, Europe and North America, the leisure industry's 'supernovas' (Roberts, 2004: 112), is what this book largely focuses on.

The growth of sports mega-events

Since 1992, when the Summer and Winter Olympic Games took place in the same year for the last time, there has been a two-year cycle of sports mega-events.[3] The Summer Olympic Games occupies the same year as the European Football Championship, organized by the Union of European Football Associations (UEFA), whilst the Winter Olympics shares its year with the FIFA football World Cup finals and the Commonwealth Games. Despite the decision of the Olympic Programme Commission of the IOC in July 2005 to reduce the number of sports from 28 to 26 from the 2012 Olympics, it is evident that the size of the event, as well as the enthusiasm to host and participate in sports mega-events like the Olympic Games and the FIFA World Cup has grown in the past twenty years.[4] At the 1984 Summer Olympics in Los Angeles 140 countries were represented, 6797 athletes competed, and 221 events took place in 23 sports. By 2004 in Athens 201 countries were involved and 11,099 athletes took part in 301 events in the 28 Olympic sports (Malfas *et al.*, 2004: 210; www.athens2004.com). The expansion and growing attraction of mega-events has been for three main reasons (as Whitson and Horne also suggest).

First, new developments in the technologies of mass communication, especially the development of satellite television, have created unprecedented global audiences for events like the Olympics and the World Cup. Since the 1960s, US broadcasting networks have substantially competed to 'buy' the Olympic Games. Next in order of magnitude of rights payments is the consortium representing the interests and financial power of Europe's public broadcasters, known as the European Broadcasting Union (EBU) that buy the rights to transmission in Europe. Media rights fees are also paid by the Asian broadcasters (including Japan and South Korea) and national media organizations, such as CBC and CTV in Canada. So in addition to the US$300 million paid by the US corporation NBC to the International Olympic Committee in 1988 (for the Seoul Summer Olympics), the EBU paid just over US$30 million and Canada paid just over US$4 million for media broadcasting rights. By 2008 (the Beijing Summer Olympics) NBC will pay US$894 million, the EBU will pay over US$443 million, and Canadian broadcasters will pay US$45 million just for the rights to transmit pictures of the action (Coakley and Donnelly, 2004: 382; Westerbeek and Smith, 2003: 91).

Table 1: US Broadcasters and Olympics Television Rights (US$m) 1960–2012

Year	Summer Games			Winter Games		
	Place	Network	Amount	Place	Network	Amount
1960	Rome	CBS	0.39	Squaw Valley	CBS	0.05
1964	Tokyo	NBC	1.5	Innsbruck	ABC	0.59
1968	Mexico City	ABC	4.5	Grenoble	ABC	2.5
1972	Munich	ABC	7.5	Sapporo	NBC	6.4
1976	Montreal	ABC	25.0	Innsbruck	ABC	10.0
1980	Moscow	NBC	72.0	Lake Placid	ABC	15.5
1984	Los Angeles	ABC	225.0	Sarajevo	ABC	91.5
1988	Seoul	NBC	300.0	Calgary	ABC	309.0
1992	Barcelona	NBC	401.0	Albertville	CBS	243.0
1994				Lillehammer	CBS	295.0*
1996	Atlanta	NBC	456.0			
1998				Nagano	CBS	375.0
2000	Sydney	NBC	705			
2002				Salt Lake City	NBC	545.0
2004	Athens	NBC	793§			
2006				Turin	NBC	614
2008	Beijing	NBC	894			
2010				Vancouver	NBC	820**
2012	London	NBC	1.181bn			

* From 1994 Summer and Winter Games have been staged in different years, allowing US TV to spread the burden of raising advertising revenue over two years.

§ NBC paid $2.3 bn for rights to the 2004, 2006 & 2008 Games after the merger of ABC & CBS in 1995.

** NBC agreed to pay just over $2bn for the rights to 2010 and 2012.

(Sources: Whannel 1992; Toohey & Veal 2000; www.Olympicmarketing.com – accessed 6 June 2003; IOC (2006) 2006 Marketing Fact File available at www.olympic.org – accessed 11 June 2006).

Similarly to the Olympic Games since the 1980s the FIFA Football World Cup has attracted substantial media interest and commercial partners. The Football World Cup is a huge media event. The resources made available for the communications systems, the enormous media centres, and the amounts paid by national broadcasting systems to televise the event provide ample evidence for this. At the Football World Cup Finals co-hosted by South Korea and Japan in 2002 for example each Local Organizing Committee (LOC) was responsible for arranging its own media facilities, infrastructure and services (Horne and Manzenreiter, 2002b). In order to reach the global television audience the World Cup was serviced by two International Media Centres (IMCs), one in Korea and one in Japan. The Korean IMC was in the COEX exhibition centre in Seoul, which at 37,000 square metres actually offered a larger area than the IMC in Paris for the whole of the previous World Cup in 1998. The Japanese IMC was in the Pacifico Yokohama Exhibition Hall and was a little over half the area (20,000 square metres). In addition, at each of the ten stadia in the two countries there were Stadium Media Centres.

In the case of the Olympic Games, TV rights accounted for 53 per cent (US$2.229 billion) of total revenue, followed by sponsorship (34 per cent, US$1.459 billion), ticketing (11 per cent, US$441 million) and merchandizing (2 per cent, US$86.5 million) in the period 2001–2004 (www.olympic.org, accessed 13 January 2006). Jacques Rogge, president of the International Olympic Committee (IOC), told *The Financial Times* in May 2005 that he expected total television rights for the Olympic Games to rise to US$3.5 billion by 2012. Not surprisingly, therefore, representatives of the media easily outnumber the athletes – in Sydney in 2000 there were 16,033 (press and broadcasting) reporters and during the Winter Olympic Games in Salt Lake City in 2002 there were 8730 reporters covering the performances of 2399 athletes (Malfas *et al.*, 2004: 211).

With respect to the Football World Cup, in 1990 sales of television rights were estimated to amount to US$65.7 million (41 per cent), sales of tickets for US$54.8 million (34 per cent) and sales of advertising rights for US$40.2 million (25 per cent). Twelve years later the world TV rights (this time excluding the US) for the 2002 and 2006 Football World Cup Finals were sold for US$1.97 billion. This was a six-fold increase on the US$310 million paid by the EBU for the three tournaments held in the 1990s.

The second reason for the expansion of mega-events is the formation of a sport-media-business alliance that transformed professional sport generally in the late 20th century. Through the idea of packaging, via the tri-partite model of sponsorship rights, exclusive broadcasting rights and merchandizing, sponsors of both the Olympics and the football World Cup events (see Tables 2 and 3) have been attracted by the association with the sports and the vast global audience exposure that the events achieve.

The two largest sports mega-events have lead the way since the 1980s in developing the transnational sport-media-business alliance worth considerable millions of dollars. According to the IOC, international sponsorship revenue for

Table 2: *TOP Sponsors (The Olympic Programme/Partner Programme) 1988–2008*

TOP-1 1988 Seoul	TOP-2 1992 Barcelona	TOP-3 1996 Atlanta	TOP-4 2000 Sydney	TOP-5 2004 Athens	TOP-6 2008 Beijing	Commercial Sector
Coca-Cola	Coca-Cola	Coca-Cola	Coca-Cola	Coca-Cola	Coca-Cola	soft drinks
Kodak	Kodak	Kodak	Kodak	Kodak	Kodak	photographic
Sports Illustrated/Time	Sports Illustrated/Time	Time Inc.	Time Inc.	Time Inc.		media
VISA	VISA	VISA	VISA	VISA	VISA	credit cards
	Bausch & Lomb	Bausch & Lomb				optical, dental
		Xerox	Xerox	Xerox		photocopying
Brother	Brother					typewriters
Philips	Philips					audio & TV
3M	3M					magnetic tapes
Federal Express	United States Postal Service (USPS)	United Parcel Service	United Parcel Service			couriers
Matsushita (Panasonic)	Matsushita (Panasonic)	Matsushita (Panasonic)	Matsushita (Panasonic)	Panasonic	Panasonic	audio & video
	Ricoh					fax
	Mars					food
		IBM	IBM			data processing
		John Hancock	John Hancock	John Hancock	John Hancock	insurance
			Samsung	Samsung	Samsung	communication
			McDonald's	McDonald's	McDonald's	fast-food
				Swatch	Swatch	timing, scoring
				Atos Origin		IT services
					Sema	IT services
					General Electric	communication
					Lenovo	computing

Sources: Miguel de Moragas Spa et al (1995) *Television in the Olympics* London: John Libbey, p. 29; Kristine Toohey & Tony Veal (2000) *The Olympic Games: A social science perspective*, Oxford: CABI, p. 108; www.olympic.org (accessed 13 January 2006).

Table 3: *FIFA World Cup Partners 1990–2006*

1990 Italy (9)	1994 U.S.A. (11)	1998 France (12)	2002 Korea/Japan (15)	2006 Germany (15)	Commercial Sector
Coca-Cola	Coca-Cola	Coca-Cola	Coca-Cola	Coca-Cola	soft drinks
Gillette	Gillette	Gillette	Gillette	Gillette	men's toiletries
Fuji	Fuji	Fuji	Fuji Film/ Fuji Xerox	Fuji Film	photographic
Philips	Philips	Philips	Philips	Philips	audio & television
JVC	JVC	JVC	JVC		audio & television
Canon	Canon	Canon			photography
Mars	Snickers	Mars			food
Vini Italia					wine
Anheuser-Busch		Casio*	Budweiser	Budweiser	beer/calculators
	MasterCard	MasterCard	MasterCard	MasterCard	credit cards
	McDonald's	McDonald's	McDonald's	McDonald's	fast-food restaurants
	Energizer				batteries
	General Motors	General Motors			automobiles
		Adidas	Adidas	Adidas	sports wear
			KT/NTT		telecommunications
			Hyundai	Hyundai	automobiles
			Toshiba	Toshiba	electrical goods
			Avaya	Avaya	communications
			Yahoo!	Yahoo!	internet services
				Continental	car tyres
				DeutscheTelekom	telecommunications
				Emirates	air transport

* French legislation placed restrictions on alcohol advertising and Budweiser sold their rights to Casio.
Sources: John Sugden & Alan Tomlinson (1998) *FIFA and the contest for world football* (Polity), pp. 92–93; http://fifaworldcup.yahoo.com (17/01/02, 10:05 p.m.); *FIFA Magazine* May 2004 Number 5 p. 82.

the 1980 Summer and Winter Olympics was nil (*Marketing Matters*, 2000: 1). The idea of selling exclusivity of marketing rights to a limited number of sponsoring partners began in Britain in the 1970s with Patrick Nally and his associate, Peter West, as the media agency WestNally. In the early 1980s the idea was taken up by Horst Dassler, son of the founder of Adidas, and at the time chief executive of the company. With the blessing of the then FIFA President Joao Havelange, Dassler established the agency ISL Marketing in 1982. Later in the 1980s ISL linked up with the International Olympic Committee (IOC), presided over by Juan Antonio Samaranch. It was ISL that established TOP, or 'The Olympic Programme', in which a few select corporations were able to claim official Olympic worldwide partner status. Whilst the TOP programme supports the Olympic Movement internationally, sponsorship agreements by Olympic host cities create even further opportunities for making money. Hence for the 2008

Olympics in Beijing, organizers have created three additional tiers of support at the national level (Beijing 2008 Partner, Sponsor and (exclusive) Supplier). In light of the enormous attraction of the Chinese market, it is not surprising that revenues from national sponsorship arrangements are likely to be considerably more than those from the TOP programme. There are at least three beer companies acting as sponsors at different levels in 2008. As Sugden and Tomlinson (1998 p. 93) note in relation to the World Cup, 'Fast foods and snacks, soft and alcoholic drinks, cars, batteries, photographic equipment and electronic media, credit sources – these are the items around which the global sponsorship of football has been based, with their classic evocation of a predominantly masculinist realm of consumption: drinking, snacking, shaving, driving'.

The third reason why interest in hosting sports mega-events has grown (as Hall and Horne and Whitson also note) is that they have become seen as valuable promotional opportunities for cities and regions. John Hannigan (1998) has identified the growth of 'urban entertainment destinations' (UEDs) since the 1980s as one of the most significant developments transforming cities throughout the developed world. Hannigan argues that the 'fantasy city' of the late 20th and early 21st century has been formed by the convergence of three trends. Firstly, through the application of the four principles of efficiency, calculability, predictability and control (or 'McDonaldization' as Ritzer, 1993, described it), there has been a rationalization of the operation of the entertainment industries. Secondly, theming, as exemplified by the Disney Corporation (or 'Disneyization', see Bryman, 2004), produces new opportunities for commercial and property developers in urban areas. Thirdly, accompanying synergies between previously discrete activities, such as shopping, dining out, entertainment and education, lead to 'de-differentiation – what some analysts regard as a feature of 'post-modernization'.

These trends, alongside the pursuit of enhanced, or even 'world class', status by politicians and businesses, raise questions for some analysts about the social distribution of the supposed benefits of urban development initiatives, including festivals, spectacles and mega-events. Which social groups actually benefit, which are excluded, and what scope is there for contestation of these developments, are three important questions that are often ignored (Lowes, 2002). Gruneau (2002: ix–x) argues that local politicians and media often focus on the interests and enthusiasms of the developers, property owners and middle-class consumers as 'synonymous with the well-being of the city'. As a result, sectional interests are treated as *the* general interest, and ongoing 'class and community divisions regarding the support and enjoyment of spectacular urban entertainments' are downplayed, if not ignored altogether (Gruneau, 2002: ix–x).

Compounding the problem is the fact that developers have often been able to obtain public subsidies from central and sub-central governments, while the same governments have been cutting back on social welfare spending. Both neoliberal (and in the United Kingdom what might be called after Tony Blair's New Labour project) 'neo-labour', political ideas have meant different objectives for community development, and different definitions of the public good. The growth of the 'global sport-media-tourism complex' (Nauright, 2004: 1334) also leads in some respect to greater secrecy and lack of transparency on the part of the organizations involved. For Zygmunt Bauman (1998: 8) this impact on democratic processes of consultation and discussion is part of the 'Great War of Independence from Space' begun in the last quarter of the 20th century. There has been 'a consistent and relentless wrenching of the decision-making centres, together with the calculations which ground the decisions such centres make, free from territorial constraints – the constraints of locality'.

What is the attraction of sports mega-events?

The 'legacies' – whether social, cultural, environmental, political, economic or sporting – are the greatest attraction but also form part of the 'known unknowns', of sports mega-events (Horne, 2007). They create the 'allure of global games' – perhaps especially for developing economies (Black & van der Westhuizen, 2004). At the same time it seems evident that forecasts of the benefits are nearly always wrong. Notwithstanding Holger Preuss's (2004) economic 'commonsense', noted by Gratton *et al.* in their chapter, since the Montreal Olympics in 1976 especially (as Whitson and Horne point out) a major public and academic concern in considerations of sports mega-events has been the gap between the forecast and actual impacts on economy, society and culture. Whilst the general academic consensus regarding the impacts of mega-events is that there are both positive and negative outcomes, a review of the enormous amount of literature on the socio-economic, socio-cultural, physical and political impacts of Olympic Games, concludes that 'economic benefits are the prime motive' for interests involved in hosting them (Malfas *et al.*, 2004: 218). The positive impacts on employment (or rather unemployment), additional spending in the community hosting an event, visiting tourist/spectator numbers, the 'showcase effect' (Hiller, 1989: 119) of media coverage on an event locality, and some (usually unspecified) impact on the social condition of the host community, are the main claims made for hosting mega-events.

As Munoz's chapter illustrates, Barcelona'92 is often cited as an exemplary Olympic Games. The Games attracted public investment of US$ 6.2 billion that helped redevelop the city and the province of Catalonia (Malfas *et al.*, 2004: 212). Unemployment in Barcelona fell compared with the rest of Spain and the European average. Yet Munoz also notes some of the downside to this success story. In a detailed economic analysis of the resources, financing and impact of the Olympics Brunet noted that 'Barcelona '92 was unusual' (Brunet, 1995: 15). Only one other Olympics (Tokyo in 1964) had generated more direct investment. Improvements in transportation, particularly 'the circulation of motor vehicles' (Brunet, 1995: 20) was one of the major impacts of the Olympics on the urban infrastructure of Barcelona. The newly built Olympic Village also opened up the coast to the city in a way that had not occurred before. Brunet (1995: 24) estimated that there was an overall permanent employment effect of 20,000 extra jobs and that the Olympics acted as 'a protective buffer against the economic crisis' that affected much of the rest of Europe in the late 1980s and early 1990s (Brunet, 1995: 23). There was some indication also that the citizens of Barcelona took advantage of the new sports infrastructure that was left after the event. The overall legacy of the '92 Olympics, however, focuses on the transformation of the urban and economic environment of Barcelona. Despite Brunet's findings questions about the quality, and duration, of the jobs created in Barcelona have been raised. The majority of the jobs created were actually low paid and short-term (Malfas *et al.*, 2004: 212). Sydney 2000 was also proclaimed by the then IOC President, Juan Antonio Samaranch, as 'the best Olympics ever', yet similar concerns about the actual distribution of the social and economic benefits and opportunity costs of hosting that Games linger, as Hall's chapter notes (see also Lenskyj, 2002).

The FIFA World Cup in 2002 was the first ever to be staged in Asia. Predictions of an additional one million sports tourists to watch the FIFA World Cup in Japan and South Korea in May and June 2002 proved to be wildly optimistic. Japan attracted only 30,000 more visitors and South Korea reported similar visitor numbers as in the previous year (Horne and Manzenreiter, 2004: 197, see also Matheson and Baade, 2003). In this respect there are several comparisons to be drawn between the study of sports mega-events and the analyses of Bent Flyvbjerg and his associates into the planning of *megaprojects* – such as major bridges, tunnels, canals, public transport schemes and prestige buildings. Their research findings suggest that promoters of multi-billion dollar megaprojects, including sports stadia and other infrastructure, may often consistently, systematically and self-servingly mislead governments and the public in order to get projects approved (see Flyvbjerg *et al.*, 2003: 11–21 and 32–48 esp.).

The tendency to overstate the potential economic, as well as social, benefits of stadium developments and hosting sports events has been detailed by several academic researchers from the UK and the USA (see contributions to Gratton and Henry eds., 2001a). With respect to megaprojects there is a similar fantasy world of underestimated costs, overestimated revenues, underestimated environmental impacts and over-valued economic development effects. As Flyvbjerg *et al.* (2003: 7) suggest, more often than not 'power play, instead of commitment to deliberative ideals, is often what characterizes megaproject development'. In this context it is important briefly to review debates about the impacts of sports mega-events.

Debates about the impacts of sports mega-events

Debates about the impacts of sports mega-events – about the distribution of the opportunity costs and benefits of hosting sports events and using sport as a form of social and economic regeneration – are best understood within the broader political/economic/ideological context in which the debates have taken shape. Claims and counter-claims are issued, with the emphasis of advocates typically on the *economic* impacts of hosting sports events (Roberts, 2004: 116–120, UK Sport, 1999). As the UK Sport report *Measuring Success 2* noted, major international spectator events generate 'significant economic activity and media interest' (UK Sport, 2004: 11). The chapter by Gratton *et al.*, which derives from this research, demonstrates how these conclusions are reached. But how that economic activity is distributed – before, during and after the event – and who actually benefits, remain key questions posed by those sceptical of economic impact studies. Social redistribution versus growth machine arguments about sports mega-events such as the Olympic Games revolve around the spin-offs and 'legacies'.

After a mega-event has finished, questions start to be raised about the popular belief that sport can have a positive impact on a local community and a regional economy. Sport has been seen as a generator of national and local economic and social development. Economically it has been viewed as an industry around which cities can devise urban regeneration strategies. Socially it has been viewed as a tool for the development of urban communities, and the reduction of social exclusion and crime. Whilst hypothetical links exist between sport activities/facilities and work productivity, participation, self-esteem, quality of life, employment, and other variables, not as much rigorous research has been done as might be expected given the claims made. Often research has been conducted in advance of sports mega-events on behalf of interested parties. As Gratton and Henry (2001b: 309) suggest, 'In general, there has been inadequate measurement' of final and intermediate outputs as well as inputs.[5]

In the UK and Australia, the main stimuli for using sport for economic regeneration has been the hosting of international sporting events. In response to urban decline, Glasgow, Sheffield, Manchester and Birmingham have invested heavily in the sports infrastructure so that each has a portfolio of major sports facilities capable of holding major sports events.[6] In addition, three of them have been designated as a 'National City of Sport'. While the World Student Games held in Sheffield in 1991 was entered into without any serious impact study, it produced a loss of £180million, and the resulting debt has added 'just over £100 to annual council tax bills and will not be repaid until 2013' (www.strategy.gov.uk/2002/sport/report). Following several failed bids to host the Olympics in the 1980s and 1990s, and the embarrassment of having to relinquish the opportunity to host the World Athletics Championship in 2005, UK cities aimed to host smaller major sports events. The generally trouble-free success of the European football championship held in England in 1996 and the Commonwealth Games staged in Manchester in 2002 provided positive support for those with the aspiration to try again for one of the 'megas'. This, plus the enthusiasm of key politicians in an era of 'cultural governance', undoubtedly underlay the decision to put London forward in the race to stage the 2012 Olympics (Fairclough, 2000).[7]

In Australia (as Hall's chapter reveals) a similar strategy of using sports events to promote tourism and regeneration has been adopted at state level – states provide cities with the funds to bid for international sports events. Several Australian cities (including Adelaide, Melbourne, Brisbane and Sydney) used sport as part of an economic development strategy in response to city/state rivalry – to establish a strong tourism industry. As Schimmel also notes, cities in the USA have placed a huge investment in the infrastructure – such as stadium developments for the big four professional team sports. Such efforts at 'urban boosterism' saw more and more cities competing to offer professional teams facilities. Teams sat back and let bidding cities 'bid up the price'. By the end of the 1990s there were 30 major stadium construction projects in progress – nearly one-third of the total professional sports infrastructure in the USA. The total value was estimated at US$9 billion (Gratton and Henry, 2001b: 311).

Reviewing these attempts to use sport as a means of urban regeneration in the USA, Europe and Australia Gratton and Henry (2001b: 314) concluded, 'the potential benefits . . . have not yet been clearly demonstrated'. Some places have been successful in harnessing social and urban regeneration plans to the sports mega-event. In this respect, as we have already noted, Barcelona was acclaimed throughout Europe and the rest of the world as how to do it. But even apparent winners have created problems for themselves. The Centre on Housing Rights and Evictions (COHRE) investigating displacement, or forced evictions, resulting from the Olympic Games and other major international events estimates that 700,000 people were evicted to make way for the 1988 Seoul Olympics and 300,000 have already been forced to move ahead of the 2008 Beijing Games (http://www.cohre.org/downloads/Achieving_Housing_for_All.pdf). Evictions are anticipated in the east end of London before 2012. In Barcelona 400 homeless people were subject to control and supervision during the 1992 Games (Cox *et al.*, 1994) and competition between high-income and low-income residents for the low-cost housing, promised after the Olympic athletes left town, soon resulted in the most affluent gaining most. Most of the apartments that comprised the 'Nova Icaria' project were sold on the open market, contrary to a previously announced aim of subsidizing housing for those on low incomes (see Hughes, 1992: 39–40 and Vázquez Montalbán, 1990/1992: 6–7). Similarly in Sydney, before the 2000 Olympics, property prices and rent increases in the vicinity of Homebush Bay, primarily occupied by low-income tenants, lead Lenskyj (2002) critically to assess the claim made by IOC President Samaranch that the Sydney Olympics were the best ever (see also Cox, 1999). Arguably, therefore, increased social polarization also remains one of the major legacies of mega-events.

Cashman (2003) identifies four periods during which the impact of the summer games on Olympic host cities is usually most open for debate. During the preparation of the bid and competition to win the right to host mega-events such as the Olympic Games 'bidding wars' are particularly apparent (also see Sugden and Tomlinson, 2002, on the bidding wars surrounding the 2006 FIFA

World Cup). This is when overestimated benefits and underestimated cost forecasts are likely to be stated with most conviction and yet often prove to be wildly inaccurate. An email circulated by British Prime Minister Tony Blair, a month before the decision was made about the 2012 Summer Olympics, claimed, amongst other things, that, 'A London victory on 6 July would mean: thousands of new jobs, a boost to tourism across the UK, the chance to host athlete preparation camps up and down the country' (tony.blair@reply-new.labour.org.uk).

We have already noted that claims about the impact of mega-events on employment need to be treated very warily. The key questions to be asked are, what kind of jobs are to be created – part-time or full-time, temporary or permanent, and for whom? In the case of the 2012 Olympics, athlete preparation camps are most likely to be in the South east of England near where the vast majority of Olympic events are to take place. These locations can also be subject to bidding wars, for example as happened in Japan during the 2002 World Cup, when local authorities proffered lucrative inducements to national football associations of teams competing in the competition to establish training camps (Horne and Manzenreiter, 2004). As regards tourism, once again specific areas of the UK/South east England are likely to benefit, whilst displaced non-sports tourists may defer their visit to the capital during the event. Clashes with other sports fixtures and cultural events (for example cricket Test matches and the Edinburgh festivals) in August 2012 appear inevitable and will therefore likely lead to a reduction in visitors to them.

Despite changes of personnel and rules, considerable secrecy and lack of transparency continue to pervade the undemocratic organizations that run sports mega-events (Hoberman, 1995; Krüger, 1993). Those that challenge this, or write about it critically, may become *persona non grata* to the mega-event organizers. Certainly there has been an increasing reliance on protecting the image of the Olympics, the host city and the IOC in the past 15 years through the employment of public relations companies (*The Guardian Sport section,* 22 September 2005: 2).

Another focus of research is the impact of mega-events on the culture, beliefs and attitudes of the host population (exemplified here in the chapters by Cornelissen and Swart, Marivoet, and Whitson and Horne). During the mega-event the identities of local people are meant to conform to the (generally) positive stereotypes contained in pre-event publicity and the opening ceremonies. A mega-event is not only about showing off a city to the world but also about putting the global on show for the locals (especially in the case of marginal cities, see Whitson, 2004). Mega-events thus invite the people of a host city – and even a host nation – to take on new identities as citizens of the world. The hosting of sports mega-events, such as the Football World Cup Finals, provides multiple meanings for different groups of agents – as they happen, when they have taken place and, perhaps especially, as they are being bid for. Advocates of hosting mega-events will deploy a range of discursive strategies to win over public opinion internally.

In the case of semi-peripheral or developing societies, colonial and neo-colonial ties have shaped and continue to shape external relationships with sports mega-events as well. Neither the continents of Africa nor South America have yet staged an Olympic Games. The unsuccessful bid by Cape Town to host the 2004 Olympic Games was the first African bid for the Games (Swart and Bob, 2004). Cornelissen (2004) notes how discourse about 'Africa' was used ideologically, by both South Africa and Morocco, during the competition to host the 2010 Football World Cup that was eventually resolved in favour of the former in May 2004. The South African bid estimated massive benefits from the event, which many consider will be impossible actually to achieve[8]. In the final bid document, twelve locations were named as sites to host matches but, as in Japan and Korea in 2002, there are likely to be several of these that do not obtain 'the requisite levels of tourism' (Cornelissen, 2000: 1307). As Cornelissen and Swart note in their chapter, this has now been reduced to ten but, even so, it remains likely that under-utilization of the facilities built will mean that not all localities will obtain the benefits promised.

Flyvbjerg (2005) has noted that mega-projects *can* be completed on schedule and within budget – the Guggenheim Bilbao Museum, the Pompidou Centre, and even further back the Empire State Building and the Eiffel Tower are examples of this. But the vast majority of mega-projects are not delivered anywhere nearly on time or within their estimated cost (*The Economist* 11 June 2005: 65–66).[9] It is becoming so evident that cost overruns are predictable that certain sections of government, as well as academics such as Flyvbjerg, have begun to consider this more seriously. The Department for Transport in the UK, for example, commissioned Flyvbjerg to investigate procedures for dealing with, in classic British understatement, 'optimism bias' in transport planning (Flyvbjerg, 2004). When it comes to actually staging mega-events, such as the Olympics, one of the persistent public concerns is whether monuments can turn into 'white elephants' and end up costing considerably more than they are worth to maintain, as happened most notoriously in Montreal in 1976, but also in Atlanta, Sydney and Athens.[10]

The kind of detailed case study conducted by Mark Lowes (2002) of community opposition to another spectacular urban sports event – the Molson Indy Vancouver – provides one model for alternative research into sports mega-events. He focuses attention on the limits and possibilities of local resistance to attempts to relocate the motor racing event into public space. Such opposition coalitions are one of the unacceptable practices to organisations running mega-events that have to be managed. In this respect Lenskyj has suggested that the IOC has become more like a 'transnational corporation' that has increasingly exploited 'young athletes' labour and aspirations for its own aggrandisement and profit' (Lenskyj, 2000: 195). The local mass media's economic interest in sport mega-events turns journalists from reporters into impresarios, from potential whistle blowers into cheerleaders. The hosting and staging of sports mega-events may help to create bourgeois playgrounds but the long-term benefits are unevenly shared.

The politics of sports mega-events

We can summarize the discussion so far, and those of several of the contributors to this volume, by stating that sports mega-events are a significant part of the experience of modernity, but they cannot be seen as a panacea for its social and economic problems. Hence there is a need to maintain an independent position to assess these events. As Flyvbjerg suggests, the key weapons against a culture of covert deceit surrounding mega-projects are transparency, accountability and critical questioning from independent and specialist organizations. Rather than simply become cheerleaders for them, boosters, rather than analysts, academics equally need to reflect critically on the effects, both economic and beyond economic impacts, that sports mega-events have. As Flyvbjerg *et al.* (2003: 108) note, 'there is no such thing as an entirely private venture for investments' with 'the magnitude and consequences' of mega-projects. The same is certainly true for sports mega-events such as the Olympics and the FIFA World Cup. Hence Bruce Kidd's (1992b: 154) observation (cited by Whitson and Horne) that 'Mega-projects like the Olympic Games require a tremendous investment of human, financial and physical resources from the communities that stage them', reminds us that they need to be the subject of public debate and accountability.

In the past twenty years government sports policy – concerning regulation, consumer protection and sports promotion – has developed in a context of the spread of neo-liberal economic ideology and globalization (Horne, 2006). This has produced a change in the relationship between sport and the state. Different states use sport for different non-sports ends – economic development and social development, nation building and signalling ('branding the nation') and to assist in economic and political liberalization (Black and van der Westhuizen, 2004). As Houlihan (2002: 194) notes the 'willingness of governments to humble themselves before the IOC and FIFA through lavish hospitality and the strategic deployment of presidents, prime ministers, royalty and supermodels' is a reflection of the value that governments now place on international sport. The promoters of sports mega-events – the Olympics and the World Cup especially – in turn rely on two agencies. On the one hand the media are essential, since without the media, sports mega events would not be able to attract the public's attention and corporate sponsorship. On the other hand, without the thousands of volunteers who work for free, the games would not be able to 'go on' (see Nogawa, 2004 for an analysis of volunteers during the 2002 World Cup in Japan and Korea). The state constructs what is and what is not legitimate sports practice and in doing so effectively determines what the sports consumers' interest is. The state also creates the framework within which partnerships between local authorities, voluntary sports and commercial organizations operate. The neo-liberal state may have 'less responsibility for direct service delivery' of sport but it has retained, if not actually expanded, its influence because of the other agencies' dependency on state resources (Houlihan, 2002: 200). Hence the state remains the place to campaign – whether it is over inequalities and social exclusion, the regulation of mega-events, consumer politics, human rights or environmental risks in sport.[11]

The sociological significance of sports mega-events

If the bulk of this introduction has so far indicated the social, economic and political significance of sports mega-events, what are the reasons why sociologists and other social scientists should be interested in analysing them? What can social scientists learn from studying them? We suggest that detailed analysis of sports mega-events, such as the football World Cup and the Summer Olympics, enables consideration of several overlapping and intersecting issues of contemporary social scientific interest. These issues include: centre-periphery relationships related to governance in world sport (Sugden & Tomlinson, 2002), power relations between nation states, supranational sport associations and the sports business (Butler, 2002), the media-sport-business connection (Jennings with Sambrook, 2000), and the cultural production of ideologies needed to cover emergent fissures when 'the circus comes to town' (Horne and Manzenreiter, 2004a).[12]

Graham Scambler (2005: 189) suggests that sports mega-events can only be fully comprehended through adopting a multidimensional 'jigsaw' theoretical model of social reality derived from the work of Habermas and the critical realism of Bhaskar. This would take into account five sets of logics and relations: the economy and relations of class, the state and relations of command, patriarchy and relations of gender, tribalism and relations of ethnicity, and honour and relations of status. Whilst we applaud the ambition to incorporate so many aspects of the contemporary lifeworld in this model for a reflective, critical sociology of sport, we consider that the ideas of other leading social theorists, including Bourdieu and Giddens in terms of understanding sport as practice and sport as spectacle in the hypercommodified world of disorganized, global capitalism also remain underdeveloped.[13]

Elsewhere we have discussed the promise of Bourdieu's ideas for analysing sport and globalization (Horne and Manzenreiter, 2004b) and one of us has outlined the promise of some of Giddens' conceptions with another colleague (Horne and Jary, 2004). Bourdieu's conception of sport as a relatively autonomous field or space of body practices with their own logic and histories created a distinctive school of research, especially, but not exclusively in France (see Pociello, ed., 1981). Other writers have noted the specific theoretical insights that Bourdieu's sociological concepts offer to the study of sport and the body (Giulianotti, 2005; Tomlinson, 2004; and Shilling, 1993). It is not our ambition here, however, to promote one particular theory or mould a synthetic sociological theory of sport (or anything else) and thus resolve the issues emerging from 'multi-paradigmatic rivalry'. We would suggest that synthetic theories in themselves are not very helpful, as they tend to close down debate. Arguably greater advances are possible through a more eclectic theoretical approach. Whilst there are obvious incompatibilities between Bourdieu and Giddens, for instance, the ambition to generate a sociology of sport that investigates novel 'empiricities' is common to both.

What is required, if better multinational transdisciplinary research is to develop, some of which is evidenced in this collection, are methodological pluralism and theoretical openness. Theory should be seen as a process, not an accomplishment. Theoretical oppositions, or dualisms, should be mobilized to address certain substantive concerns, rather than argued away. Like Eric Dunning (1999) our argument is that 'sport matters'. Unlike him, we would place greater emphasis on the variability of sports' impact on different people at different times and places. The overall social significance of sport is conjunctural. Sport has become more of an integral part of the 'economies of signs and space' of late capitalist modernity in the past twenty years, but it has not always been so. Therefore a discontinuist thesis of historical development, rather than a developmental one, such as figurational sociology provides, is arguably a more accurate model. This is consistent with Pierre Bourdieu's concern, made with reference to Elias, that 'historical analysis of long-term trends is always liable to hide critical breaks' (Bourdieu and Wacquant, 1992: 93). Sport can best be viewed as a contested cultural terrain. Sport, and leisure in general, do matter, but not for all the people and not all the time. Studies of contestation and fluctuations in the relationship between sport and economic, political and social power, contained in this collection, demonstrate some aspects of this variability in significance.

Sports mega-events provide novel ways in which research into national and cultural identity, mobility, and individualization can be approached, as our contributors indicate. Insofar as sports mega-events reflect contemporary socioeconomic conditions study of them highlights matters pertaining to the 'cultural turn' applied to sociology and the sociology of sport. The 'cultural turn' is connected to debates about modernity, lifestyles and identity concerning the shifting relationship between the state and the capitalist market, above and below the national level, the transformation of the meaning of citizenship, and the implications of these developments for personal and social identities. Research into sports mega-events can provide insights into three main dynamics of this contemporary consumer society – globalization, increased commodification and growing inequality.[14] Sports mega-events also bring large groups of people together in collective displays of devotion and celebration. As the chapters by Manzenreiter and Marivoet, in particular, indicate, the adoption of symbols, especially flags, songs and team shirts, act as signs of social inclusion in expressive displays of sportive nationalism. Yet challenges to national identity are also manifest in contemporary patterns of elite athletic talent migration that contribute in no small part to the difficulties in defining national allegiances. Additionally the global division of labour in sport means that some local and national sporting differences may be erased by the economic dominance of certain regions and leagues (eg, Europe and football, the USA and basketball).

The dominance of transnational companies and media conglomerates in terms of the sponsorship and marketing of sports mega-events also creates the conditions in which leading athletes become stars, celebrities and brands (Smart, 2005; Whannel, 2002).

Sports mega-events have been largely developed by undemocratic organizations, often with anarchic decision-making and a lack of transparency, and more often in the interests of global flows rather than local communities. In this respect they represent a shift of public funds to private interests. Such organizations represent part of the ideological assault on citizenship that has occurred since the 1980s, which prefer global consumers to local publics. This emphasis on economic liberalization also has its corollary in discourses about human rights and political liberalization. But, as Xu's chapter suggests, the contradiction between these two is often resolved in favour of economic liberalism. Whether it be through the removal of surplus populations and the socially marginal from host sites and venues, the construction of highly gender specific male cultural centres, or the re-affirmation of the hierarchical ranking of nations through sport performances, sports mega-events can contribute to the naturalization of social inequalities. Sports mega-events promise (albeit brief) moments of 'festive intercultural celebration' (Kidd, 1992a: 151). Yet, as we have suggested here, it would be a failure of the social scientific imagination to be seduced by the allure of mega-events.

Conclusion – forming a new research agenda for sports mega-events

The chapters that follow are arranged into three sections that indicate broad sub-divisions in the study of sports mega-events – their role in capitalist modernity, glocal politics, and as a feature of power, spectacle and the urban environment. The chapters all indicate areas where further research is needed, whilst those by Roche and Gratton and his colleagues explicitly state some of the research questions about sport mega-events that might be specifically investigated in the future. What kind of mark do we hope this book leaves on sports mega-event discourses in the future?

An Olympic Games or a football World Cup involves competing groups of players with different interests and capital. As academics we too are players in the game, and generally as Giulianotti (2005: 159) notes, 'no player argues for the game's complete abolition; the most radical argue for reinventing the system that produces the game's rules, procedures and distribution of capital'. It is true to say that almost all sports politics is reformist rather than revolutionary. Those involving 'occidental modernity's core urban mega-events' (Scambler, 2005: 69) are no different. The main axis of concern about sports mega-events, however, has swung from their political use to their economic use in the past twenty-five years, when the Los Angeles Olympics witnessed an accelerated 'incorporation of sporting practice into the ever-expanding marketplace of international capitalism' (Gruneau, 1984: 2).

So what are the key themes and issues we consider worth further exploration in future research into sports mega-events? Firstly, in keeping with the reformist politics mentioned above, more accurate evaluations, social impact assessments and full public consultation before submitting bids is required if mega-events, as mega-projects, are to retain public support and become more democratically accountable achievements (Flyvbjerg *et al.*, 2003). Greater institutional checks and balances to control costs, including the formulation of penalties for transgression, such as financial penalties for cost overruns, as well as environmental and social impact assessments need to be developed on the basis of independent research. This book does not outline such checks and balances but may, it is hoped, contribute to their development by raising awareness of the existence of research-based criticism of non-economic, as well as economic, aspects of sports mega-events. Secondly, as Schimmel indicates in her chapter and as was witnessed barely 24 hours after the announcement that London had been selected to host the 2012 Summer Olympic Games in July 2005, security issues are likely to come more to the fore in production of sports mega-events. Heightened concerns about risk and the nature of globalization in its 'uncertainty' phase (Robertson, 1992: 58–9) will form a substantial research theme in future studies of sports mega-events.

Thirdly, whether the focus is on the business of sport in a globalizing world (involving the global trade in sports goods, services, sponsorship and team and property ownership), the mediation of mega-events by transnational media conglomerates and new technologies, or the shifting balance between public and private financing of sport, commodification and the heightened spectacularization of sport through sports mega-events will remain central concerns of research (see Kellner, 2003 on the 'sports media spectacle'). Fourthly, and last but by no means least, the social function, meanings and processes involved in the stimulation of new social movements and opposition coalitions, as well as volunteers and spectators, engaged with sport and sports mega-events will continue to require further analysis from independent social researchers. In these and other ways, social scientific analysis of sport and sports mega-events will develop in the future.

Notes

1 This chapter draws in part on sections of Horne (2007).
2 For another illustration of the importance of the media to sports mega-events see many of the contributions to the special edition of the *International Review for the Sociology of Sport* 'Sports Mega-Events', Volume 35, No. 3, 2000.
3 The Winter Olympic Games is roughly one-quarter the size of the Summer Games in terms of athletes and events and so some might argue that it is not a true 'mega' (Matheson and Baade 2003). It certainly qualifies as a 'second order' major international sports event. The UEFA European Football Championship is in a similar category, as Marivoet outlines in her chapter.
4 Between 1980 and 2000 seven new sports and 79 events were added to the programme of the Summer Olympics. 28 sports have featured in the Summer Olympics since 2000, although the

rare decision to scale down the number to 26 (removing baseball and softball after the 2008 Olympics) was made in July 2005 (www.olympic.org/uk). After 1998 the FIFA World Cup Finals expanded from 24 to 32 football teams.

5 One of the main problems regarding the assessment of the costs and benefits of mega events relates to the quality of data obtained from impact analyses. Economic impact studies often claim to show that the investment of public money is worthwhile in the light of the economic activity generated by having professional sports teams or mega events in cities. Yet economic benefits are often expressed in terms of both net income *and* increased employment, whereas in fact increased employment results *from* additional income, not as well as. Economic impact assessments of mega events also rely on predictions of expenditure by sports tourists, and again research shows that such studies have often been methodologically flawed. The real economic benefit of visitor numbers and spending is often well below that specified because of 'substitution', 'crowding out' and unrealistic use of the economic 'multiplier' factors. Another measure of economic impact – on the creation of new jobs in the local economy – has often been politically driven to justify the expenditure on new facilities and hence the results are equally questionable – see Matheson and Baade 2003 and Crompton (n.d.).

6 Partly in the light of London's successful bid for the 2012 Olympic Games, the Scottish Executive endorsed the bid by Glasgow to host the Commonwealth Games in 2014 in 2005, although the final decision is not expected until November 2007.

7 Fairclough describes 'cultural governance' as 'governing by shaping or changing the cultures of the public services, claimants and the socially excluded, and the general population" (Fairclough, 2000, p. 61). This form of governance has featured in the political system of the United Kingdom for the past 26 years. Cultural governance also 'implies an increased importance for discourses in shaping the action – managing culture means gaining acceptance for particular representations of the social world, ie, particular discourses' (Fairclough, 2000, p. 157). In this respect sport has become a most important feature of government intervention and regulation. This importance has been reflected in a number of initiatives and publications. Thus Tony Blair has continued the style of politics inherited from Margaret Thatcher, and to a lesser degree John Major. The Thatcher Government(s) between 1979 and 1990, for example, explicitly sought to create an 'enterprise culture' in which social and political well-being would be ensured not by central planning or bureaucracy but through the enterprising activities and choices of autonomous businesses, organizations and people. 'Enterprise' was a potent concept because it conveyed not just how organizations should operate but also how individuals should act – with energy, initiative, ambition, calculation and personal responsibility. The enterprising self was thus a calculating self, about her or him self and on her or him self. That the 'enterprising self' also appears to be a description of an active sports person is no coincidence. It is not unusual to find a particular kind of figure held up in high esteem at specific historical moments.

8 77,400 permanent jobs, income of 2 per cent of South Africa's GDP and additional income from tax of US$ 550 million (Cornelissen, 2004: p. 1297).

9 Two recent examples of escalating costs and delays in megaprojects in Britain are the re-building of Wembley Stadium and the new Scottish Parliament building. After Wembley was chosen as the site of the new national stadium in 1997, delays and cost overruns have been a regular feature of the project. Initially costed at £185 million. Work on the site was due to start in 1999 by when the stadium was expected to cost £475 million. In fact work did not get underway until September 2002 when the figure had reached £752 million – making it the most expensive sports stadium in the world. At the time of writing (February 2006) the rising costs of steel and other delays to completion have lead some people in the construction industry to estimate that the final total cost will be close to £1 billion. It is still not certain however when it will be open for business. Such was the outcry about the spiralling costs associated with the building of the new Scottish Parliament building at Holyrood in Edinburgh that an inquiry was established. Originally estimated at between £10 and £40 million in the devolution legislation passed in 1997, costs rose to £55 million (1998), £109 million (1999), £195 million (2000) and £374 million (2003). The building was finally opened in 2004 at a cost of £431 million (www.holyroodinquiry.org).

10 The phrase 'white elephant' is purported to derive from the practice of the King of Siam (modern Thailand) to deal with threats to his rule by giving these sacred and therefore purely symbolic, but expensive animals to rivals. The cost of maintaining the animal was more than they were worth.

11 One of us has suggested elsewhere that the major issues in the study of sport in consumer culture are 1. 'commodification' and trends in the global sports goods and services market, 2. 'consumerization' and the growth of sports coverage in the media, especially its role in the process of creating consumers out of sports audiences and fans, 3. 'commercialization' and the importance of sponsorship and advertising for contemporary sport, 4. 'cultural governance' and the changing role of government in the regulation, (consumer) protection and promotion of sport, 5. 'lifestylization', or how much, as a result of increasing consumerization, has the role of sport in the construction, maintenance and challenging of lifestyles and identities altered, and 6. 'inequality' – how consumerization is reflected in social divisions in patterns of involvement and participation in sport. These issues amount to a research agenda for the sociology of sport that considers consumer processes and politics more centrally than it has done to date (Horne, 2006).

12 See Veal & Toohey 2005 for a substantial bibliography of writing on the Olympic Games that includes much of this research.

13 Whilst there are obviously several alternative theoretical approaches in the sociology of sport, it is not our intention to argue for one or other of these here. As one of us has noted elsewhere (Horne, 2006, pp. 15–16), it was sports historian Allen Guttmann who once observed (in relation to the figurational sociology of Dunning and Elias) that 'no key turns all locks'. Nonetheless, as can be seen from several of the contributions to this collection, many social scientists recognize there is a need to approach the study of sport and sports mega-events in consumer culture with considerable emphasis placed on the production of consumption, as much as the meanings or pleasures of consumption.

14 In these economies the body is more than an instrument for producing material goods and getting things done. The body, including the sporting and physically active body, is now portrayed as an object of contemplation and improvement, in the spectacular discourses of the mass media, the regulatory discourses of the state and in peoples' everyday practices (or 'body projects'). Contemporary advertisements for commercial sport and leisure clubs in the UK combine the discourses of both medical science and popular culture in such phrases as 'fitness regime', 'problem areas like the bottom or the stomach', 'consultation' and 'fix'. By exhorting potential consumers/members to 'Flatten your tum and perk up your bum' and reassuring us that 'Gym'll fix it', regulatory control of the body is now experienced through consumerism and the fashion industry. Sport has thus become increasingly allied to the consumption of goods and services, which is now the structural basis of the advanced capitalist countries through discourses about the model, (post-) modern consumer-citizen. This person is an enterprising self who is also a calculating and reflexive self. Someone permanently ready to discipline her- or himself – through crash diets, gymnastics, aerobics, muscle toning, tanning, strip-waxing, and cosmetic ('plastic') surgery (including breast enlargement and cellulite reduction) as well as sporting physical activity – in order to fit in with the demands of advanced liberalism (Horne, 2006).

References

Bauman, Z. (1998) *Globalization* Cambridge: Polity.

Black, D. & van der Westhuizen, J. (2004) The allure of global games for 'semi-peripheral' polities and spaces: a research agenda In *Third World Quarterly* Vol. 25, No. 7: pp. 1195–1214.

Bourdieu, P. (1999) The State, Economics and Sport in H. Dauncey and G. Hare (eds) *France and the 1998 World Cup* London: Frank Cass pp. 15–21.

Bourdieu, P. (1998) The Olympics-An Agenda for Analysis in P. Bourdieu *On Television and Journalism* London: Pluto pp. 79–82.

Bourdieu, P. (1993) How can one be a sportsman? In P. Bourdieu *Sociology in Question* London: Sage pp. 117–131.

Bourdieu, P. (1990) Programme for a sociology of sport in P. Bourdieu *In Other Words* Cambridge: Polity pp. 156–167.

Bourdieu, P. & Wacquant, L. (1992) *An Invitation to Reflexive Sociology* Cambridge: Polity.

Brunet, F. (1995) 'An economic analysis of the Barcelona '92 Olympic Games: resources, financing, and impact', Centre d'Estudis Olimpics i de l'Esport, Barcelona: Universitat Autònoma de Barcelona. (available at http://olympicstudies.uab.es/pdf/od006_eng.pdf)

Bryman, A. (2004) *The Disneyization of Society* London: Sage.

Butler, O. (2002) Getting the Games: Japan, South Korea and the co-hosted World Cup in J. Horne & W. Manzenreiter (eds) *Japan, Korea and the 2002 World Cup* London: Routledge pp. 43–55.

Cashman, R. (2003) Impact of the Games on Olympic Host Cities, Centre d'Estudis Olimpics, Universitat Autònoma de Barcelona. (Spanish language version available at http://www.blues.uab.es/olympic.studies/pdf/FL8_spa.pdf)

Chapin, T. (2002) 'Identifying the real costs and benefits of sports facilities'. Lincoln Institute of Land Policy Working Paper. (available at http://www.lincolninst.edu/pubs/dl/671_chapin-web.pdf)

Coakley, J. & Donnelly, P. (2004) *Sports in Society* Toronto: McGraw-Hill Ryerson.

Cornelissen, S. (2004) 'It's Africa's turn!' The narratives and legitimations surrounding the Moroccan and South African bids for the 2006 and 2010 FIFA finals *Third World* Quarterly Vol. 25, No. 7: pp. 1293–1309.

Cox, G. (1999) *Ready, Set, Go: Housing, Homelessness and the 2000 Olympics*, Sydney: Shelter New South Wales.

Cox, G. Darcy, M. & Bounds, M. (1994) *The Olympics and Housing: A study of six international events and analysis of the potential impacts of the Sydney 2000 Olympics*, Campbelltown, New South Wales: University of Western Sydney and Shelter New South Wales.

Crompton, J. (n.d.) *Measuring the Economic Impact of Visitors to Sports Tournaments and Special Events* (available at http://www.rpts.tamu.edu/faculty/EconomicImpact.pdf)

Crompton, J. (2001) Public subsidies to professional team sport facilities in theUSA. In C. Gratton & I. Henry (eds) *Sport in the city* London: Routledge pp. 15–34.

Dunning, E. (1999) *Sport Matters* London: Routledge.

Fairclough, N. (2000) *New Labour, New Language?* London: Routledge.

Flyvbjerg, B. (2005) Design by deception: The politics of megaproject approval, *Harvard Design Magazine*, no. 22, pp. 50–59.

Flyvbjerg, B. in association with COWI (2004) *Procedures for Dealing with Optimism Bias in Transport Planning* London: Department for Transport.

Flyvbjerg, B., Bruzelius, N. & Rothengatter, W. (2003) *Megaprojects and Risk* Cambridge: Cambridge University Press.

Giulianotti, R. (2005) *Sport, a critical sociology* Cambridge: Polity.

Giulianotti, R. (ed.) (2004) *Sport and modern social theorists* Basingstoke: Palgrave.

Gratton, C. & Henry, I. (eds) (2001a) *Sport in the city* London: Routledge.

Gratton, C. & Henry, I. (2001b) Sport in the city. Where do we go from here? In Gratton, C. & Henry, I. (eds) *Sport in the city* London: Routledge, pp. 309–314.

Gruneau, R. (2002) Foreword In M. Lowes *Indy Dreams and Urban Nightmares* Toronto: Toronto University Press, pp. ix–xii.

Gruneau, R. (1984) Commercialism and the modern Olympics in A. Tomlinson and G. Whannel (eds) *Five Ring Circus: Money, power and politics at the Olympic Games* London: Pluto pp. 1–15.

Hall, C. M. (2001) Imaging, tourism and sports event fever: the Sydney Olympicsand the need for a social charter for mega-events. In: C. Gratton & I. Henry (eds) *Sport in the city* pp. 166–183.

Hannigan, J. (1998) *Fantasy City* London: Routledge.

Hiller, H. (1989) Impact and image: the convergence of urban factors in preparing for the1988 Calgary Winter Olympics in G. Syme *et al.* (eds) *The Planning and Evaluation ofHallmark Events* Aldershot: Avebury, pp. 119–131.

Hoberman, J. (1995) Toward a Theory of Olympic Internationalism *Journal of SportHistory* 22 (1): 1–37.

Horne, J. (2006) *Sport in Consumer Culture* Basingstoke: Palgrave.

Horne, J. (2007) The Four 'Knowns' of Sports Mega-Events In *Leisure Studies (Forthcoming)*.

Horne, J., Jary, D. & Tomlinson, A. (1987) (eds) *Sport, Leisure and Social Relations* London: Routledge & Kegan Paul/ Sociological Review Monograph No. 33.

Horne, J. & Jary, D. (2004) Anthony Giddens: Structuration Theory, and Sport and Leisure in R. Giulianotti ed. *Sport and modern social theorists* Basingstoke: Palgrave pp. 129–144.

Horne, J. & Manzenreiter, W. (2004a) Accounting for mega-events: forecast and actual impacts of the 2002 Football World Cup Finals on the host countries Japan and Korea In *International Review for the Sociology of Sport* 39 (2): 187–203.

Horne, J. & Manzenreiter, W. (2004b) Football, culture, globalisation in W. Manzenreiter and J. Horne (eds) *Football Goes East: business, culture and the people's game in China, Japan and South Korea* London: Routledge pp. 1–17.

Houlihan, B. (2002) Political involvement in sport, physical education and recreation in A. Laker (ed.) *The Sociology of Sport and Physical Education* London: Routledge pp. 190–210.

Hughes, R. (1992) *Barcelona* New York: A. Knopf.

Jennings, A. with Sambrook, C. (2000) *The Great Olympic Swindle* London: Simon & Schuster.

Kellner, D. (2003) *Media Spectacle* London: Routledge.

Kidd, B. (1992a) The culture wars of the Montreal Olympics *International Review for the Sociology of Sport* 27(2): 151–161.

Kidd, B. (1992b) The Toronto Olympic Commitment: Towards a Social Contract for the Olympic Games *Olympika* 1 (1): 154–167.

Krüger, A. (1993) Book review of J. Boix & A. Espada *El deporte del poder: vida y milagro de Juan Antonio Samaranch* (Madrid: Ediciones temas de hoy, 1991), In *The International Journal of Sports History*, 10, August: 291–293.

Law, C. (1994) *Urban Tourism* London: Mansell.

Lenskyj, H. (2002) *The Best Olympics Ever? Social impacts of Sydney 2000* Albany, NY: SUNY Press.

Lenskyj, H. (2000) *Inside the Olympic Industry: Power Politics and Activism* Albany, NY: SUNY Press.

Lowes, M. (2002) *Indy Dreams and Urban Nightmares* Toronto: Toronto University Press.

Madrigal, R., Bee, C. & LaBarge, M. (2005) Using the Olympics and FIFA World Cup to Enhance Global Brand Equity in J. Amis & T.B. Cornwell (eds) *Global Sport Sponsorship* Oxford: Berg, pp. 179–190.

Malfas, M., Theodoraki, E. & Houlihan, B. (2004) Impacts of the Olympic Games as mega-events *Municipal Engineer* 157 (ME3): 209–220. (available at http://www.extenza-eps.com/TELF/doi/pdf/10.1680/muen.157.3.209.49461).

Manzenreiter, W. & Horne, J. (2005) Public Policy, Sports Investments and Regional Development Initiatives in Contemporary Japan In J. Nauright and K. Schimmel (eds) *The Political Economy of Sport* London: Palgrave, pp. 152–182.

Marketing Matters (2001) *Marketing Matters: The Olympic Marketing Newsletter*, No. 19, July (available at http://multimedia.olympic.org/pdf/en_report_273.pdf).

Matheson, V. & Baade, R. (2003) Mega-Sporting Events in Developing Nations: Playing the Way to Prosperity? Working Papers 0404, College of the Holy Cross, Department of Economics (available at http://ideas.repec.org/p/hcx/wpaper/0404.html).

Nauright, J. (2004) Global games: culture, political economy and sport in the globalised world of the 21st century In *Third World Quarterly* 25(7): 1325–1336.

Nogawa, H. (2004) An international comparison of the motivations and experiences of volunteers at the 2002 World Cup in W. Manzenreiter and J. Horne (eds) *Football Goes East: business, culture and the people's game in China, Japan and South Korea* London: Routledge pp. 222–242.

Pociello, C. (ed.) (1981) *Sports et Societe: approche socio-culturelle des pratiques* Paris: Editions Vigot.

Preuss, H. (2004) *The Economics of Staging the Olympics: A Comparison of the Games 1972–2008* Cheltenham: Edward Elgar.

Ritzer, G. (1993) *The McDonaldization of Society*, Newbury Park, Ca: Pine Forge.

Robertson, R. (1992) *Globalization: social theory and global culture* London: Sage.

Roberts, K. (2004) *The Leisure Industries* London: Palgrave.

Roche, M. (2000) *Mega-events and modernity* London: Routledge.

Scambler, G. (2005) *Sport and Society: history, power and culture* Maidenhead: Open University Press.

Shilling, C. (1993) *The Body and Social Theory* London: Sage.

Smart, B. (2005) *The Sport Star: Modern sport and the cultural economy of sporting celebrity* London: Sage.

Sugden, J. & Tomlinson, A. (2002) International power struggles in the governance of world football: the 2002 and 2006 World Cup bidding wars In J. Horne & W. Manzenreiter (eds) *Japan, Korea and the 2002 World Cup* London: Routledge, pp. 56–70.

Syme, G., Shaw, B., Fenton, D. & Mueller, W. (1989) *The Planning and Evaluation of Hallmark Events* Aldershot: Avebury.

Swart, K. & Bob, U. (2004) The seductive discourse of development: the Cape Town 2004 Olympic bid *Third World Quarterly* Vol. 25, No. 7: pp. 1311–1324.

Tomlinson, A. (2004) Pierre Bourdieu and the Sociological Study of Sport: Habitus, Capital and Field in R. Giulianotti ed. *Sport and modern social theorists* Basingstoke: Palgrave pp. 161–172

Tomlinson, A. & Young, C. (eds). (2005) *National Identity and Global Sports Events* Albany, NY: SUNY Press.

UK Sport (2004) *Measuring Success 2* London: UK Sport.

UK Sport (1999) *Measuring Success* London: UK Sport.

Vázquez Montalbán, M. (1990/1992) *Barcelonas* London: Verso.

Veal, A. J. & Toohey, K. (2005) *The Olympic Games: A bibliography* Sydney: School of Leisure, Sport and Tourism, University of Technology, Sydney, available at http://www.business.uts.edu.au/lst/downloads/olympic_bib_update2.pdf

Vigor, A., Mean, M. & Tims, C. (eds) (2004) *After the Gold Rush: A sustainable Olympics for London* London: Institute for Public Policy Research (IPPR)/Demos.

Whitson, D. (2004) Bringing the world to Canada: 'the periphery of the centre' In *Third World Quarterly* Vol. 25, No. 7: pp. 1215–1232.

Whannel, G. (2002) *Sports Media Stars* London: Routledge.

Witt, S. (1988) Mega events and mega attractions. In *Tourism Management* 9 (1): 76–77.

Young, K. & Wamsley, K. (eds) (2005) *Global Olympics: Historical and sociological studies of the modern games* Oxford: Elsevier.

Internet sites

http://www.cohre.org/downloads/Achieving_Housing_for_All.pdf – The Centre on Housing Rights and Evictions (COHRE).

http://www.olympic.org/uk/index_uk.asp – The official website of the Olympic movement.

Part 1
Sports Mega-Events, Modernity and Capitalist Economies

Mega-events and modernity revisited: globalization and the case of the Olympics

Maurice Roche

In *Mega-Events and Modernity* (2000)[1] I reviewed the history, politics and sociology of the two great popular cultural mega-event genres at the heart of 19th and 20th century international public culture, namely Worlds Fairs or Expos and Olympic Games. The genres were analysed in relation to the growth of national and global dimensions of cultural organization in modernity. This chapter provides an opportunity to reflect on the themes and interests in that study. In particular it allows for some reflections on the relevance of 'modernity' understood as 'globalization' for mega-events, a theme which was undeveloped in the book. In order to explore the Olympic sport mega-event as a significant case of globalization, the chapter focuses on its mediated and media-event aspects.

Introduction

Understanding globalization processes and dynamics, and thus the potential for 'global society', is one of the greatest social scientific challenges of our period; and controlling globalization, or indeed even steering it, through the development of forms of global governance, is one of the greatest political challenges we face in the 21st century. The urgency and scale of these challenges has been tragically underscored in recent times by the Islamic extremist terror attacks on the USA on September 11th, 2001, and by the violence of the wars and further terrorism unleashed by this event. 'Globalization' is a relatively recently developed concept in social scientific discourse, referring to a social reality which is variously defined and politically contested. Nevertheless in one way or another in the social sciences we all now work in the shadow of the realities of globalization, and, whether explicitly or implicitly, in relation to the analysis of globalization as a distinctive intellectual paradigm. This is as true in sport and Olympic studies, as it is in academic studies in all other sectors of contemporary society and culture. This chapter aims to reflect on this situation from the perspective of an interest in sport mega-events and the Olympics in particular.

Among other things it asks what the study of sport mega-events and the Olympics has got to learn from the study of globalization. But equally it asks what the general study of globalization and of the development of global society has got to learn from the study of sport mega-events and the Olympics.

To explore these concerns the discussion takes three main steps. The first section considers two alternative interpretations of the concept of globalization relevant to the understanding of global sport mega-events, namely 'basic' and 'complex' perspectives. The second section considers the Olympics as a globally mediated (particularly a televised) event. And the final section considers aspects of the new research agenda facing the international social scientific community in understanding contemporary sport mega-events such as the Olympics as global media events.

Sport, the Olympics and globalization

To preface the discussion we can briefly note some relevant comments of Greek European Affairs Minister George Papandreou, speaking some years ago about the Athens 2004 Olympics which his government helped to organize. 'We hope to revive some of the ancient traditions, bringing in a cultural aspect which is very important, but also bringing in the 'Olympic Truce'. In a new century, where we live in the global village, the Olympic Games is the one event which brings people together in the world. Not just governments, but citizens of the world, and the man in the street through television and the media in this one local festival' (Papandreou, 1998, quoted in Maguire, 1999: 144).

Understandably in relation to an Olympic Games to be held in the historic city of Athens, Papandreou pointed to the deep Hellenic and European cultural and civilizational legacy from which the modern Olympic movement draws. In addition, however, he pointed to the present and to the relevance to the 21st century of what are historically relatively recent, late 20th century, developments and legacies in the modern Olympics, notably the global televising of the Games and the Olympic Truce project. In doing so he characterized the present social context of the Olympics in global society terms, as a 'global village' in which people are 'citizens of the world'. This chapter aims to review and to reflect on the Olympics as a globally mediated event, in relation to the broader context of the coterminous development of global society in our times through processes of globalization.

I share the analytic view of those who believe that, for good or ill, a distinctive global level of social organization and governance is beginning to emerge as we enter the 21st century, even if this is ideologically contested by neo-local and anti-globalization forces, and even if it is currently weak, fitful and uneven. From a normative perspective it seems to me that more global organization and governance, albeit of a democratic and socially responsible kind, are very much needed. This is not least in order to build the capacity to protect an increasingly threatened global environment and also to promote and to begin to give substance to the universalism embodied in the values of peace, human rights and social justice. The fact of globalization sets the terms of reference for any credible contemporary analysis of the combination of facts and ideals involved in cultural movements such as the Olympics. So what guides my review and reflection on the Olympic movement, here and elsewhere, is the problem of how constructively to interpret the Olympic movement's long-standing if often blemished idealism, particularly given the adaptive capacity it has always appeared to possess throughout the 20th century and which it is currently displaying again in the contemporary era of globalization.

Sport studies, media studies and other hybrid sub-disciplinary offspring such as media-sport studies, have traditionally taken the nation-state and national identity as a key point of reference and context. This is not surprising since the modern mass press and mass sports, together with, of course, the modern Olympic movement, emerged as part of a wave of 'invented traditions' (Hobsbawm, 1983; Roche, 2000a) in popular culture associated with nation-building at the end of the 19th century. In recent years, however, we have seen a new wave of sport and media-sport studies which show a developed 'post-national' awareness of the global-level and globalization processes as well as the nation-state level as key social contexts, and which illustrate the importance of this global theme in research and analysis[2]. Understandably, given the global aspirations of the events they analyse, this awareness of global society and globalization, is also present in Olympic studies and in football World Cup studies[3]. While sport and Olympic studies, however, are becoming more concerned to study globalization, mainstream globalization analysis has yet to discover sport as a relevant social phenomenon. With the exception of a very few writers who occasionally made passing reference to the global cultural significance of the Olympics (eg, Robertson, 1992: 179; Lechner & Boli, 2005: ch.1), globalization theorists seem to have had a blind spot when it comes to international sport culture. Reference to international sport and the Olympics is notably absent from many major analyses of globalization and of global culture[4]. In addition, seminal studies of globalization in relation to the media also, curiously, have little or nothing to say about the distinctive global mediatisation involved in the televising of major sport and Olympic events[5]. More of an academic dialogue is evidently needed between sport and Olympic studies on the one hand and globalization studies on the other, and hopefully this chapter might, among other things, make a small contribution to promoting this.

From a sociological perspective the notion of 'society' can be said, among other things, to refer to the experiential, interactional and institutional differentiation and interconnection of the economic, cultural and political dimensions and spheres of community life, particularly, but not exclusively, as exemplified in the modern nation-state form of community life. The notion of 'global society' and the processes of globalization which can be argued to be promoting it in our times can thus be analysed as having distinctive economic, cultural and political dimensions. Contemporary globalization is being particularly driven by the uneven but interconnected techno-economic dynamics of capitalist market-building and of science-based technological change. These dynamics are evidently influential in contemporary sport culture generally in terms of such factors as the incessant pressures of commercialization and medi-atization, and also the incessant development and application of performance-enhancing medical and material technologies. For the purposes of this chapter, however, I will focus more on the cultural and political dimensions of global-ization rather than the techno-economic dimension. So in considering Olympic Games events as being, among other things, globally mediated through televi-sion, my emphasis will be on understanding the Olympics as an element in the development of global culture.

A common view of 'globalization' in academic, political and public dis-courses and also in the academic discussions noted above is what I will refer to as the 'basic globalization' perspective. This involves some or all of a set of four main assumptions or theses. Firstly this view assumes that globalization is a deterministic process (involving the techno-economic dynamics noted above) which can be barely resisted by social and political organizations such as nation-states. Secondly it assumes that it requires the promotion of standardization and uniformity in all spheres of life. Thirdly, in addition and related to these two factors, it assumes that through the impacts of mass communications and trans-port technologies, globalization involves a historically unprecedented experience of 'one world' and of 'compression' of social space and time. Fourthly it assumes that globalization impacts are mainly felt at the national rather than sub- or trans-national levels.

This provides one perspective from which to consider the changing social context and role of the Olympics. This perspective implies a view of the Olympics which emphasizes such things as: the deterministic influences of techno-economic change on the Olympics, the Olympics as a cultural carrier of these globalising forces and a disseminator of a standardizing and uniform form of sport culture, the Olympic Games events themselves as involving the periodic compression of social space-time and the promotion of 'one world' awareness, and the impacts of the globalising features of the Olympics particularly on host nations, but also on international society as a world of participating nations. No doubt each of the assumptions in this perspective has some grounds in reality and some application to the understanding of the social nature, impacts and legacies of the Olympics. In this chapter, however, I want to suggest that globalization is a more complex process, and to argue that the social legacy and adaptive potential of the Olympics need to be understood in these more complex terms.

Generally what we can call the 'complex globalization' perspective suggests that, firstly, as against the techno-economic determinism thesis, globalization also involves the possibility for collective agency and influence by political and cultural collectivities such as nations and international organizations and move-ments. Secondly as against the standardization thesis, this perspective suggests that globalization can also involve differentiation and particularization. Sometimes this is referred to as 'glocalization' in recognition of the idea that localities like cities can connect more strongly with global economic and cultural circuits, and thus be more strongly globalized, by emphasizing and building up their 'unique place' characteristics, as for instance in relation to the global tourism industry. Thirdly, as against the time-space compression thesis, this perspective suggests that globalization can also involve the reconstruction of temporal and spatial distance and differences. Finally, as against the prioritization of national-level impacts, the complex globalization perspective suggesting that globalization impacts and collective agency response to them, can also be seen to operate at sub-national levels, eg, cities and city-regions, and trans-national levels, eg, world regions and their organization, such as the European Union (Telo eds., 2001; Schirm, 2002; Garnet, 2004; possibly also continental spheres influenced by historical 'civilizational' – eg, religious – differences, Huntington, 2002) as well as at national level. The new global social constellations being formed by complex globalization (eg, by the glocalization of social spaces and places and by the multi-layering of levels of governance and social organization (Brenner, 1999) provide reference points, for instance, for currently influential images and theories of global society as a multi-polar 'network society' which attempt to address, grasp and model this complexity (eg, Castells, 1996)[6].

This chapter suggests that the differences between the basic and complex perspectives on globalization are useful terms of reference when attempting to understand the Olympics in relation to contemporary social change. Also it suggests that the social significance and role in global society of the Olympic Games, both as a mass mega-event phenomenon and as an international movement, is better seen in terms of the complex rather than the basic globalization perspectives. That is the Olympics are best seen, albeit against a background of basic globalization processes, in terms of more complex globalization processes of differentiation and agency – particularly time and space differentiation, and particularly through the agency, individual and collective, of Olympic media audiences, host cities and the movement itself as a corporate political actor.

Olympic television and 'the global village'

Sport and Olympic culture (particularly televised international sport events) provide a special and arguably unique sphere and system of social organization and of cultural events and exchanges in which some of the international, transnational and universal dimensions of human society in the contemporary period can be experienced in dramatic, memorable and significantly trans-linguistic forms of communication both by performers and by media spectators. Sport mega-events in the contemporary period, in particular the two leading examples of the Olympic Games and the football World Cup competition – because they have been regularly televised 'live' to hundreds of millions, sometimes billions, of people in most of the world's nations since the advent of

31

satellite communications and particularly since the early 1980s – are also, by definition, 'media events' (Dayan & Katz, 1992). As such, for at least a generation they have given a tangible reality to the well known concept, first introduced in the 1960s by the legendary media analyst Marshall McLuhan (albeit inappropriately given television's technical limitations at the time), of 'the global village' (McLuhan, 1960).

The Olympic movement discourse of 'Olympism' involves the communication and promotion of universalistic ideals about peace and education. Mass public acceptance of such normative universalism may or may not be achieved. Whether it is or not, the simultaneous world-wide mass spectatorships involved in mediated sport mega-events like the Olympics are sociological realities. They create a unique cultural space and provide unrivalled opportunities to dissolve spatial and temporal distance, to participate in a notional global community, and to promote, albeit transitorily but recurrently, individual and collective experiences of 'globality' or 'one world' awareness[7]. There are no comparable opportunities for ceremonial and celebratory televisual evocations of 'globality' in conventional international politics around institutions such as the United Nations, which is possibly why the UN has been generally warm and positive in its relationship with the Olympic Movement in recent years (Roche, 2000: ch.7). While there are periodic international collective experiences in major acts of terrorism, wars, disasters and other such events these are typically negative and frightening, unpredictable and rare. Television systems remain significantly national in content and there is very little in the international televisual 'global village' to compare with the positive and celebratory, predictably recurrent and relatively frequent character of sport mega-events such as the Olympic Games as media events.

The televising and international broadcasting of Olympic Games events, at least in the last two decades, arguably produces special periodic instances of a 'global village' in which 'the whole world watches' games played on the 'global commons'. As we noted earlier in Papandreou's comments about the Athens 2004 Olympics, the 'global village' concept appears in contemporary Olympic policy discourse. Olympic TV, seen as such a global 'media event', could be said to illustrate elements of the 'basic globalization' perspective. That is, from this perspective, firstly the events can be said, on the one hand, to promote universalistic values (Olympic values) and, on the other hand, to promote cultural standardization both directly (eg, the spread of international sport organization and 'sport (consumer) culture'), and indirectly (through their commercialization) through the marketing vehicle they provide for global brands and consumer culture (particularly, although not exclusively, American versions of these things, as elements of 'Coca-Colonization' and 'McDonaldization', Ritzer, 1998, 1999). Secondly, from this perspective, the global broadcasting of the 'live' Olympic media-event can be said to exemplify space-time compression. That is, with due allowance for over-emphatic simplification, 'the whole world' can be said to watch 'the same thing at the same time', and thus in some sense to be in communication or at least to co-exist and be co-present in 'the same (mediated) place' at 'the same (mediated) time', a global 'here and now'. What light does Olympic TV research throw on these claims?[8]

In favour of the basic globalization perspective's 'standardization' thesis the structure and content of Olympic Games, and thus the content of Olympic TV broadcasts, have evidently come to have highly repetitive and ritualistic features. Olympic opening and closing ceremonies and medal presentation ceremonies are tightly controlled and rule-governed by the IOC and its Charter; they are seen as valued rituals and are subject to a traditional ceremonial choreography which Olympic TV programming must represent. Nevertheless every Games is also, in important respects, a unique event in which the standardized elements are interpreted and represented in ways which are particular to the host nation and city. Also, in favour of the space-time compression thesis, no doubt literally 'the whole world' does not watch the live televising of, say, the Opening Ceremony of the Olympic Games. Nevertheless it is reasonable to acknowledge that – even allowing for some exaggerations in the estimates – a large and rising proportion of the world's population does do so, (estimated at around 1 billion for the Seoul and Barcelona Games in 1988 and 1992, 2 billion for the Atlanta Games in 1996, and 3.5 billion for the Sydney and Athens Olympics). Of course, that said, the quality of the audience experiences of these mass publics – how people view these broadcasts and what they make of them – is another matter. As with the unequal distribution of viewing (and of access to viewing) between nations and world regions, it cannot be read off from these aggregate quantitative data.

Substantial and systematic empirical media case studies were conducted into the Olympic Games of LA 1984 (Rothenbuhler, 1988, 1989), Seoul 1988 (Larson & Park, 1993; also Rivenburgh, 1992), and Barcelona 1992 (Spa, Rivenburgh & Larson, 1995). Less comprehensive and more specialist media studies were conducted on the 1994 Lillehammer Winter Olympics (Puijk ed., 1996; Puijk, 1999), the 2000 Sydney Olympics (Rowe, 2000; Wilson, 2000, 2002) and the 2002 Salt Lake City Winter Olympics (Friedrich, Mikos & Stiehler, 2002). In addition the IOC and UNESCO have supported research conferences and colloquia on the topic of the Olympics and the media (eg, Jackson & McPhail, eds., 1989). Each of the main empirical studies indicated has its strengths and weaknesses not least in terms of their coverage of the three main dimensions of media processes – production, content and reception. The Los Angeles study was mainly a piece of audience research into responses to Olympic TV, while the Seoul and Barcelona studies mainly focused on analyses of the production and content dimensions of Olympic TV (although the Barcelona study also contained a limited amount of audience research). Each of these studies, perhaps particularly the Seoul study, generated some interesting theoretical interpretations and reflections relevant to globalization analysis and media-sport analysis which have been reviewed elsewhere (eg, Roche, 2000: ch.6, 2002c). Among other things they suggest that there are significant differences in national broadcasters' production of Olympic TV programming and in audience responses as between different nations and other differential social contexts[9]. To these extents the world which is constituted in the periodic and recurrent mass watching of Olympic TV is not particularly well captured in the image of a unitary 'global village'.

Generally speaking these Olympic TV studies tend to support the argument, as against the basic globalization view of standardization, that Olympic TV retains important differentiating and particularising aspects. Not unsurprisingly some of these aspects relate to the role of nations and nationalism in the Olympic movement, and to the opportunities Games media events provide periodically to re-assert and re-configure national identities and differences, albeit in the context of an otherwise globalising world order. World regional inequalities are also noted in Olympic TV studies as relevant differentiating factors. Also, connected with the differentiating and particularizing characteristics of nationalism and world regional inequalities, the Olympic TV studies tend to suggest that to characterize the experience of watching 'live' Olympic TV in terms of 'one world', global co-presence and other aspects of space-time compression misrepresents the diversity and complexity of that experience. In terms of both of these aspects Olympic TV is better understood in the terms of a 'complex globalization' rather than a 'basic globalization' perspective. And this is also the case in terms of the other complex globalization features noted earlier, namely 'agency' (here nationalistic agency) as against determinism, and the 'glocalisation' (national-level and also world regional) that Olympic Games events involve. That said, nevertheless some kind of shareable global community experience, some sense of simultaneous co-presence (consistent with the national and other differentials and particularities noted in the studies), can be said to be evoked in Olympic TV. Arguably this is connected with a sense of collective memory and history, the intertwining of national and global narratives, which has come to be associated with the Olympics in the perceptions of publics world-wide.

New agendas in global sport mega-event research

In analysing and researching sport mega-events our interest may lie either in using the sport mega-event field to contribute to globalization analysis or, less ambitiously, in developing this field further for its own sake. Either way the research noted in this chapter indicates significant gaps and needs in our information and knowledge-base. These issues ought to be addressed if the field of Olympic and international sport research is to develop adequately from a sociological and global society-oriented perspective. This is particularly so in that dimension of it concerned with sport mega-events as media-events and as mediatized forms of cultural experience. If we are to seriously face up to the challenges of Olympic research in our period, and contribute to the understanding of the Olympics as an event in a changing global culture, we need a qualitatively new and improved level of cross-national studies, particularly media studies.

Ideally this would involve multi-national networks and teams, given that the scale of the empirical work is beyond the capabilities of isolated scholars and nationally located researchers. It would need to involve systematically comparative methodologies both quantitative and qualitative, and to be conducted over medium-term time-frames (eg, spanning at least two Summer Games events). The research team coordinated by Miguel de Moragas Spa and his colleagues through the Olympic Studies Centre at Barcelona has provided an indication of the way ahead (Moragas Spa, Rivenburgh & Larson, 1995). Their study of media aspects of the production, content and reception of the 1992 Barcelona Olympics was pioneering in this respect. It set new standards and pointed the way. But, as the team themselves were the first to admit, this study had its own limitations (including perhaps the fact that it was restricted to a study of only one Games event). In any case it was conducted over a decade ago and nothing like it seems to have been attempted at Atlanta in 1996 or for Sydney in 2000 or Athens 2004. In our era of globalization, international research communities in such socially significant and growing areas as sport and media studies surely need to be doing better than this.

In terms of the contemporary mediation of sport events, and in addition to television studies, we also need to take full account of the socio-cultural significance and changes involved in the diffusion of new media technology, particularly the Internet (Castells, 2001). The internet at its current stage of development and usage is not capable of creating a 'global village'-type of impact in relation to mega sport events comparable with live global television. This is partly because the main current platform for internet access, personal computers, while they are widely diffusing in the global 'North', are not widely diffused in the global 'South'. It is also partly because the quality of 'video streaming' available on PCs is technologically limited and not comparable with TV images unless, which is still a minority case in many Northern countries, the personal computers are run using high capacity broadband cable networks. And finally it is partly because mega-event franchising governing bodies, notably the IOC and FIFA, have restricted internet companies' capacities to 'netcast' live events for fear of undermining the exclusivity arrangements reached with their main paymasters in major television networks, and for which these networks are prepared to pay premium prices. Since each of these conditions, however, is likely to be subject to significant change in the short- to medium-term future, it is clear that time is beginning to run out on satellite television technology's exclusive capacity to create a version of 'the global village' at mega sport events. The internet potentially offers more individually-tailored and interactive experiences of 'the same' global event. This will undoubtedly change the research agenda facing the international sport and Olympic studies community into the medium term future in many ways. In the terms outlined in this chapter, this is likely to involve shifting it further towards an appreciation of the heuristic relevance of a complex rather than a basic globalization paradigm.

The discussion in this chapter suggests that a new agenda needs to be developed concerned with the changing nature of the 'global village' achieved by the world-wide televising of the Olympic Games (together with its additional dissemination by 'video streaming' in the related medium of the internet). We need to recognize and address the challenges of the gaps and needs which currently exist in this key sector of Olympic and international major sport event research, both for their own sake. We also need it for the sake of decisively improving the quality of evidence-based sport and Olympic policy-making in future, given the well-known inadequacies of the decision-making processes which have historically tended to dominate in the mega-event field (Roche, 1992a, b, 1994, 2000 passim), namely intuitive decision-taking and policy-making, whether of the 'visionary' or 'blind gamble' kind. In my view the time is getting overdue for the international sport and Olympic studies community to begin to develop ambitious and internationally coordinated plans for medium-term duration projects studying globalization-relevant aspects of future Olympic Games events.

How well placed is the research community to meet these kind of challenges and to engage in research with these sorts of characteristics? Fairly good bases of official information for each Games event have been produced by each Olympic organizing committee in their main post-event reports and also in their other information provision activities before, during and after the event. This has been accumulating as an information resource in the Olympic movement for both event organizers and academics. Also from a journalistic perspective, there is often good conventional media reporting and analysis using event organizers' 'on-the-record' information services, together with some notable if inevitably controversial occasional exercises in investigative journalism undertaken without much assistance from official or 'on-the-record' sources (Simson and Jennings, 1992; Jennings, 1996; Jennings with Sambrook, 2000). There is the theoretically under-informed and often methodologically questionable tradition of sport event economic impact studies which cities have often used to guide them in bidding for and planning sport mega-events (Roche, 1992a). Some action has been undertaken by the IOC to improve the quality of this kind of research incorporated in the plans of cities bidding for the Olympic Games and the knowledge and technology transfer between current and future host cities (eg, see Dubi, Hug & van Griethysen, 2003; also Moragas Spa, Kennet & Puig, eds., 2003 in general). In addition there are the media-sport studies we have noted in this chapter. Finally there are distinct and valuable traditions of individual inquiry and scholarship in the fields of Olympic and international sports studies, particularly from historical and ethnographic perspectives. All of these sorts of sources and others have at last begun to be accumulated in the growing international network of specialist Olympic research centres such as those in Canada, the USA, Australia, Spain and also recently in the UK. All of that being said, however, it seems to me that currently we seem to be somewhat under-resourced and unprepared to face the challenges of longitudinal, international and interdisciplinary research indicated above which are necessary given the evolving, global, mediated and multi-dimensional characteristics of such sport mega-events as the Olympic Games.

The kind of research effort outlined earlier would, no doubt, need support from relevant national and international (eg, the UN and the EU) social science research funding authorities, from the IOC, from Games event organizing committees and perhaps also from the major media companies involved. Progress in achieving this particular 'wish list' unfortunately does not seem to have been a feature of the Athens Olympic Games held in 2004, just as it wasn't a feature of Atlanta 1996 or Sydney 2000. It would be a sad comment, however, on the capacity and aspirations of the international scholarly and research communities operating in this area of contemporary social and cultural studies if they were unable to make at least some progress in this direction if not by the time of the Beijing Olympics in 2008 then at least by the time of the London Olympics in 2012.

Conclusion

In this chapter I have taken the position that the development of a global level of social organization through processes of globalization is one of the dominant sociological realities and political challenge of our times and of the 21st century, just as the development of the nation-state level was the dominant reality for much of the 19th and 20th centuries. In earlier periods the social role of the Olympic Games events, of the Olympic event cycle and of the movement which organizes them, needed to be understood in relation to, among other things, the sociology and politics of nations, particularly the nation-building of host nations, and the motivations of participant nations in terms of the presentation and recognition of national identities. Comparably in the contemporary period the social roles, and thus the potential social legacies, of the Olympics, need to be seen – in addition to their national implications for nation states – in relation to the contemporary realities of globalization and global society-building. On this basis the chapter aimed briefly to review and reflect on aspects of the Olympics which are relevant to this, specifically the emergence of the Olympics as a globally mediated event since the 1980s.

Two frameworks were briefly outlined for understanding contemporary globalization processes and for discussing these legacies, namely perspectives which conceptualised globalization in 'basic' and 'complex' terms. These discussions suggested that the social significance and role in global society of the Olympic Games, both as a mass mega-event phenomenon and as an international movement, is better seen in terms of the complex rather than the basic globalization perspective. That is the Olympics are best seen, albeit against a background of basic globalization processes, in terms of more complex globalization processes of differentiation and agency – particularly time and space differentiation (as against simplistic time-space compression assumptions), and particularly through the agency, individual and collective, of Olympic media audiences, host cities and the movement itself as a corporate political actor (as against simplistic deterministic assumptions). This discussion provided the basis both for an outline of some key aspects of the new agenda facing Olympic mega-event research in the contemporary period, and also for some proposals to begin implementing this agenda in a new generation of internationally coordinated sport mega-event research projects.

Notes

1 Roche 2000; also see 1992a, 1992b, 1994, 1999, 2001a, 2001b, 2002a, 2002b, 2003, 1998 ed.
2 eg, Rowe *et al.* 1994, Rowe 1996, 1999, Maguire 1999, Boyle & Haynes 2000, Miller *et al.* 2001, Brookes 2002.
3 For Olympic studies see eg, Larson & Park 1993, Roche 2000a, 2002c, Rowe 2000, also IOC 1996; and for football World Cup studies see eg, Sugden & Tomlinson 1998, Giulianotti 1999, Horne & Manzenreiter 2002, Sandvoss 2003.
4 On globalization see eg, Albrow 1996, Castells 1996, Hirst & Thompson 1996, Spybey 1997, Held *et al.* 1999, Bauman 1999, Giddens 1999, Beck 2000, Waters 2001; on global culture see Lechner & Boli 2005, Tomlinson 1999, Featherstone ed. 1990. For an IOC view of globalization see IOC 1996: ch. 1.
5 eg, Barker 1997, Herman & McChesney 1997.
6 For fuller discussion of these alternative globalization analyses and frameworks, and of the role of sport mega-events in them, see Roche 2000:ch. 8 and 2002c.
7 For analyses of the socio-historical significance of 'globality' or awareness of the world as a singular place rather than as an aggregate of spatially and politically distinct and separate places and territorially-based nation-state societies see Robertson 1992 and Albrow 1996.
8 For further discussion beyond this chapter see Roche 2000 ch.6 and 2002c.
9 For further discussion of media aspects of the Olympics see MacAloon 1984, 1989, Real 1996a, 1996b, 1996c, 1996d, 1998 and Tomlinson 1996.

References

Albrow, M. (1996) *The Global Age*. Cambridge: Polity.
Barker, C. (1997) *Global Television*. Oxford. Blackwell.
Bauman, Z. (1999) *Globalization: The Human Consequences*. Cambridge: Polity.
Beck, U. (2000) *What is Globalization?* Cambridge: Polity.
Brookes, R. (2002) *Representing Sport*. London: Arnold.
Boyle, R. & Haynes, R. (2000) *Power Play: Sport, Media and Popular Culture*. Harlow: Pearson Education.
Brenner, N. (1999) 'Globalization as reterritorialisation: The re-scaling of urban governance in the European Union', *Urban Studies* 36 (3): 431–451.
Castells, M. (1996) *The Information Age, Vol.1 – The Rise of Network Society*. Oxford: Blackwell.
Castells, M. (2001) *The Internet Galaxy*. Oxford: Oxford University Press.
Dayan, D. & Katz, E. (1992) *Media Events*. London: Harvard University Press.
Dubi, C., Hug, P-A. & van Griethysen, P. (2003) 'Olympic Games management; From candidature to the final evaluation, an integrated management approach', in M. Moragas, C. Kennett & N. Puig (eds.) *The Legacy of the Olympics Games 1984–2000*. Lausanne: IOC, 403–414.
Featherstone, M. (ed.) (1990) *Global Culture: Nationalism, Globalization and Modernity*. London: Sage.
Friedrich, J., Mikos, L. & Stiehler, H-J. (2002) 'Salt Lake City Games 2002: Olympic rituals and intercultural frames in the age of the sport-media complex'. Unpublished paper presented at the IAMCR conference, 22nd–26th July, Barcelona.

Garnet (2004) (The GARNET project), EC Framework 6, 'Global Governance, Regionalisation and Regulation: the role of the EU', coordinated by the Centre for the Study of Globalization and Regionalisation, Warwick University, near Coventry, UK.

Giddens, A. (1999) *Runaway World: How Globalization is Reshaping our Lives.* Cambridge: Polity.

Giulianotti, R. (1999) *Football. A Sociology of the Global Game.* Cambridge: Polity.

Held, D. *et al.* (1999) *Global Transformations.* Cambridge: Polity.

Herman, E. & McChesney, R. (1997) *The Global Media*, London, Cassell.

Hirst, P. & Thompson, G. (1999) *Globalization in Question.* Cambridge: Polity.

Hobsbawm, E. (1983) 'Mass-producing traditions: Europe, 1870–1914' in Hobsbawm, E. & Ranger, T. (eds) *The Invention of Tradition*, Cambridge: Cambridge University Press, pp. 263–307.

Horne, J. & Manzenreiter, W. (2002) 'The World Cup and television football', in J. Horne and W. Manzenreiter (eds) *Japan, Korea and the 2002 World Cup.* London: Routledge, pp. 195–212.

Huntington, S. (2002) *The Clash of Civilizations and the Remaking of World Order.* London: Free Press.

IOC (1996) *The International Olympic Committee – One Hundred Years. Vol. 3: 1972–1996.* Lausanne: IOC.

Jackson, R. & McPhail, T. (eds) (1989) *The Olympic Movement and the Mass Media.* Calgary: Hurford Enterprises.

Jennings, A. (1996) *The New Lords of the Rings.* London: Simon and Schuster.

Jennings, A. with Sambrook, C. (2000) *The Great Olympic Swindle.* London: Simon and Schuster.

Larson, J. & Park, H. (1993) *Global Television and the Politics of the Seoul Olympics.* Oxford: Westview Press.

Lechner, F. & Boli, J. (2005) *World Culture.* Oxford: Blackwell.

MacAloon, J. (1984) 'Olympic Games and the theory of spectacle in modern societies', in J. MacAloon (1984) *Rite, Drama, Festival, Spectacle.* Philadelphia: The Institute of Human Issues, 246–50.

MacAloon, J. (1989) 'Festival, Ritual and TV', in R. Jackson and T. McPhail (eds.) *The Olympic Movement and the Mass Media.* Calgary: Hurford Enterprises, Part 6, 21–40.

Maguire, J. (1999) *Global Sport.* Cambridge: Polity.

McLuhan, M. (1960) *Explorations in Communication*, ed. E.S. Carpenter. Boston: Beacon Press.

Miller, T. *et al.* (2001) *Globalization and Sport.* London: Sage.

Moragas Spa, de, M., Rivenburgh, N. & Larson, J. (1995) *Television in the Olympics.* Luton: John Libbey Media.

Moragas Spa, de, M., Kennett, C. & Puig, N. (eds) (2003) *The Legacy of the Olympics Games 1984–2000.* Lausanne: IOC.

Puijk, R. (1999) 'Producing Norwegian culture for the domestic and foreign gaze: The Lillehammer Olympic opening ceremony', in A. Klausen (ed.) *Olympic Games as Performance and Public Event: The Case of the XVII Winter Olympic Games in Norway.* Oxford: Berghahn Books, 97–136.

Puijk, R. (ed.) (1996) *Global Spotlights on Lillehammer.* Luton: John Libbey Media.

Real, M. (1996a) *Exploring Media Culture.* London: Sage.

Real, M. (1996b) 'The postmodern Olympics: Technology and the commodification of the Olympic movement', *Quest* 48: 9–24.

Real, M. (1996c) 'Is television corrupting the Olympics? Media and the (post) modern games at age 100', *Television Quarterly* Summer: 2–12.

Real, M. (1996d) 'The televised Olympics from Atlanta: A look back and ahead', *Television Quarterly* Autumn: 9–12.

Real, M. (1998) 'Mediasport: Technology and the commodification of postmodern sport', in L. Wenner (ed.) *MediaSport.* London: Sage, pp. 14–26.

Ritzer, G. (1998) *The McDonaldization Thesis.* London: Sage.

Ritzer, G. (1999) *Enchanting a Disenchanted World: Revolutionizing the Means of Consumption.* London: Sage.

Rivenburgh, N. (1992) 'National image richness in US-televised coverage of South Korea during the Seoul Olympics', *Asian Journal of Communication* 2 (2): 1–39.

Robertson, R. (1992) *Globalization; Social Theory and Global Culture.* London: Sage.

Roche, M. (1992a) 'Mega-events and micro-modernization', *British Journal of Sociology* 43: 563–600.

Roche, M. (1992b) 'Mega-events and citizenship', *Vrijtijd en Samenleving* (Leisure and Society) 10 (4): 47–67.

Roche, M. (1994) 'Mega-events and urban policy', *Annals of Tourism Research* 21 (1): 1–19.

Roche, M. (1999) 'Mega-events, culture and modernity: Expos and the origins of public culture', *Cultural Policy* 5 (1): 1–31.

Roche, M. (2000) *Mega-Events and Modernity. Olympics and Expos in the Growth of Global Culture.* London: Routledge.

Roche, M. (2001a) 'Modernity, cultural events and the construction of charisma: Mass cultural events in the USSR in the interwar period', *Cultural Policy* 7 (3): 493–520.

Roche, M. (2001b) Book review of A. Klausen (ed.) *Olympic Games as performance and public event, Culture, Sport and Society* 4 (3).

Roche, M. (2002a) 'The Olympics and "global citizenship"', *Citizenship Studies* 6 (1): 165–181.

Roche, M. (2002b) 'The Europeanisation of football'. Unpublished paper, available from the author, Dept. Sociology, Sheffield University, Sheffield, UK.

Roche, M. (2002c) 'Olympic and sport mega-events as media-events. Developing the globalization paradigm'. Unpublished paper presented at 'The Olympics and Globalization', 6th International Symposium, International Centre for Olympic Studies, 17th–18th October, University of Western Ontario, Canada.

Roche, M. (2003) 'Mega-Events and time: On time structures in global society', *Time and Society* 12 (1): 99–126.

Roche, M. (ed.) (1998) *Sport, Popular Culture and Identity*. Aachen: Meyer & Meyer Verlag.

Rothenbuhler, E. (1988) 'The living room celebration of the Olympic Games', *Journal of Communication* 38 (4): 61–81.

Rothenbuhler, E. (1989) 'Values and symbols in orientations to the Olympics, *Critical Studies in Mass Communication* 6: 138–157.

Rowe, D. (1996) 'The global love-match: sport and television', *Media, Culture and Society* 18: 565–582.

Rowe, D. (1999) *Sport, Culture and the Media: The Unruly Trinity*. Buckingham: Open University Press.

Rowe, D. (2000) 'Global media events and the positioning of presence', *Media International Australia* Number 97, November, (special edition 'The Olympics: Media, Myth and Madness'): 11–22.

Rowe, D. *et al.* (1994) 'Global sport? Core concern and peripheral vision', *Media, Culture and Society* 16 (4): 661–675.

Sandvoss, C. (2003) *A Game of Two Halves: Television Football, Television and Globalization*. Routledge: London.

Schirm, S. (2002) *Globalization and the New Regionalism: Global Markets, Domestic Politics and Regional Cooperation*. Cambridge: Polity Press.

Simson, V. & Jennings, A. (1992) *The Lords of the Rings: Power, Money and Drugs in the Modern Olympics*. London: Simon & Schuster.

Spybey, T. (1997) *Globalization and World Society*. Cambridge: Polity.

Sugden, J. & Tomlinson, A. (1998) *FIFA and the Contest for World Football*. Polity: Cambridge.

Telo, M. (ed.) (2001) *European Union and New Regionalism*. Aldershot: Ashgate.

Tomlinson, A. (1996) 'Olympic spectacle: Opening ceremonies and some paradoxes of globalization', *Media, Culture and Society* 18 (4): 583–602.

Tomlinson, J. (1999) *Globalization and Culture*. Cambridge: Polity.

Waters, M. (2001) *Globalization*. Routledge: London

Wilson, H. (2000) 'Hosting the Olympic broadcast (Sydney 2000)', *Media International Australia* No. 97, November, (special edition 'The Olympics: Media, Myth and Madness'): 23–34.

Wilson, H. (2002) 'Studying the web: Lessons from the Sydney Olympics'. Unpublished paper presented at the IAMCR annual conference, 22nd–26th July, Barcelona.

The economic impact of major sports events: a review of ten events in the UK

Chris Gratton, Simon Shibli, and Richard Coleman

Introduction

Over recent years there has been a marked contrast between the discussions around the economic impact of major sports events in North America on the one hand and most of the rest of the world on the other. In the USA the sports strategies of cities in the USA have largely been based on infrastructure (stadium) investment for professional team sports, in particular, American football, baseball, basketball, and ice hockey. Over the last decade cities have offered greater and greater incentives for these professional teams to move from their existing host cities by offering to build a new stadium to house them. The teams sit back and let the host and competing cities bid up the price. They either move to the city offering the best deal or they accept the counter offer invariably put to them by their existing hosts. This normally involves the host city building a brand new stadium to replace the existing one which may only be ten or fifteen years old. The result is that at the end of the 1990s there were thirty major stadium construction projects in progress, around one-third of the total professional sports infrastructure, but over half of all professional teams in the USA have expressed dissatisfaction with their current facilities.

Baade (2003) argues that since 1987 approximately 80 per cent of the professional sports facilities in the United States will have been replaced or have undergone major renovation with the new facilities costing more than $19 billion in total, and the public providing $13.6 billion, or 71 per cent, of that amount. The use of taxpayers money to subsidize profit-making professional sports teams is justified on the basis that such investment of public money is a worthwhile investment since it is clearly outweighed by the stream of economic activity that is generated by having a professional sports team resident in the city. Such justifications are often backed up by economic impact studies that show that the spending of sports tourists in the host city more than justifies such a public subsidy. Crompton (1995, 2001) has illustrated that such studies have often been seriously methodologically flawed, and the real economic benefit of such visitor spending is often well below that specified in such studies. This is particularly the case given the need for such huge infrastructure investment needed to attract the professional teams.

In Europe, however, city sport strategies have concentrated more on attracting a series of major sports events, such as World or European Championships, again justified on the economic impact generated through hosting such events. Whereas many American sports economists (eg, Baade, 1996; Noll & Zimbalist, 1997; Coates & Humphreys, 1999) now consistently agree that studies show no significant direct economic impact on the host cities from the recent stadium developments, it is not so evident that European style hosting of major sports events is not economically beneficial to the host cities. This chapter looks at ten major sports events, all World or European Championships hosted by UK cities over recent years, all of which have been studied by the current authors. The difference from the North American situation is that these events move around from city to city in response to bids from potential host cities and in all ten cases did not require specific capital infrastructure investment to be staged but rather were staged in existing facilities. Before we look at these events, however, we briefly review the literature on the economic importance of major sports events. The biggest by far of such events is the summer Olympic Games, in particular in the infrastructure investment required to host the event, and the next section is devoted just to that event before the literature relating to all other major sports events is considered.

The economic importance of the summer Olympic Games

Despite the huge sums of money invested in hosting the summer Olympics, there has never been an economic impact study of the type described in this paper to assess the economic benefits of hosting the event. Kasimati (2003) summarized the potential long-term benefits to a city of hosting the summer Olympics: newly constructed event facilities and infrastructure, urban revival, enhanced international reputation, increased tourism, improved public welfare, additional employment, and increased inward investment. In practice, however, there is also a possible downside to hosting the event including: high construction costs of sporting venues and related other investments, in particular in transport infrastructure; temporary congestion problems; displacement of other tourists due to the event; and underutilized elite sporting facilities after the event which are of little use to the local population.

Kasimati (2003) analysed all impact studies of the summer Olympics from 1984 to 2004 and found, in each case, that the studies were done prior to the Games, were not based on primary data, and were, in general, commissioned by proponents of the Games. He found that the economic impacts were likely to be inflated since the studies did not take into account supply-side constraints such as investment crowding out, price increases due to resource scarcity, and the displacement of tourists who would have been in the host city had the Olympics not been held there. Although no proper economic impact study using primary data has ever been carried out for the summer Olympics, Preuss (2004) has produced a comprehensive analysis of the economics of the summer Olympics for every summer Olympics from Munich 1972 using secondary data, and employing a novel data transformation methodology which allows comparisons across the different Olympics.

Despite collecting a massive amount of secondary data, Preuss's conclusion on the estimation of the true economic impact of the summer Olympics is the same as Kasimati's: 'The economic benefit of the Games . . . is often overestimated in both publications and economic analyses produced by or for the OCOG [Organizing Committee of the Olympic Games] . . . multipliers tend to be too high and the number of tourists is estimated too optimistically' (Preuss, 2004: 290). Preuss, however, does make some strong conclusions from his analysis. He shows, for instance, that every summer Olympics since 1972 made an operational surplus that the OCOG can spend to benefit both national and international sport. Popular stories in the mass media relating to massive losses from hosting the Olympics have nothing to do with the Games' *operational* costs and revenues. Rather it is to do with the *capital infrastructure investments* made by host cities on venues, transport, accommodation and telecommunications. These are investments in capital infrastructure that have a life of possibly 50 years or more and yet many commentators count the full capital cost against the two to three weeks of the Games themselves. Preuss points out that in strict economic terms this is nonsense:

> it is impossible and even wrong to state the overall effect of different Olympics with a single surplus or deficit. The true outcome is measured in the infrastructural, social, political, ecological and sporting impacts a city and country receive from the Games. (Preuss, 2004: 26)

Estimating the true economic impact of a summer Olympic Games properly therefore requires a huge research budget in addition to the other costs associated with the Games. Research needs to start several years before the Olympics and continue several years after they have finished. So far nobody has been willing to fund such research. There is increasing research output, however, relating to other major sporting events.

The economic importance of other major sports events

The study of hallmark events or mega-events became an important area of the tourism and leisure literature in the 1980s. The economic benefits of such events have been the main focus of such literature, although broader based multidisciplinary approaches have been suggested (Hall, 1992; Getz, 1991). Within the area of mega-events, sports events have attracted a significant amount of attention. One of the first major studies in this area was the study of the impact of the 1985 Adelaide Grand Prix (Burns, Hatch & Mules, 1986). This was followed by an in-depth study of the 1988 Calgary Winter Olympics (Ritchie, 1984;

Ritchie & Aitken, 1984, 1985; Ritchie & Lyons, 1987, 1990; Ritchie & Smith, 1991).

Mules and Faulkner (1996) point out that hosting major sports events is not always an unequivocal economic benefit to the cities that host them. They emphasize that, in general, staging major sports events often results in the city authorities losing money even though the city itself benefits greatly in terms of additional spending in the city. They cite the example of the 1994 Brisbane World Masters Games which cost Brisbane A$2.8 million to put on but generated a massive A$50.6 million of additional economic activity in the state economy. Mules and Faulkner's basic point is that it normally requires the public sector to be involved in the role of staging the event and incurring these losses in order to generate the benefits to the local economy:

> This financial structure is common to many special events, and results in the losses alluded to above. It seems unlikely that private operators would be willing to take on the running of such events because of their low chance of breaking even let alone turning a profit. The reason why governments host such events and lose taxpayers' money in the process lies in spillover effects or externalities. (Mules & Faulkner, 1996: 110)

It is not a straightforward job, however, to establish a profit and loss account for a specific event. Major sports events require investment in new sports facilities and often this is paid for in part by central government or even international sports bodies. Thus, some of this investment expenditure represents a net addition to the local economy since the money comes in from outside. Also such facilities remain after the event has finished acting as a platform for future activities that can generate additional tourist expenditure (Mules & Faulkner, 1996).

Increasingly, sports events are part of a broader strategy aimed at raising the profile of a city and therefore success cannot be judged simply on a profit and loss basis. Often the attraction of events is linked to a re-imaging process and, in the case of many cities, is invariably linked to strategies of urban regeneration and tourism development (Bianchini & Schengel, 1991; Bramwell, 1995; Loftman & Spirou, 1996; Roche, 1994). Major events if successful have the ability to project a new image and identity for a city. The hosting of major sports events is often justified by the host city in terms of long-term economic and social consequences, directly or indirectly resulting from the staging of the event (Mules & Faulkner, 1996). These effects are primarily justified in economic terms, by estimating the additional expenditure generated in the local economy as the result of the event, in terms of the benefits injected from tourism-related activity and the subsequent re-imaging of the city following the success of the event (Roche, 1992).

Cities staging major sports events have a unique opportunity to market themselves to the world. Increasing competition between broadcasters to secure broadcasting rights to major sports events has led to a massive escalation in fees for such rights which, in turn, means broadcasters give blanket coverage at peak times for such events, enhancing the marketing benefits to the cities that stage them.

Methodology

The ten events under survey are detailed in Table 1. All but one of them, the 2002 World Snooker Championship (which was a contract for the host city, Sheffield), were studied as part of a UK Sport funded research project to estimate the economic impact of the events. UK Sport is the body responsible in the UK for a 'World Class Events Programme' that supports sports governing bodies in their attempts to bring major sports events to the UK. Financial support is provided from lottery funding for both the bidding process and the staging of the event if the bid is successful. Two of the events studies (the World Boxing Championships in Belfast, and the World Half-Marathon Championships in Bristol) were joint contracts with both UK Sport and the host cities (ie, Belfast and Bristol).

The ten studies featured in this chapter were conducted using essentially the same methodology. This, therefore, provides the added value of having a dataset in which the events are comparable. It is the results of cross event comparability and the issues arising from such comparisons upon which this chapter is

Table 1: *Major sports events surveyed in the U.K.*

Year	Event	Abbreviation	Host City
1997	World Badminton Championships	WBC	Glasgow
1997	European Junior Boxing Championships	EJBC	Birmingham
1997	European Junior Swimming Championships	EJSC	Glasgow
1998	European Short Course Swimming Championships	ESCSC	Sheffield
1999	European Show Jumping Championships	ESJC	Hickstead
1999	World Judo Championships	WJC	Birmingham
1999	World Indoor Climbing Championships	WICC	Birmingham
2001	World Amateur Boxing Championships	WABC	Belfast
2001	World Half Marathon Championships	WHM	Bristol
2002	World Snooker Championship	WSC	Sheffield

primarily concerned. The methodology employed in the economic impact studies was divided into ten stages, which can be summarized as follows:

- Quantify the proportion of respondents who live in the host city and those who are from elsewhere;
- Group respondents by their role in the event, eg, spectators, competitors, media, officials etc;
- Establish basic characteristics of visitors, eg, where they live and composition of the party;
- Determine the catchment area according to local, regional, national or international respondents;
- Quantify the number of visitors staying overnight in the host city and the proportion of these making use of commercial accommodation;
- Quantify how many nights those using commercial accommodation will stay in the host city and what this accommodation is costing per night;
- Quantify for those staying overnight (commercially or otherwise) and day visitors, the daily spend in the host city on six standard expenditure categories;
- Quantify what people have budgeted to spend in the host city and for how many people such expenditure is for;
- Establish the proportion of people whose main reason for being in the host city is the event;
- Determine if any spectators are combining their visit to an event with a holiday in order to estimate any wider economic impacts.

Much of this analysis was undertaken using a standard questionnaire survey to interview key interest groups at an event and the data collected was then analysed using a specialist statistical software package and spreadsheets to calculate the additional expenditure in the host economy.

Multipliers

It is the direct impact attributable to *additional expenditure* that this research concentrated upon, in order to allow for meaningful comparisons between events. That is to say, the comparisons do not include induced impact derived from the application of multipliers to the additional expenditure calculations. To do so would be to compare host economies rather than specific events, as multipliers are specific to a given economy. Moreover, the information needed to establish a multiplier for a given local economy is not always readily available. As a result, historically, consultants have used highly technical and ambitious multipliers that are not empirically based and are often 'borrowed' from other sectors (eg, construction), or other economies. This 'borrowed' type of multiplier analysis can be considered only a poor approximation at best and any findings are most likely to be erroneous – not least because the multiplier is unique to the prevailing local economic conditions and, to reiterate, this type of research is about *comparing events and not economies*. Most of John Crompton's criticisms of poor methodology in the carrying out of economic impact studies of major events are related precisely to the incorrect choice or use of multipliers (see Crompton, 1995, 2001).

Results

Absolute impact

Graph 1 details the absolute additional expenditure directly attributable to staging each of the ten events. The most significant economic impact is attributable to the 2002 World Snooker Championship closely followed by the 1997 World Badminton Championships. Both these events took place over a two-week period and this extended period for the events did lead to higher economic impact. The World Half Marathon Championships was different from the other events in the sense that it did not take place in a stadium or fixed seating area and there were no tickets sold for spectators. Consequently the crowd at this event has been estimated in conjunction with the local organizing committee, city authority and the police. This estimate of the number of spectators, which has been used to calculate the economic impact, is on the conservative side.

In five of the ten events, the additional expenditure generated in the host economies exceeded £1.45m, which might be termed a 'major' impact. Although the majority of the events detailed in Graph 1, however, could be described as 'major' in the sporting calendars of those who organize the events, closer inspection of the figures reveals that it does not follow that a 'major event' in sporting terms necessarily equates with having a 'major' economic impact. For example, although the two swimming events, the 1997 Junior Swimming Championships in Glasgow and the European Short Course Swimming Championships in Sheffield, were both European Championships, they made a relatively small contribution to the economy of the host cities.

In a similar manner to the word 'major', the words 'world championships' do not necessarily mean that there will be a large downstream economic impact. The 1997 World Badminton event generated economic impacts of £2.2 million, whereas the 2001 World Half Marathon and 1999 World Indoor Climbing Championship generated more modest impacts of £584,000 and £398,000 respectively.

Impact per day

Although the absolute economic impact attributable to a given event is important in quantifying the overall benefit that an event might have, it is a somewhat flawed basis for comparison as the duration of events is invariably different. For example, the World Badminton Championships took place over 14 days and the World Half Marathon was over inside one and a half hours. Thus in order to make a standardised comparison of the economic impact attributable to events it is useful to examine the economic impact *per day* of competition. The results of this analysis are shown in Graph 2.

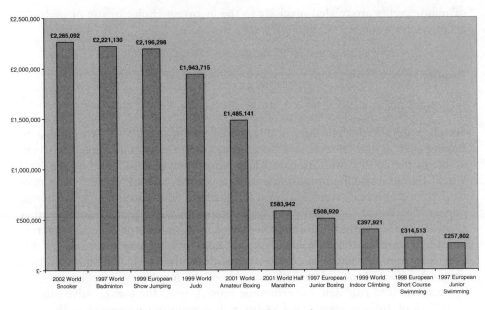

Graph 1: *Economic impact of 'major' sports events.*

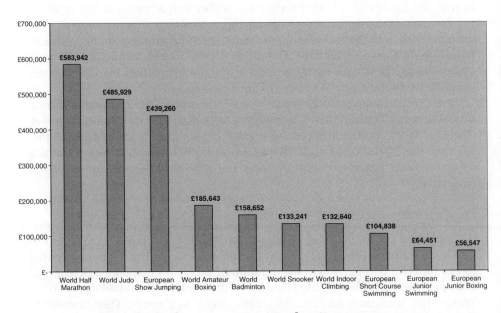

Graph 2: *Daily economic impact of major sports events.*

In Graph 2 we see that the events with the highest absolute economic impact, The World Badminton Championships and the World Snooker Championship, are only fifth and sixth in importance in relation to economic impact per day and it is the World Half Marathon Championship which is most important on this measure, where the daily impact and the absolute impact are identical, closely followed by the World Judo Championships and European Show-Jumping Championships.

Visitor and organizational spend

Generating economic impact is not UK Sport's rationale for attracting major events to the UK. As previously suggested, however, it is a useful device by which to justify the funding of an event in economic terms. Therefore in order to be able to forecast economic impact it is essential to understand the components that create economic impact. In broad terms these can be identified as:

- Organizational expenditure, ie, expenditure made directly by the organizers of an event in the locality where the event is taking place.
- Competitor or delegation expenditure, ie, expenditure made directly by those taking part in the event and their support staff in the locality where the event is taking place.
- Other visitor expenditure ie, expenditure made directly by those people involved with an event other than the organizers and delegations. Other visitor groups include officials, media representatives and spectators.

In the interest of simplicity the three types of expenditure can be collapsed into two categories, ie, organizational expenditure and visitor expenditure (delegation and other visitor expenditure combined). Using the ten events in the sample, the relative amounts of expenditure attributable to organizational and visitor expenditure can be seen in Graph 3.

Graph 3 indicates that for all except one of the events (the European Junior Boxing Championships), the economic impact attributable to organizational expenditure was a minor part of the total economic impact with a highest percentage score of 26% (World Amateur Boxing Championships) and a lowest percentage score of 0% in the European Junior Swimming (not illustrated). The European Junior Boxing Championships was a relatively small event which did not attract significant numbers of spectators.

For the events included in this sample, the vast majority of the economic impact (greater than 80%) was caused by visitors and therefore it is logical to concentrate the subsequent secondary analyses on visitor expenditure. The reason why the majority of events in this research have relatively low levels of organizational expenditure is because they were all events that took place within existing facilities and existing infrastructure. There was no need to build or upgrade existing facilities and therefore virtually all expenditure incurred by organizers was on revenue items necessary for the operational running of the event.

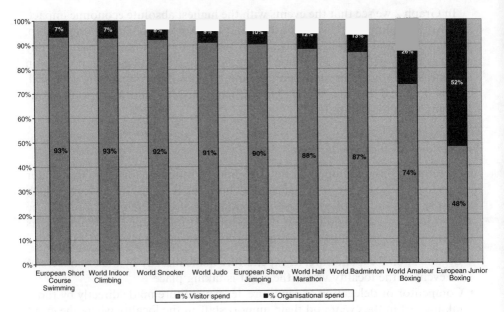

Graph 3: *The relative proportions of visitor and organizational spending at major sports events.*

Visitor expenditure

At this point it is worth disaggregating total visitor expenditure into its component parts of spectator, competitor (delegation) expenditure and other visitor expenditure. In 1997 the six events studied were illustrated along a continuum of 'spectator' to 'competitor and others'. Using the results of the ten events studied since 1997, this continuum can be upgraded to indicate the composition of visitor expenditure at an event. The revised continuum is shown in Graph 4 and this disaggregates the expenditure of 'others' from that of 'competitors'.

From Graph 4 it can be seen that at five of the ten events featured, the majority (at least 51%) of the economic impact can be attributed to spectators and these would be categorized as 'spectator driven' events. By contrast, at the remaining events the economic impact was driven by other groups (principally competitors), in particular at the two swimming events. The Short Course and Junior Swimming events are characterized by having large numbers of competitors staying in commercial accommodation and relatively small numbers of spectators (990 and 640 admissions respectively) most of whom are either the friends or families of the competitors; such events are categorized as 'competitor driven'.

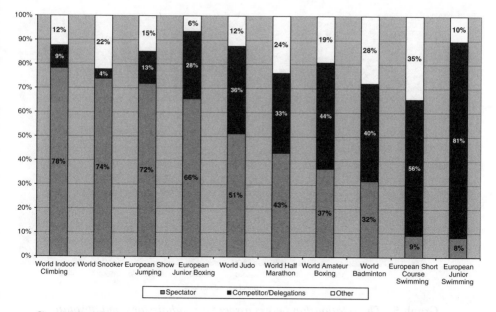

Graph 4: *The continuum between spectators' and other visitors' expenditure.*

Key determinants of economic impact

In order to investigate the relationship between the absolute scale of an economic impact and the number of people who generated it, we now examine economic impact against the total number of spectator admissions as shown in Graph 5. This does not include events which were not staged in stadiums and where the spectator admissions were approximations, as there were no audience data available (eg, the World Half Marathon). Graph 5 indicates that there is a very high correlation ($r = 0.91$) between the number of spectator admissions at an event and the economic impact attributable to that event. Therefore it can be concluded that if economic impact is an important consideration in determining whether or not to support an event, then the number of spectators is the principal determinant of absolute economic impact. As a consequence of this finding it can be concluded that in elite level sport (ie, the type of event likely to be supported by UK Sport), 'competitor driven' events are unlikely to generate as much economic impact in absolute terms compared with 'spectator driven' events.

It could be argued that if all or most of the spectators attending an event were local people, then the economic impact attributable to that event would be relatively small as there would be only a small net change in the economy ie, most expenditure would be 'deadweight'. In order to investigate this possibility

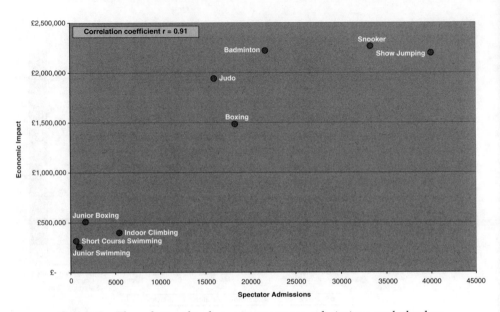

Graph 5: *The relationship between spectator admissions and absolute economic impact.*

further, we examine the relative proportions of local to non-local admissions as detailed in Graph 6.

According to Graph 6, there was only one instance of local admissions exceeding those of non-local people: the World Half Marathon Championships. The World Half Marathon had 55% of spectators from the local area. This was a direct result, however, of the Bristol Half Marathon running alongside the elite event, hence there were many people from Bristol supporting family and friends in the mass participation event. Moreover, of the remaining events, the event organizers at the European Show Jumping and the World Amateur Boxing interfered with the market conditions, in that significant numbers of complimentary tickets were passed to local people in order to increase the attendance at the events. Hence it is reasonable to conclude that the majority of spectators to events come from outside the local area and this therefore confirms the earlier assertion that absolute economic impact is critically dependent on the number of spectators attending an event – a point emphasized still further when one considers that the correlation between non-local admissions and absolute impact while still high (r = 0.87), is not as high as the correlation using total spectator admissions.

The key points emerging from this initial results section can be summarized as follows:

• The most appropriate way to compare the economic impact attributable to various events is on an economic impact per day basis;

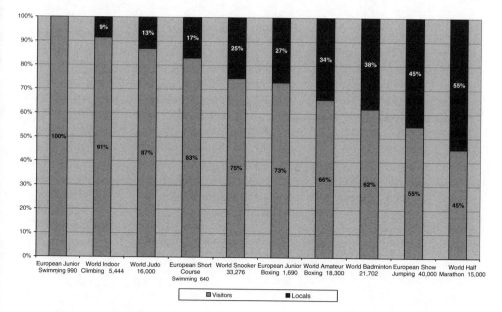

Graph 6: *The relative proportions of non-local and local spectators at events.*

- Spectator driven events are likely to have a higher economic impact than competitor driven events;
- The key determinant of total economic impact is the number of spectators attending an event;
- For most major sporting events, visitors from outside the immediate area are likely to account for the majority of admissions.

Additional benefits

The Balanced Scorecard approach to event evaluation

This final section may interest event organizers and practitioners, as well as social scientific analysts, in that it acknowledges that the benefits associated with events are far reaching and not merely confined to economic impacts. This section uses the 'Balanced Scorecard' approach to event evaluation (see Figure 1) developed from original work at Harvard Business School.

Apart from an event's economic impact, additional aims and benefits might arise in the form of media value linked to coverage at home or internationally. Moreover, linked to such coverage may be place marketing benefits for key aspects of the host city or area, which could ultimately impact upon tourism by increasing the number of visitors to the area in future as a result of media coverage afforded to an event. Public perceptions of places can also improve as a

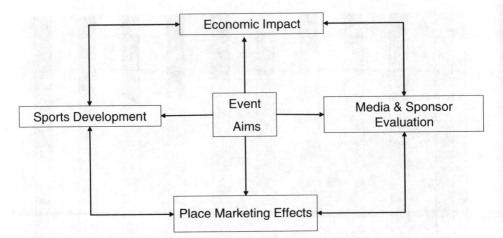

Figure 1: *The 'Balanced Scorecard' approach to evaluating events.*

result of people's experiences at major sports events, which in turn might lead to repeat visits as evidenced by qualitative feedback from spectators at some of the events. Furthermore, an immediate benefit of staging an event might involve some form of sports development impact which could encourage more people to take up a sport being showcased. The long-term effect of any increase in participation could be tracked, although it may be difficult to prove causality. To illustrate some of these points, examples are drawn from three events: the European Short Course Swimming Championship, World Amateur Boxing and World Half Marathon.

Examples of additional benefits

Apart from revealing an economic impact on Sheffield of almost £315,000, the research into the European Short Course Swimming Championships at the time also audited the public profile by analysing the television coverage of the event. In addition to the UK television coverage the event was also shown across Europe in Germany, Finland, Italy and Croatia. Audience data and broadcasts were confirmed by the Broadcasters' Audience Research Board (BARB) and calculations using industry standard methodologies were made relative to:

- Percentage Share: The proportion of people watching a given programme expressed as a function of the total number of people watching television at that time.
- Television Rating (TVR): This is the key performance indicator of the size of an audience for any given programme. TVR is expressed as the percentage of all the people in a country with access to a television actually watching the programme or programme segment in question.

Table 2: *Television coverage of the European Short Course Swimming Championships*

Indicator	UK	Other European	Total
Number of Programmes	6	12	18
Total Duration (Minutes)	369	718	1,087
Cumulative Audience (000s)	5,451	2,522	7,973
Highest Share Achieved	23.0%	9.8%	23.0%
Highest TVR Achieved	4.9%	9.0%	9.0%

Using the five countries from which the broadcast and audience data were available, the European Short Course Swimming Championships attracted a cumulative audience of 7,973,000 of which 5,451,000 were UK viewers as summarized in Table 2.

The data has two practical applications:

- For event promoters, in order to acquire a greater appreciation of the commercial value of the event in terms of related advertising and sponsorship sales. Commercial revenues contribute to the operating costs of an event and hence achieving value for money is the key when advertising and sponsorship sales are being made.

- For host venues, advertisers and sponsors, who can evaluate the return on their investment. For example, the total value of the Sheffield City Council support of the event was £25,000. This can be traded off against the value of the place marketing achieved. Using the data in Table 2, a degree of quantitative evaluation of place marketing can be made. A 'Sheffield National City of Sport' advertising board was on display at pool deck level alongside the advertising board of the main sponsor (Adidas). Using sponsorship industry standard methodology, it is relatively easy to calculate the proportion of the 1,087 broadcast minutes during which the board was on full view promoting the city of Sheffield.

The World Amateur Boxing Championships in Belfast achieved a total cumulative audience of 6.6 million in the UK, which included 330,000 young people under the age of 16 (ie, potential for a sports development impact). Across 13 programmes (mainly on BBC2), the event was screened for a total of 551 minutes (9 hours 11 minutes), with live feed and highlights screened to more than 20 countries. The UK viewing figures peaked at 2.06 million with the audience share at this point being 22%.

Based on analyses of the television coverage using specialist sponsorship evaluations, estimates suggested that a major sponsor enjoyed media exposure worth £51,014 in the UK alone. Data such as this provides a sound baseline against which sponsors can assess the extent to which they have achieved a return on their investment. In this instance the sponsor invested £63,000 and in return they received exposure that would have cost more than £51,000 to purchase in the commercial marketplace, ie, 81% of their total investment. In addition to UK television coverage, broadcasters from other countries also bought the rights to screen the event and thus there would be additional media value obtained for the sponsor from this worldwide exposure. Although the worldwide television exposure was not analysed in this instance, it is possible to access the audience data as demonstrated by the European Short Course Swimming Championships example, or alternatively where this is not possible, sponsorship evaluation companies can apply a 'rate card' based on a flat rate for 30 seconds of advertising time on a particular channel.

A similar methodology can be adopted in order to estimate the place marketing effects associated with television coverage. At the World Half Marathon, Bristol City Council was responsible for underwriting the event and for a significant proportion of the running costs. In return the place marketing benefits linked to the exposure of the 'Bristol' brand, amounted to a notional £42,000 of exposure. In order to maximize any place marketing benefits for a particular location, event organizers should consider working closely with the host broadcaster in order to ensure the showcasing of key local attractions as the backdrop to human-interest features around the event coverage. Sheffield City Council used such human interest features (known as 'postcards') to great effect during a major snooker event in 2002 such that the combined place marketing effects for the city were a notional £3.2 million, ie, the commercial cost of the exposure created by the event, based on the cost/1000 viewers of a 30 second television commercial.

Apart from media value and place marketing, the 'Balanced Scorecard' approach also refers to sports development effects and these were analysed during the research at the World Amateur Boxing in Belfast. In the run-up to and during the championships a community development programme with boxer Wayne McCulloch entitled 'Train with Wayne' provided young children and potential future champions with the opportunity to become involved in the sport of boxing. Up to 100 youngsters participated during the televised build up to the Championship. During the event 'Come and Try It' sessions were enhanced by concessionary tickets to the event, school visits and discount packages. Furthermore, training for potential young boxers was also strengthened through the involvement of 300 local volunteers in the event, training for technical officials, time-keepers, judges, medical personnel and competition managers. This event has therefore left a broad legacy of enhanced skills which maybe used to maintain the impetus provided by the staging of the event.

As well as the economic impact attributable to the World Amateur Boxing (£1.49m), the profile of Belfast as a city of world-class sport was enhanced through the marketing of the event and the televisual exposure of the 'Belfast' brand throughout the world. Collectively, the boxing and the previous success of the World Cross Country Championships provided the catalyst to formulate an events strategy for Northern Ireland, designed to help re-image the Province through sport.

In summary, given the complex aims and objectives increasingly associated with major sports events, in future more detailed analysis and evaluation will be necessary to satisfy the needs of different partners. Adopting a methodology linked to (for example) the 'Balanced Scorecard' could move beyond simple economic impact studies, to include TV, media and sponsorship evaluations as well as sports development, home soil advantage and other legacies.

Conclusions

This chapter has provided a detailed overview of ten economic impact studies undertaken at major sports events, all World or European Championships, in the UK since 1997. Each study represents a value-for-money appraisal of an event, by quantifying the net change in the host economy that is directly attributable to the event and measurable in cash terms using detailed audit trails. The evidence presented vindicates (in economic terms) the decisions made by UK Sport to use Lottery funding via the World Class Events Programme to attract many of the events. Moreover, the detailed database of event evaluations possessed by UK Sport provides the evidence to inform future strategic decisions relative to the type of events that the UK may consider bidding for in years to come. According to such evidence and in order to maximize potential economic impact, the following should be considered prior to bidding:

- The ability of the event to attract people from outside the host area and thereby reduce the 'deadweight' percentage of those attending;
- Generally the greater the absolute number of spectators the more significant the economic impact and junior events are likely to have the smallest impacts as they rarely attract many spectators;
- The economic impact is not necessarily a function of the status of an event in world sporting terms;
- The number of days of competition and the availability of local commercial accommodation to allow visitors to extend their dwell times in the host area.

Beyond the development of the economic impact model, this chapter has demonstrated how the event evaluations have evolved and should continue to evolve in order to better understand the likely legacies of events long after any medals have been presented. These legacies could be in terms of media value, place marketing effects for the host area, as well as sports development impacts which may stimulate young people to get more involved in sport. The evidence presented above suggests that the European model of attracting major sports events to cities that do not require additional infrastructure investment in order to host the event can generate significant economic benefits to the host cities.

References

Baade, R.A. (1996) 'Professional sports as catalysts for economic development', *Journal of Urban Affairs* 18 (1): 1–17.

Baade, R.A. (2003) 'Evaluating subsidies for professional sports in the United States and Europe: A public sector primer', *Oxford Review of Economic Policy* 19 (4): 585–597.

Bianchini, F. & Schengel, H. (1991) 'Re-imagining the city', in J. Comer and S. Harvey (eds) *Enterprise and Heritage: Crosscurrents of National Culture*. London: Routledge, 214–234.

Bramwell, B. (1995) 'Event tourism in Sheffield: A sustainable approach to urban development?' Unpublished paper. Sheffield: Sheffield Hallam University, Centre for Tourism.

Burns, J.P.A., Hatch, J.H. & Mules, F.J. (eds) (1986) *The Adelaide Grand Prix: The Impact of a Special Event*. Adelaide: The Centre for South Australian Economic Studies.

Coates, D. & Humphreys, B. (1999) 'The growth of sports franchises, stadiums and arenas', *Journal of Policy Analysis* 18 (4): 601–624.

Crompton, J.L. (1995) 'Economic impact analysis of sports facilities and events: eleven sources of misapplication', *Journal of Sport Management* 9 (1): 14–35.

Crompton, J.L. (2001) 'Public subsidies to professional team sport facilities in the USA', in C. Gratton and I. Henry (eds) *Sport in the City: The Role of Sport in Economic and Social Regeneration*. London: Routledge, 15–34.

Getz, D. (1991) *Festivals, Special Events, and Tourism*. New York: Van Nostrand Reinhold.

Hall, C.M. (1992) *Hallmark Tourist Events: Impacts, Management and Planning*. London: Belhaven Press.

Kasimati, E. (2003) 'Economic aspects and the Summer Olympics: a review of related research', *International Journal of Tourism Research* 5: 433–444.

Loftman, P. & Spirou, C. (1996) 'Sports stadiums and urban regeneration: the British and United States Experience'. Paper to the conference *Tourism and Culture: Towards the 21st Century*. Durham, September 1996.

Mules, T. & Faulkner, B. (1996) 'An economic perspective on major events', *Tourism Economics* 12 (2): pp 107–117.

Noll, R. & Zimbalist, A. (eds) (1997) *Sports, Jobs & Taxes*. Washington, DC: The Brookings Institution.

Preuss, H. (2004) *The Economics of Staging the Olympics: A Comparison of the Games 1972–2008*. Edward Elgar: Cheltenham UK.

Ritchie, J.R.B. (1984) 'Assessing the impact of hallmark event: conceptual and research issues', *Journal of Travel Research* 23 (1): 2–11.

Ritchie, J.R.B. & Aitken, C.E. (1984) 'Assessing the impacts of the 1988 Olympic Winter Games: the research program and initial results', *Journal of Travel Research* 22 (3): 17–25.

Ritchie, J.R.B. & Aitken, C.E. (1985) 'OLYMPULSE II – evolving resident attitudes towards the 1988 Olympics', *Journal of Travel Research* 23 (3): 28–33.

Ritchie, J.R.B. & Lyons, M.M. (1987) 'OLYMPULSE III/IV: a mid term report on resident attitudes concerning the 1988 Olympic Winter Games', *Journal of Travel Research* 26 (1): 18–26.

Ritchie, J.R.B. & Lyons, M.M. (1990) 'OLYMPULSE VI: a post-event assessment of resident reaction to the XV Olympic Winter Games', *Journal of Travel Research* 28 (3): 14–23.

Ritchie, J.R.B. & Smith, B.H. (1991) 'The impact of a mega event on host region awareness: a longitudinal study', *Journal of Travel Research* 30 (1): 3–10.

Roche, M. (1992) 'Mega-event planning and citizenship: problems of rationality and democracy in Sheffield's Universiade 1991', *Vrijetijd en Samenleving* 10 (4): 47–67.

Roche, M. (1994) 'Mega-events and urban policy', *Annals of Tourism Research* 21 (1): 1–19.

Urban entrepreneurship, corporate interests and sports mega-events: the thin policies of competitiveness within the hard outcomes of neoliberalism

C. Michael Hall

Mega-events, otherwise referred to as hallmark or special events, are major fairs, festivals, expositions, cultural and sporting events which are held on either a regular or a one-off basis (Hall, 1992). Mega-events have assumed a key role in urban and regional tourism marketing and promotion as well as wider urban and regional development strategies. Nations, regions, cities and corporations have used mega-events to promote a favourable image in the international tourist, migration and business marketplace (Ritchie & Beliveau, 1974; Law, 1993, 2000; Malecki, 2004). Mega-events are therefore one of the means by which places seek to become 'sticky' (Markusen, 1996) – that is attract and retain mobile capital and people – through place enhancement and regeneration and the promotion of selective place information (Hall, C.M., 2005a, b).

Mega-events are therefore an extremely significant component of place promotion because they may leave behind social, economic and physical legacies which will have an impact on the host community for a far greater period than that in which the event took place. For example, when asked as to the 'most likely legacy' of the 1994 Victoria Commonwealth Games in Canada a readers' poll in *Monday Magazine* ranked debt, new pool, higher taxes, increased tourism, and higher real estate prices as being the Games' legacies (McCaw, 1994). Such a lay assessment of the effects of hosting a mega-event may well be quite astute. Mega sports events such as the Olympic Games have been associated with large-scale public expenditure, the construction of facilities and infrastructure, and urban redevelopment and revitalization strategies which may have undesirable long-term consequences for public stakeholders although significant short-term gains for some corporate interests (Hall, 1992; Essex & Chalkley, 1998; Eisinger, 2000).

Mega-events can be regarded as one of the hallmarks of modernity and have long managed to integrate industrial and corporate interests with those of government with respect to urban development and imaging. Arguably this is historically most clearly seen in the hosting of World Fairs and Expositions. For example, Bailey (1987: 68) observed that the Great Exhibition at the Crystal Palace of 1851 was a concrete pivot of the change 'whereby leisure in its modern form became progressively more plentiful, more visible, more sought after and more controversial', with the Great Exhibition fusing commercial recreation with educational instruction and industry. Nevertheless, Olds (1988: 14) recognized, 'World Fairs are not merely overgrown amusement parks or simple trade fairs. They play a multitude of roles both explicit and implicit'. 'The fairs were not only selling goods, they were selling ideas: ideas about the relations between nations, the spread of education, the advancement of science, the form of cities, the nature of domestic life, the place of art in society' (Benedict, 1983: 2). Furthermore, they were an opportunity for nations to improve their image in an increasingly market conscious and economically competitive world. For example, according to Armstrong (1986: 11), 'the first international exhibition, the Great Exposition of the Works of Industry of All Nations, held in Hyde Park London, in 1851 was held because, as Prince Albert stated, "It was the only way to out-do the French"'.

World Fairs, however, do not have the international impact that they used to have, in either economic or imaging terms (Dungan, 1984; Rubalcaba-Bermejo & Cuadrado-Roura, 1995; Rydell, Findling & Pelle, 2000). The reduced profile of World Fairs needs to be seen within the context of increased attention given to mega-events other than fairs or expositions. The relative decline of importance of World Fairs and Exposition has gone hand-in-hand with the growth in the significance of sports mega-events for urban and regional growth and place competition (Malecki, 2004; McCallum, Spencer & Wyly, 2005). Arguably such a shift in the relative significance of mega-events is related to globalization of the media along with space-time compression associated with technological developments in transport and communication which have provided increased commercial impact for sports events. Such developments have meant that the 'market reach' of a mega-event has become greater than ever before and whereas until the age of global television it would take weeks or months for people to experience a mega-event, and to travel to such events, this can now occur in the space of hours with the event beamed to a global live audience. Indeed, it is impossible to separate the growth of corporate and government interest in the hosting of mega-events and the media discourse on place competitiveness from the commercialization of sport on a global scale and advances in communication technology (Whitson, 1998; Barney, Martyn & Wenn, 2002; Coles, 2003). Even so, as Short *et al.* (2000) observed, despite the continuing internationalization of sports and the global nature of the Olympics and other such events, in-depth analysis of their urban impact has been largely neglected in the globalization literature.

Undoubtedly, the connection between professional sports and media does contribute to the attractiveness of hosting sports mega-events (Hiller, 2000; Jones, 2001; Malecki, 2004). According to Tomlinson (1996: 585) the competition of and for the Olympics attests to 'the intensifying symbiosis of top-level performance sport and television'. Even the International Olympic Committee stated after the 1992 Games' spectacular ratings success that 'it is through television that the world experiences the Olympics' (Tomlinson, 1996: 583). Sports spectatorship via the media has led to increased corporate interest in sponsoring sporting events and competitions, often on an exclusive basis in order to 'place' products through advertising both in stadia as well as on television and other media. For example, in the case of the 2006 football World Cup in Germany although almost three million tickets were issued for the 64 matches, the worldwide television audience was estimated before the competition to be an average of half a billion people per match (Starck, 2005). The World Cup was also forecast to provide a direct tourist spend of approximately 1.5 billion euros, yet the size of such visitor impact was regarded as less than that which will be gained by forms that provide sporting goods, broadcasts, communication technology and other products and services provided by World Cup sponsors (Starck, 2005).

The implications of the growth of the media impact of the hosting of mega-events have not been isolated to corporate sponsorship. Indeed, corporate interests now dominate not just the scheduling of events but also their development, planning and regulation (Whitson, 1998; Law, Harvey & Kemp, 2002). For example, because of the desire for exclusivity for their products, event sponsors are increasingly demanding exclusivity for their products not only inside stadia with respect to advertising and retails sales but also in the host cities. In the case of the 2006 Football World Cup in Germany, 'official provider' licenses meant that German beer or sausage would not be available in stadia as beer and fast food rights were held by Anheuser Busch and McDonald. Because of the agreements with host cities, however, as part of the event bid the arrangements for the World Cup meant that in the supposedly 'public' places of the twelve host cities, the winning sponsors had the right to pitch their products exclusively when matches were on (Hall, A., 2005). Perhaps not surprisingly, such a situation led to substantial protests from German companies particularly as the bid for the Cup was partly justified by the supposed economic benefits it would bring to Germany and host cities. As Niclas Stucke, president of a German trade association for fairs stated, 'There won't be any German products on sale in the marketplaces of the towns where matches are being held . . . You can get Coca-Cola, American beer and McDonald's but that will be it. German products will be locked out' (cited in Hall, A., 2005).

Nevertheless, the regulation of 'public' space during the hosting of mega-events is nothing new, with events such as the Commonwealth Games, the Olympics and the America's Cup typically having specific government legislation passed to assist not only the fast-track developing of event related infrastructure but also to regulate the activities and behaviours of visitors to event sites in order to meet the requirements for a 'successful' hosting of the event (Chalkley & Essex, 1999). For example, in the case of the 2000 Sydney Olympics the New South Wales state government passed legislation in 1995 which meant that Sydney residents lost their right to initiate a court appeal under environment and planning legislation against the proposed Olympic projects. Further legislation passed under the New South Wales Government's *Olympic Co-ordination Authority Act* allowed, somewhat ironically given the green image which was an integral part of the Games bid (SOCOG, 1996), all projects linked with the Games to be suspended from the usual Environmental Impact Statements requirements (Totaro, 1995). Invariably, however the success of an event is defined in terms of the economic impact of the event and the media exposure of event hosts, not a broad notion of community wellbeing although such wellbeing may usually be used as a justification to host mega-events (Cochrane, Peck & Tickell, 1996; Whitson, 2004), with sport often being upheld as a mechanism for social and economic development. Despite the rhetoric, however, of the value of sport mega-events for economic competitiveness and development there is little research on the actual regenerative potential of investment in sport, or the long-term benefits to local communities of sports events-led investment strategies (Gratton, 1999; Coalter, Allison & Taylor, 2000; Hall, 2004). The vast majority of economic impact studies have simply estimated the value of the sports industry, rather than addressed issues of regeneration *per se* (Leisure Industries Research Centre, 1997). For example, Coalter, Allison & Taylor (2000: 6.4) report on a study of the economic importance of sport in Lincoln and Stone in the United Kingdom which concluded that 'although many claims are made for the contribution that this sector makes in terms of economic welfare, these are frequently based on assertion rather than concrete evidence. There is a need for a more systematic evaluation process to underpin strategies of support for sport both generally and in the region'. Unfortunately, such evaluation processes are generally not forthcoming and, where they are conducted, the findings are often not encouraging in terms of the original expectations for sports-generated economic development (Hall, 1992, 2001; Crompton, 1995; Page & Hall, 2003). Despite such misgivings a number of cities have embarked on large-scale sporting developments associated with regeneration strategies usually in relation to the hosting of major sports events such as the Olympics (eg, Sydney, Barcelona, London), the Commonwealth Games (eg, Manchester, Melbourne), or even the World Student Games (eg, Sheffield).

Indeed, Gratton (1999: 16) argues that the commercial sports sector 'is the lead sector in any strategy of economic regeneration based on sports-related industry. This is mainly due to the substantial economic benefits in terms of the sector's contribution to the generation of employment, the value of consumer expenditure, the investment opportunities and the "foot-loose" nature of the industries within the sector'. The capacity of business interests to shift capital in order to take advantage of mega-event opportunities has been long recognized, with the vast majority of firms attracted by mega-events tending to only relocate in the short-term unless they are also involved with long-term infrastructure management (Hall, 1992). Therefore, it is perhaps not surprising that a strong link has been forged between transnational capital and global sports events that provide a basis for the creation of partnerships between local and transnational interests.

The creation of coalitions between economic interests in the bidding and hosting of mega-events is reflective of Molotch's (1976) theorization of the city as a growth machine in which 'the desire for growth provides the key operative motivation toward consensus for members of politically mobilized local elites, however split they might be on other issues' (1976: 310). Such pursuit of growth is regarded as shaping not only the local political system but also the pattern of urban development in which museums, sports teams, convention centres and mega-events become an integral part of urban re-imaging strategies and place competitiveness.

> The athletic teams in particular are an extraordinary mechanism for instilling a spirit of civic jingoism regarding the 'progress' of the locality. A stadium filled with thousands (joined by thousands more at home before the TV) screaming for Cleveland or Baltimore (or whatever) is a scene difficult to fashion otherwise. This enthusiasm can be drawn upon . . . in order to gain general acceptance for local growth-oriented programs (Molotch, 1976: 315).

Indeed, the desire to be competitive is often integral to gaining public acceptance of bids to host mega-events by private interests. According to Law (1993: 107), the mega event 'acts as a catalyst for change by persuading people to work together around a common objective and as fast track for obtaining extra finance and getting building projects off the drawing board. This is not without its problems, since some would argue that it gives priority to development issues over those of welfare. The physical aspect of this strategy is that it has been linked with inner city regeneration and in particular with that of the city centre.' However, place competition has the potential to be a zero-sum game. As Harvey (1989: 12) commented

> Many of the innovations and investments designed to make particular cities more attractive as cultural and consumer centres have quickly been imitated elsewhere, thus rendering any competitive advantage within a system of cities ephemeral . . . Local coalitions have no option, given the coercive laws of competition, except to keep ahead of the game thus engendering leap-frogging innovations in lifestyles, cultural forms, products and service mixes, even institutional and political forms if they are to survive.

Imaging a city through the organization of spectacular urban space by, for example, hosting a mega-event, is therefore a mechanism for attracting mobile capital and people (of the right sort) in a period of intense inter-urban competition and urban entrepreneurialism in which neoliberalism has become one of the major frameworks by which the experience of urban development is understood.

Neoliberalism promotes market-led economic and social restructuring which produces, among other things, a more general orientation of economic and social policy to the private sector's 'needs' (Jessop, 2002). In the case of urban redevelopment this has typically meant the development of structures and powers of governance that are opaque and unaccountable to public stakeholders and participation (Owen, 2002). Neoliberalism therefore structures ideas about and the objectives set for community development, definitions of the public good, and definitions of citizenship that 'create wider distinctions than ever before between the "citizen" and the "consumer" and which of these ought to be the focal point of urban public life' (Lowes, 2004: 71). The fusion of urban entrepreneurialism with neoliberalism therefore provides the ideological justification for place-competitive re-imaging strategies including the hosting of sports mega-events while such events also provide an example of the manner in which 'local neoliberalisms' are embedded within wider networks and structures of neoliberalism (Peck & Tickell, 2002). Indeed, the competitiveness hegemony is such that according to some economic analysts, 'the critical issue for regional economic development practitioners to grasp is that the creation of competitive advantage is the most important activity they can pursue' (Barclays, 2002 cited in Bristow, 2005).

Sports mega-events emerge as central elements in place competition in at least three ways. First, the infrastructure required for such events is usually regarded as integral to further economic development whether as an amenity resource or as infrastructure. Second, the hosting of events is seen as a contribution to business vitality and economic development. Thirdly, the ability to attract events is often regarded as a performance indicator in its own right of the capacity of a city or region to compete. Indeed, such competition can lead public-private growth coalitions to seek to coerce and co-opt interests in an attempt to control the mega-event agenda, particularly at the bidding stage. To quote Harvey (1993: 9), 'Coercion arises either through interplace competition for capital investment and employment (accede to the capitalist's demands or go out of business; create a "good business climate" or lose jobs) or more simply, through the direct political repression and oppression of dissident voices (from cutting off media access to the more violent tactics of the construction Mafias in many of the world's cities)'.

In the case of the Sydney bid for the 2000 Olympics, the former New South Wales State Premier, Nick Greiner (1994: 13), argued that 'The secret of the success was undoubtedly the creation of a community of interest, not only in Sydney, but across the nation, unprecedented in our peacetime history'. The description of a 'community of interest' is extremely apt, as such a phrase indicates the role of the rather narrow community, in the form of elite interests, which direct and influence hallmark event proposals (Hall, 1992). In particular, the Sydney media played a critical role in creating the climate for the bid (McGeoch, 1994). As Greiner (1994: 13) stated:

> Early in 1991, I invited senior media representatives to the premier's office, told them frankly that a bid could not succeed if the media played their normal 'knocking role' and that I was not prepared to commit the taxpayers' money unless I had their support. Both News Ltd and Fairfax subsequently went out of their way to ensure the bid received fair, perhaps even favourable, treatment. The electronic media also joined in the sense of community purpose.

The Sydney Olympic experience of a combination of coercion and co-option to reduce public opposition to both the bidding process and the hosting of mega-events was to be repeated in the state of Victoria with respect to the hosting of the Formula One Australian Grand Prix. The Victorian Grand Prix Act exempted the Grand Prix and its track construction from environmental impact studies, and pollution and planning controls. The Act also exempted all agreements with the international promoters of the event from the state Freedom of Information Act. As Lowes (2004: 77) noted, the Act 'effectively removed the Grand Prix event from all the usual checks and balances which ordinarily protect the public by ensuring that no single arm of government is inordinately powerful or unaccountable'. Indeed, the Act was specifically designed to reduce debate, as indicated in a news release from the office of the Deputy Premier and Minister responsible for the Grand Prix, Pat McNamara, which stated, 'The Grand Prix Act has been principally designed to ensure that the over 400,000 spectators who attend this event over four days won't have their fun spoiled by political protest groups' (October 26, 1995). Indeed, the attitude of the then Victorian State Government towards opposition to the state government's sports and events growth agenda well illustrates the desire of growth coalitions to stifle debate.

The Victorian Parliamentary Opposition Leader asked Premier Jeff Kennett if he would 'instigate a full, open and public inquiry into the suitability of Albert Park for the Grand Prix compared to other sites, such as Sandown and Phillip Island?' As Lowes (2004) notes, Kennett's reply was unequivocal and worth quoting at length:

> The Leader of the Opposition is absolutely predictable in everything he asks. That is such a stupid question; even Clyde Holding would not have asked it. Clyde Holding, a former Opposition leader, did not once ask such a stupid question, and he went on to higher office! [. . .] *There will be no further review. The only people who ever ask for committees or reviews are those who cannot make decisions* [italics added]. That is exemplified by the stupid question that the Leader of the Opposition asked today (Victoria Parliament Hansard, May 6, 1994; also cited in Lowes, 2004: 80).

Significantly, however, criticism of the value of mega-events is founded not just on their role within neoliberal competitive discourse but also upon their actual economic contribution. For example, debate has been substantial over the economic benefits of the Formula One Grand Prix held in Melbourne. According to Tourism Victoria (1997: 24), the 1997 Grand Prix 'was watched by an estimated overseas audience of more than 300 million people . . . total attendance at the race was 289,000 over the four days . . . An independent assessment of the 1996 . . . Grand Prix indicated that it provided a gross economic benefit to the Victorian economy of $95.6 million and created 2,270 full year equivalent jobs'. In contrast, a thorough evaluation of the Grand Prix by Economists at Large and Associates (1997: 8) for the Save Albert Park Group concluded the following about the claim of $95.6 million of extra expenditure:

- It was a misrepresentation of the size of the economic benefit;
- The claimed gross benefits are overstated or non-existent; and
- Ironically, compared with what might have been achieved, Victorians were poorer when they could have been wealthier if the government had chosen a more 'boring' investment than the Grand Prix.

Yet the lack of robust assessments of sporting mega-events is not confined to Australia. Such is the strength of the mythology of event benefits for growth that in the case of Toronto's unsuccessful bid for the 2008 Summer Olympics only one councillor out of the 55 members of the Toronto City Council voted against the Olympic bid proposal even though they only had a 20 page background document to the proposal in terms of information. When city councillors voted on the project, they did not have: an estimate of the cost of bidding for the Games; a list of the names of the backers of 'BidCo', the private corporation that was heading up the Olympic bid; a reliable estimate of the cost of staging the Games; a plan for the public participation process, the environmental review process or the social impact assessment process; or a detailed financial strategy for the Games (Hall, 2003). Yet an unquestioning belief in the competitive benefits of hosting such large scale events is the norm and not an exception (Hall, 1992; Coates & Humphreys, 1999; Teigland, 1999; Tranter & Keefee, 2004; Whitson, 2004).

It is therefore perhaps not surprising that in their review of event-specific evaluations, Coalter, Allison & Taylor (2000: 6.7) concluded, that 'there is little evidence about the medium to long-term economic effects of such sports event-led economic regeneration strategies . . . In particular, there is a lack of available data on the *regenerative impact* of sports investments on local communities.' Nevertheless, despite such caution sport and sport-related tourism continues to be integral to regeneration strategies (Hall, 2004). For example, as part of its regional strategy the Northwest Development Agency (NWDA) in the UK state 'NWDA will help to capture and support a long-term programme of arts, sport and cultural events with engendering pride and raising aspirations. It brings in and helps to retain the more skilled and talented members of the community – people whose leadership skills are needed to sustain the capacity of every community' (2000: 34). More significantly for sports tourism they later go on to claim

> Quality infrastructure for sport, arts and museums can help to build the region's image and is part of the package needed to attract and retain those with the highest levels of talent and skill. These facilities are major tourist and visitor attractions too. The NWDA together with partners will identify the strategic gaps required to strengthen the region's position and image within the context of an action plan for viable new investment. The action plan will consider the need for new facilities, new investment, and improvements to existing facilities (NWDA, 2000: 50).

Undoubtedly, facilities can generate employment, particularly through the construction phase, and may generate some employment in the longer-term though in the case of event employment much of it will be part-time or casual and low-skilled. Integral, however, to the successful contribution of such facilities to job recreation will be the extent to which facilities have a policy to train and employ people from within the target area. Unfortunately, as Hiller (2000: 455) noted with respect to the unsuccessful Cape Town bid to host the Summer Olympic Games, 'the idea of harnessing a mega-event to a broader urban agenda that moves beyond the interests of finance capital, developers, inner-city reclamation and the tourist city is a relatively new idea'.

Corporate interests have substantially contributed to the desire of public-private urban growth coalitions to host sporting mega-events which by definition are a scarce resource. Such efforts, even if they are not successful, direct media attention to the cultural capital of cities that aspire to be 'world class' (Whitson & Macintosh, 1993; Waitt, 1999; Whitelegg, 2000; Eisinger, 2000; Lowes, 2002) and further reinforce not only the discourse of interurban competition but also its lived experience. Sports mega-events have therefore become integral to the entrepreneurial strategies of cities seeking to gain competitive advantage in the global economy. They provide an excellent example of the way the production of state and urban public policy has become less concerned with the evaluation of public policies within their own terms of reference than with the macro-policy context and the neoliberal policy problems of competitiveness resulting in what Peck (2001) aptly describes as 'thin policies/hard outcomes'.

Yet the sustainability of place competitive strategies, let alone its real benefits are increasingly questionable. Swyngedouw (1992) noted that the 'frenzied' and 'unbridled' competition for cultural capital results in over-accumulation and the threat of devaluation. Even Kotler, Haider & Rein (1993), who provide the standard case text for place marketing, acknowledged that 'the escalating competition . . . for business attraction has the marks of a zero-sum game or worse, a negative-sum game, in that the winner ultimately becomes the loser' (1993: 15). The desire to host sport mega-events and the requirements of having constantly to develop new and upgrade existing sports and visitor infrastructure has meant that cities 'face the possibility of being caught in a vicious cycle of having to provide larger subsidies to finance projects that deliver even fewer public benefits' (Leitner & Garner, 1993: 72). Yet even in such situations where corporate interests clearly benefit more than the public, such is the strength of the neoliberal discourse of competitiveness and the 'necessity' to become a place in which capital 'sticks' that the desirability to host sports mega-events by urban growth coalitions will remain unconstrained.

In fact to criticize the hosting of mega-events as an economic and social development mechanism is to be doubly damned. For one contends not only with the neoliberal discourse of competition and the relentless pursuit of regeneration but also with the mythologies of the social benefits of sport. Sport is extremely hard to argue against. The inherent belief of many that sport is good for you, makes for better citizens, creates pride in the community, and generates a positive image is hard to overcome (Hall, 2004). This belief and a relative lack of criticism of it means that, in terms of urban regeneration, many large-scale sport infrastructure projects and mega-events are going to continue to be funded as it provides opportunities not only for the furtherance of corporate interests but also for politicians to be seen to be 'doing something' in the face of global competition. As I have noted elsewhere, investment in accessible and affordable education, health and communications technology, along with a diversified job creation strategy is far more likely to have more long-term benefits for urban economic and social well-being than investment in elite mega-sports events and infrastructure (Hall, 2004). But given the hegemony of neoliberal discourse in the construction of the contemporary city perhaps it is just much easier to avoid these issues and watch the next World Cup finals or Olympic Games instead.

References

Armstrong, J. (1986) 'International events and popular myths', in Travel and Tourism Research Association (Canadian Chapter) *International Events: The real tourism impact, Proceedings of the 1985 Canada Chapter Conference*. Edmonton: Travel and Tourism Research Association (Canadian Chapter), 7–37.

Bailey, P. (1987) *Leisure and Class in Victorian England: Rational Recreation and the Contest for Control, 1830–1885*. London: Methuen.

Barney, R.K., Martyn, S.G. & Wenn, S.R. (2002) *Selling the Five Rings: The International Olympic Committee and the Rise of Olympic Commercialism*. Salt Lake City: University of Utah Press.

Benedict, B. (ed.) (1983) *The Anthropology of World Fairs*. London: Scolar Pres.

Bristow, G. (2005) 'Everyone's a "winner": problematising the discourse of regional competitiveness', *Journal of Economic Geography*, 5 (3): 285–304.

Chalkley, B. & Essex, S. (1999) 'Urban development through hosting international events: A history of the Olympic Games', *Planning Perspectives* 14: 369–394.

Coalter, F., Allison, M. & Taylor, J. (2000) *The Role of Sport in Regenerating Deprived Urban Areas*. Edinburgh: Centre for Leisure Research, University of Edinburgh, The Scottish Executive Central Research Unit.

Coates, D. & Humphreys, B. (1999) 'The growth effects of sport franchises, stadia and arenas', *Journal of Policy Analysis and Management* 16: 601–624.

Cochrane, A., Peck, J. & Tickell, A. (1996) 'Manchester plays games: Exploring the local politics of globalization', *Urban Studies* 33 (8): 1319–1336.

Coles, T. (2003) 'Urban tourism, place promotion and economic restructuring: the case of post-socialist Leipzig', *Tourism Geographies* 5 (2): 190–219.

Crompton, J.L. (1995) 'Economic impact analysis of sports facilities and events: eleven sources of misapplication', *Journal of Sport Management* 9: 14–35.

Dungan, Jr., T. (1984) 'How cities plan special events', *The Cornell Hotel and Restaurant Administration Quarterly* 25 (1): 83–89.

Economists At Large (1997) *Grand Prixtensions: The Economics of the Magic Pudding*. Prepared for the Save Albert Park Group, Economists At Large, Melbourne.

Eisinger, P. (2000) 'The politics of bread and circuses: building the city for the visitor class'. *Urban Affairs Review* 35: 316–333.

Essex, S. & Chalkley, B. (1998) 'Olympic Games: catalyst of urban change', *Leisure Studies* 27: 187–206.

Gratton, C. (1999) *Sports-Related Industry Study: Final Report*. Manchester: Manchester City Council and Northwest Development Agency.

Greiner, N. (1994) 'Inside running an Olympic bid', *The Australian*, 19 September: 13.

Hall, A. (2005) 'Small beer for World Cup Germans', *The Age*, February 8.

Hall, C.M. (1992) *Hallmark Tourist Events: Impacts, Management, and Planning*. London: Belhaven Press.

Hall, C.M. (2001) 'Imaging, tourism and sports event fever: the Sydney Olympics and the need for a social charter for mega-events', in C. Gratton & I. Henry (eds) *Sport in the City: The Role of Sport in Economic and Social Regeneration.* London: Routledge, pp. 166–183.

Hall, C.M. (2003) 'Packaging Canada/packaging places: Tourism, culture, and identity in the 21st Century', in C. Gaffield & K. Gould (eds) *The Canadian Distinctiveness into the XXIst Century.* Ottawa: International Council of Canadian Studies and the Institute of Canadian Studies, University of Ottawa Press, 199–214.

Hall, C.M. (2004) 'Sports tourism and urban regeneration', in B. Ritchie & D. Adair (eds) *Sports Tourism: Interrelationships, Impacts and Issues.* Clevedon: Channelview Publications, 192–206.

Hall, C.M. (2005a) *Tourism: Rethinking the Social Science of Mobility.* Harlow: Prentice-Hall.

Hall, C.M. (2005b) 'Reconsidering the geography of tourism and contemporary mobility', *Geographical Research* 43 (2): 125–139.

Harvey, D. (1989) 'From managerialism to entrepreneurialism: the transformation of urban governance in late capitalism', *Geografiska Annaler* 71B: 3–17.

Harvey, D. (1993) 'From space to place and back again: reflections on the condition of postmodernity', in J. Bird *et al.* (eds) *Mapping the Futures: Local Cultures, Global Change.* London: Routledge, pp. 3–29.

Hiller, H.H. (2000) 'Mega-events, urban boosterism and growth strategies: an analysis of the objectives and legitimations of the Cape Town 2004 Olympic bid', *International Journal of Urban and Regional Research* 24 (2): 4394–58.

Jessop, B. (2002) 'Liberalism, neoliberalism, and urban governance: A state-theoretical perspective', *Antipode* 34: 452–472.

Jones, C. (2001) 'A level playing field? Sports stadium infrastructure and urban development in the United Kingdom', *Environment and Planning A* 33: 845–861.

Kotler, P., Haider, D.H. & Rein, I. (1993) *Marketing Places: Attracting Investment, Industry, and Tourism to Cities, States, and Nations.* New York: Free Press.

Law, A., Harvey, J. & Kemp, S. (2002) 'The global sport mass media oligopoly: The three usual suspects and more', *International Review for the Sociology of Sport* 37 (3–4): 279–302.

Law, C.M. (1993) *Urban Tourism: Attracting visitors to large cities.* London: Mansell.

Law, C.M. (2000) 'Regenerating the city centre through leisure and tourism', *Built Environment* 26 (2): 117–129.

Leisure Industries Research Centre (1997) *A Review of the Economic Impact of Sport: Final Report.* Leisure Industries Research Centre, Sheffield: Sheffield Hallam University.

Leitner, H. & Garner, M. (1993) 'The limits of local initiatives: a reassessment of urban entrepreneurialism for urban development', *Urban Geography* 14: 57–77.

Lowes, M. (2002) *Indy Dreams and Urban Nightmares: Speed Merchants, Spectacle, and the Struggle over Public Space in the World-Class City.* Toronto: University of Toronto Press.

Lowes, M. (2004) 'Neoliberal power politics and the controversial siting of the Australian Grand Prix Motorsport event in an urban park', *Society and Leisure* 27 (1): 69–88.

Malecki, E.J. (2004) 'Jockeying for position: What it means and why it matters to regional development policy when places compete', *Regional Studies* 38 (9): 1101–1120.

Markusen, A. (1996) 'Sticky places in slippery space: a typology of industrial districts', *Economic Geography* 72: 293–313.

McCallum, K., Spencer, A. & Wyly, E. (2005) 'The city as an image-creation machine: A critical analysis of Vancouver's Olympic bid', *Association of Pacific Coast Geographers Yearbook* 67: 24–46.

McCaw, F. (1994) 'Best of Victoria 1994: Monday readers' poll', *Monday Magazine*, 30 June-6 July: 20.

McGeoch, R. with Korporal, G. (1994) *The Bid: How Australia Won the 2000 Games.* Sydney: William Heinemann.

Molotch, H. (1976) 'The city as a growth machine: Towards a political economy of place', *American Journal of Sociology* 82 (2): 309–332.

Northwest Development Agency (2000) *Regional Strategy.* Manchester: Northwest Development Agency.

Olds, K. (1989) 'Mass evictions in Vancouver: the human toll of Expo '86', *Canadian Housing* 6 (1): 49–53.

Owen, K.A. (2002) 'The Sydney 2000 Olympics and urban entrepreneurialism: Local variations in urban governance', *Australian Geographical Studies* 40: 323–336.

Page, S.J. & Hall, C.M. (2003) *Managing Urban Tourism*. Prentice-Hall, Harlow.

Peck, J. (2001) 'Neoliberalizing states: Thin policies/hard outcomes', *Progress in Human Geography* 25 (3): 445–455.

Peck, J. & Tickell, A. (2002) 'Neoliberalizing space', *Antipode* 34: 380–403.

Ritchie, J.R.B. & Beliveau, D. (1974) 'Hallmark events: an evaluation of a strategic response to seasonality in the travel market', *Journal of Travel Research* 14 (Fall): 14–20.

Rubalcaba-Bermejo, L. & Cuadrado-Roura, J.R. (1995) 'Urban hierarchies and territorial competition in Europe: exploring the role of fairs and exhibitions', *Urban Studies* 32: 379–400.

Rydell, R.W., Findling, J.E. & Pelle, K.D. (2000) *Fair America: World's Fairs in the United States*. Washington D.C. Smithsonian Institution Press.

Short, J. *et al.* (2000) 'From World cities to gateway cities', *City* 4 (3): 317–340.

SOCOG/Sydney Organising Committee for the Olympic Games (1996) *Environmental Guidelines*. Sydney: SOCOG.

Starck, P. (2005) 'Soccer World Cup to boost German 2006 GDP – Study', *The Guardian*, December 1.

Swyngedouw, E.A. (1992) 'The mammon quest. 'Glocalisation', interspatial competition and the new monetary order: the construction of new scales', in M. Dunford & G. Kaflakas (eds) *Cities and Regions in the New Europe*. London: Belhaven, 39–67.

Teigland, J. (1999) 'Mega-events and impacts on tourism: the predictions and realities of the Lillehammer Olympics', *Impact Assessment and Project Appraisal* 17: 305–317.

Tomlinson, A. (1996) 'Olympic spectacle: opening ceremonies and some paradoxes of globalization', *Media, Culture and Society* 18: 583–602.

Totaro, P. (1995) 'Olympic opponents denied sporting chance', *Sydney Morning Herald* December 16: 1.

Tourism Victoria (1997) *Annual Report 1996–97*. Tourism Victoria, Melbourne.

Tranter, P.J. & Keefee, T.J. (2004) 'Motor racing in Australia's Parliamentary Zone: successful event tourism or the Emperor's new clothes?' *Urban Policy and Research* 22 (2): 169–187.

Victoria Parliament Hansard (1994) May 6, Assembly 1671.

Waitt, G. (1999) 'Playing games with Sydney: Marketing Sydney for the 2000 Olympics', *Urban Studies* 36: 1055–1077.

Whitelegg, D. (2000) 'Going for gold: Atlanta's bid for fame', *International Journal of Urban and Regional Research* 24: 801–817.

Whitson, D. (1998) 'Circuits of promotion: Media, marketing and the globalization of sport', in L. Wenner (ed.) *Media Sport*. New York: Routledge, pp. 57–72.

Whitson, D. (2004) 'Bringing the world to Canada: "the periphery of the centre"', *Third World Quarterly* 25 (7): 1215–1232.

Whitson, D. & Macintosh, D. (1993) 'Becoming a world class city', *Sociology of Sports Journal* 10: 221–240.

Part 2
The Glocal Politics of Sports Mega-Events

Underestimated costs and overestimated benefits? Comparing the outcomes of sports mega-events in Canada and Japan

David Whitson and John Horne

Introduction

Since the late 1970s, and the widely publicized debts of the Montreal Olympics in 1976, a major feature of analysis of sports mega-events has been the gap between optimistic forecasts and the actual impacts of Games on the local economy, society, and culture (Vigor, Mean & Tims, 2004). That there are likely to be significant gaps between the benefits forecast for sports mega-projects, and the ensuing legacies, is now fairly predictable (Flyvbjerg, Bruzelius & Rothengatter, 2003). Advocates for mega-projects tend to make optimistic economic estimates, whilst opponents worry about public debt and about the 'opportunity costs', when public money is spent on architecturally dazzling stadia and other spectacular infrastructure. In addition to debates over cost/benefit calculations, moreover, there are debates over the social impacts of hosting an Olympic Games, especially when the legacies of Olympic facilities are of debatable value to low income residents. This chapter raises questions about the discrepancies between predicted and actual outcomes of sports mega-events, and about why hosting is so often the project of political and business elites. It also raises questions about the economic impacts of tourism, in the years after the Games are gone (Levine, 1999).

The enthusiasm to host sports mega-events has grown in the past twenty years for three related reasons. First, new developments in the technologies of mass communication, especially the development of satellite television, have created unprecedented global audiences for events like the Olympics and the FIFA World Cup. This, secondly, has meant that the television revenues available to host cities have grown exponentially since the mid-1970s. Indeed, where the television rights for Montreal 1976 sold for less than US$30 million, only eight years later the rights for the Los Angeles Olympics brought in more than $240 million, and by Sydney 2000 this had risen to over $1 billion (Roche, 2000). Thirdly, the influx of corporate sponsorship money into the Olympics which began with Los Angeles in 1984 has provided another extremely lucrative source

© The Editorial Board of the Sociological Review 2006. Published by Blackwell Publishing Ltd, 9600 Garsington Road, Oxford OX4 2DQ, UK and 350 Main Street, Malden, MA 02148, USA

of income for host cities. Together, these two 'revenue streams' – and we should remember that the strategic appeal of the Olympics to corporate sponsors is itself directly related to the size of the television audiences – have transformed the economic calculus associated with hosting the Games. A measure of the transformation is that, in the aftermath of Montreal's huge debts, Los Angeles was the only serious bidder for the 1984 Olympics. Today, in contrast, the Olympics have become an extended extravaganza of promotional opportunities and competitions to host the Games attract bids from many of the world's leading cities (Whitson, 1998; Shoval, 2002).

The legacies of mega-events: comparing the Japanese experience

For the purposes of this chapter, it is important to consider that just as sports mega-events carry connotations that are seen as useful in the selling of all manner of commercial products, so too are they seen as valuable promotional opportunities for cities and regions, showcasing their attractions to global audiences and helping to attract tourism and outside investment. This may be the case in a very particular way, moreover, for Winter Olympic hosts. Skiing is so central to the winter tourism industry that the opportunity to showcase an area's skiing in Olympic Games telecasts is widely believed to make the global reputation of a winter holiday destination. This was certainly the aspiration when Calgary staged the Olympic skiing in the Alberta Rockies in 1988, for example, and more recently, when the Salt Lake City Olympics gave Utah the opportunity to show off its ski resorts to global audiences. Similar aspirations also applied in Japan, in 1972 (Sapporo) and again in 1998 (Nagano). The fact, however, that both these destinations have succeeded in the Japanese market without ever becoming international ski destinations serves to raise questions about this hypothesis.

Recent research into the Nagano Winter Olympics and the co-hosted football World Cup in 2002 in Japan and the Republic of Korea/South Korea (Horne & Manzenreiter, 2004; Manzenreiter & Horne, 2002) offers some useful points of comparison and contrast with the Canadian experiences to be discussed below. In Japan, since at least the 1980s, local planners have believed that two general benefits follow from the promotion of sports. First, sport has been considered an important generator of local economic activity, and for the past fifteen years, Japanese cities of various sizes have enthusiastically invested in new sports facilities. In partnership with private sector beneficiaries of public spending on infrastructure, notably the construction sector, regional governments have used sports-related construction to create local economic activity. Promoters of this growth strategy include virtually all of Japan's infamous *zenekon*, or 'general contractors'. Kajima Corporation was general contractor for the four 2002 World Cup arenas: Saitama Stadium 2002, Miyagi Stadium, 'Big Swan' Niigata Stadium and Shizuoka Stadium 'Ecopa'. Other major contractors such as

Takenaka, Taisei, and the Sato Group also did important business in World Cup-related construction. In Japan, representatives of these *zenekon* are central actors in political parties, lobby groups and non-governmental organizations, giving rise to concerns about the workings of the *doken kokka* or 'construction state' (McCormack, 2002). A good example of the linkages between business and sport in Japan was the (now discredited) industrialist Tsutsumi Yoshiaki, previously one of Japan's richest men and a member of many influential sports committees. Under his presidency, the Japan National Olympic Committee was turned into a professionally run sport agency, and it was allegedly his presidency of the Japan Ski Association that drew the Morioka World Cup (1994) and the Nagano Winter Olympics to Japan (Seki, 1997: 374–395).

At the same time, it was also widely claimed that a modern sports infra-structure would have positive impacts for the quality of life of local populations, as well as enhancing the image of provincial cities. Staging sports events or having teams competing in one of Japan's professional football or baseball leagues would, it was believed, provide sources of community identification, and such intangibles were considered to be potentially helpful in reversing the migra-tion of younger Japanese from provincial cities into metropolitan centres. With respect to Japan, then, some researchers suggest that civic leaders have sought longer-term community-building and 'imaging' benefits from investment in sport, as much as immediate economic benefits (for example Harada, 2005 on the failed bid by Japan's second largest city, Osaka, to host the 2008 Olympic Games).

Despite such optimistic views of even failed hosting bids, and while the Nagano Olympics were reported to have generated a surplus of JPY 2.5 billion, the benefits of this have largely by-passed the taxpayers. The main Olympic lega-cies for the population of Nagano, for example, were a rarely used bob sled track, the 'Nagano Spiral', and the giant speed-skating venue, the 'M-Wave', a very beautiful facility (built by the Kajima Corp.) but one which has incurred heavy operational losses. Such was the construction in Nagano and the sur-rounding region before the Olympics that some of the city's population dubbed it the 'construction firm Olympics' (Wall, 1995). A new *shinkansen* (express 'bullet train') track was opened in time for the Nagano Olympics, which reduced the commuting time to and from the Tokyo area significantly, but the *local public* infrastructure created by this sports building boom was relatively inconsequen-tial. Likewise, promises to use the (co-) hosting of the 2002 World Cup as an opportunity to create infrastructure for sports development purposes came to very little. New football stadia have subsequently been used mainly for profes-sional teams, ie, for commercial sport, and one-off events and concerts, rather than as facilities for youth or the general public (Horne, 2004). Social goals, such as stemming the migration to metropolitan centres, or simply the improvements in the lives of the Japanese population that might follow from high-quality public infrastructure for sport and recreation, are still far from being accom-plished (Manzenreiter & Horne, 2005).

The politics and economics of sport in urban space

We turn, at this point, to an examination of how sports mega-projects have served the aspirations of corporate/civic elites in other parts of the world, notably Canada. John Hannigan (1998) has identified the growth of 'urban entertainment destinations' as one of the most significant developments transforming cities throughout the developed world since the 1980s, including North America and Asia. The convergence of three trends – rationalization in the entertainment industries, the theming of entertainment facilities, and synergies between previously discrete activities like shopping, dining out, spectator entertainment, and gambling – has helped to produce what Hannigan calls the postmodern 'fantasy city'. Moreover, the production of infrastructure for urban leisure has been further assisted by developments in urban politics: in particular, the growth of the 'entrepreneurial city' (Harvey, 1989) or the 'competition state' (Jessop, 2002). This has seen urban and regional governments compete with one another to offer incentives to private developers of sports and entertainment complexes, and even entire downtown entertainment districts, in the belief that this is the best (or only) way to bring investment, shopping, and vitality back to decaying downtowns (Judd, 2003). As a result, developers of professional sports venues and other upscale entertainment facilities have been able to extract public subsidies and tax holidays from governments anxious for their business, even while the same governments have been cutting back spending on social services (Noll & Zimbalist, 1997). Neo-liberal political ideologies have brought market-oriented meanings to agendas like 'community development', as well as new definitions of the public good. There has been a shift away from notions of citizenship that stressed 'social rights', towards discourses of consumerism in which citizens are positioned as individual consumers of services, and the best cities are those that have 'world class' shopping.

It is within this broader political and ideological context that debates about the costs and benefits of hosting sports events, and whether mega-events can be catalysts for social and economic regeneration, have taken shape in Canada and other 'Western' nations. In the United Kingdom, claims and counter-claims abound, with the emphasis of advocates typically on the short-term economic impacts of hosting sports events (Roberts, 2004: 116–120; UK Sport, 1999; UK Sport, 2004), while critics emphasize the social costs. There is as yet no consensus, leading Gratton and Henry (2001: 314) to propose that 'the potential benefits . . . of sport in the city have not yet been clearly demonstrated'. In North America, meanwhile, research increasingly suggests that sports mega-events channel public resources to private corporations (Judd, 2003; Baade & Matheson, 2002; Crompton, 2001; Noll & Zimbalist, 1997). Consistent with this critical stance, Australian scholars have questioned whether the people of Sydney – as opposed to local elites – benefited from hosting the 2000 Olympics. 'The irony is that government, which is meant to be serving the public interest, is instead concentrating . . . on entrepreneurial and corporate rather than broader social goals' (Hall, 2001: 180; see also Wilson, 1996).

It is in the context of competitions between cities to establish themselves as 'world class' urban entertainment destinations, competitions involving the growth aspirations of corporate/civic elites, that we proceed from here to examine the experiences of Canadian cities that have hosted Olympic Games in recent decades: Montreal in summer 1976 and Calgary in winter 1988. We will also consider developments in Vancouver, which hosted Expo '86 and will host the Winter Olympics in 2010. What we will propose in the next sections of the chapter is that Canadian cities that have sought to host an Olympic Games have all had aspirations to promote themselves on a world stage. Each has approached hosting the Olympics as an opportunity to 'bring the world to us', and to demonstrate to visitors and potential investors alike that they were economically dynamic and culturally sophisticated cities. The belief, however, that an Olympic Games leads to an economic windfall for the host city will be challenged, in light of the Canadian experience and other critical scholarship. Then, the argument that an Olympic Games (or other sports mega-event) 'repositions' a host city, by conferring on it an image as a global city, is also critically examined. In the final section, we briefly consider some of the political issues raised by investing public money in the hosting of mega-events. We challenge the view that mega-events and the developments they bring with them are always good for the 'community', or the city 'as a whole'. It will be suggested instead that bidding to host mega-events, in Canada at least, has been a project of civic and regional elites, for the good reason that these elites are best positioned to benefit from whatever economic growth materializes. There are also, however, 'opportunity costs', the effects of which are typically borne by poorer citizens. We urge, therefore, in conclusion, that Olympic hosting should be the subject of a full and inclusive public debate, in which citizens in every social location have opportunities to participate.

Do the Olympics generate economic growth? Is tourism over-rated?

It is widely assumed that hosting an Olympic Games represents an extraordinary economic opportunity for host cities (and nations), justifying the investment of large sums of public money. Yet, it is well known that hosting the Olympics resulted in huge losses and debts for the City of Montreal. When the debt is finally paid off sometime in 2006, it is estimated that hosting the Olympics will have cost Montreal well over Ca\$2 billion in capital and interest costs, without anything like commensurate benefits. It is true that in the years just before the Montreal Olympics (1974–1976), major Quebec construction and building supplies firms did very well (just like their major Japanese counterparts in the 1990s, as outlined above), while in 1976 itself, hotels and restaurants also enjoyed a banner year. Far from experiencing a post-Olympic boom, however, the economy of Montreal in the mid-1970s went into a steep decline that would last for almost two decades. Unemployment doubled between 1975 and 1982, property prices collapsed, and the number of hotel rooms in downtown Montreal declined to pre-Olympic levels (Levine, 1999).

It is necessary to situate Montreal's Olympic deficit in the political context of the times, a decade when French-speaking Canadians were seeking to redefine their relationship to Canada, and when Quebec sovereignty was very much on the political agenda. The most comprehensive study of this era in Montreal politics suggests that for Mayor Jean Drapeau, hosting global events like Expo '67 and the Olympic Games, and building *grands projets* like Habitat (for Expo) and the Olympic Stadium, was at the core of a strategy whereby Montreal would demonstrate its arrival as a 'world city' (Morin, 1998). Drapeau aspired to make Montreal a global destination for tourists, new residents, and investors, and he saw mega-events as a promising way of accomplishing this. Although Drapeau himself was not a separatist, the very strength of separatist sentiment in the early 1970s, and the threat posed by the *Front du libération de Quebec* (FLQ), made the Canadian government reluctant to provide financial support for an event that might exacerbate political divisions in Canada. Having already provided a substantial subsidy to Expo '67, the federal government feared a backlash in the rest of Canada if it were seen to be giving more money to Quebec. This meant that almost all the costs of the Olympic installations were borne by the city of Montreal, with only modest assistance from the province of Quebec. This fact distinguishes Montreal from the standard pattern in which hosting an Olympics is a shared project of national, regional, *and* city governments, with national governments typically bearing a major share of the costs.

The same climate of political uncertainty was a large factor in Montreal's subsequent economic difficulties. In November 1976, only a few months after the Olympics, a *sovereigntiste* Parti Quebecois government was elected, and even though a mandate to negotiate independence from Canada was later refused in a referendum, Quebec pushed ahead with its election promise to make French the working language of public life. This led to a flight of English speakers, a collapse in property prices, and a flight of capital to Toronto that would establish that city as Canada's financial capital. Montreal, it must be noted, has rebounded strongly since the mid-1990s. Greater political stability – along with strong federal patent protection legislation – has contributed to booming biotech and pharmaceutical industries, as well as media and telecommunications, and together these have produced strong growth in 'knowledge industry' jobs and a healthy rebound in property prices. Our point here is that over the long term, the impact of a mega-event, even one as large as an Olympics, cannot be isolated from larger political and economic events. It is also a relatively small factor in the economy of a major metropolitan centre.

Turning to Calgary, the standard view is that hosting the Winter Olympic Games in 1988 was an unqualified success. In contrast to Montreal's deficits, the Calgary Olympics recorded a profit of more than $130 million, in part a product of a business approach closely modelled on that of Los Angeles 1984. At the time Calgary enjoyed the largest revenues from television ever recorded in the history of the Winter Olympics, and significant additional revenues from corporate sponsors (for television rights revenues see the introductory chapter by Horne and Manzenreiter). Importantly, Calgary also enjoyed major financial contributions from both the federal and provincial governments. The profits from the Games have been turned into a Legacy Fund that has helped to maintain the Olympic sports facilities in good condition, and to subsidize sport development in Alberta. Nonetheless, the few scholarly studies that have examined the economic impacts of the 1988 Winter Olympics suggest that the *direct* impacts for Calgary business were not as great as official rhetoric implies.

For example, Mount & Leroux (1994) surveyed medium and small businesses that had opened or added capacity in Calgary in the year before the 1988 Winter Olympics. It was hypothesized that members of this group would have been likely to view the Olympics as good for business. Only 31 per cent, however, (mostly suppliers of goods or services to Olympic facilities) considered that the Games had benefited their businesses. Moreover, even among those who did credit the Olympics with positive effects, more than half believed that the Calgary Stampede (an annual event for which the city is well known) makes a greater contribution to the local economy. Another study found that the impact of the Olympics on public awareness of Calgary in the US (the US was the largest television audience for the Games, and the primary target market for Alberta Tourism promotions) had declined within only two years to a point where it was less than the impact of the Calgary Stampede (Ritchie & Smith, 1991). This finding is mirrored in studies that show that the effects of the Olympics on tourism to Los Angeles and Atlanta were limited to the years of the Games themselves (Baade & Matheson, 2002).

Thus, although tourism may boom in the year of a special event, growth in tourism in the years after the event is difficult to sustain, and is highly dependent on extraneous factors such as economic recessions, political concerns, or health scares (eg, SARS). Moreover, these factors apply not only in the city itself but also in the countries and regions from which tourists come. In addition, special events are also likely to have less impact on the civic economy in the longer term than annual events for which a city develops an international reputation (the Calgary Stampede, as noted, the Montreal International Jazz Festival, in the case of Montreal, or the Edinburgh Festival). The lesson here is that the economic impacts of special event tourism are usually less than advocates would suggest, and that in measuring them it is necessary to look beyond the tourist industry itself. Do they register, in other words, in the standard measures of economic growth: in business start-ups and expansions, for example, in property prices, in retail sales figures (and sales taxes collected), and job creation?

It is important, furthermore, in examining employment effects, to consider not just the number but the quality and stability of the jobs created. Statistics Canada figures indicate that average incomes in the tourist sector in Montreal actually declined between 1990 and 1995, and that jobs in the tourist industry made up 9 of the 25 lowest paying occupations in Canada. There is a counterargument that tourism provides jobs for unskilled workers; official studies, however, underscore the low earnings and productivity associated with most tourism employment (OECD 1995, and Statistics Canada 1998, both cited by Levine, 1999: 441–3). Thus, if the ultimate agenda is not just job creation but the creation of value-added jobs, thereby improving the *quality* of local employment, investing in tourism is not the most cost-effective strategy for achieving this.

A final issue in evaluating economic impacts is that the direct effects of Olympic spending are realised in the years leading up to the event, mostly in the construction and real estate sectors, and in media and advertising. In the former case, though, windfall profits are products of either infrastructure spending or property speculation, and infrastructure spending in most Olympic cities still represents public money. In the case of Japan, as we have noted above, using public funds to create opportunities for the local construction and land development industries is a normal expectation of public policy (see Horne & Manzenreiter, 2004 on 'the construction state' and sport in Japan). It must be recognized, however, that this is not the same as attracting outside investment into the community. To point this out is not to discount the possibility that the business associated with mega-events will lead to subsequent business opportunities, or to global investments in local property (the outcomes that every city hopes for). For these – indirect and often time-delayed – outcomes to occur on any scale, however, usually require other developments (in Vancouver, for example, Asian immigration) of a kind such that precise cause-and-effect relationships are difficult to demonstrate.

For Baade & Matheson (2002), then, the conclusion to be drawn is that cities must be realistic in weighing what the Olympics demand of them in terms of investment in infrastructure, against the benefits likely to be realized after the Games are over. Many of the economic impact studies that predict impressive benefits from Olympics are, in their view, optimistic in their assumptions: in the growth multipliers they use, and in their failure to account for 'leakage' of revenues to transnational suppliers of services (notorious in tourism). The latter represents money that is rarely spent in the community itself. Almost never, moreover, are 'opportunity costs' introduced into the equation. Baade & Matheson (2002: 145) conclude, therefore, that 'the Olympics industry is by its nature exceptional in terms of its infrequency, and the particular and immediate demands it makes on a host economy . . . [and it] can have a permanent impact only to the extent that its infrastructure demands translate into permanent uses . . . [and do not] divert scarce capital and other resources from more productive uses'.

The 'world class' city: place promotion and civic identity

If the economic legacy of hosting major Games is as problematic as the above suggests, why then do cities and nations seek so assiduously to host them? For despite a long history of cost over-runs – illustrated most recently in Athens, the most costly Olympics ever at 9 billion Euro (£6.25 billion), 2. 4 billion Euros over budget, (*The Guardian*, 13 November 2004: 18), there is no shortage of candidate cities.[1] For Canadian cities, on the periphery of international cultural attention until well into the 20th century, the staging of global mega-events has offered a way of putting themselves 'on the map', and showcasing their attractions to international visitors and potential investors. For Montreal's Mayor Drapeau, as we have noted, not only were events like Expo '67 and the 1976 Olympics envisaged as catalysts for major investments in public and private construction. Just as important, the positive global exposure it was envisaged that Montreal would receive from these events, both among visitors and the millions more who would see and read about the city in the international media, would confer on Montreal the status of a 'world class' city. A decade later, Expo '86 in Vancouver and the 1988 Winter Olympics in Calgary offered these two western Canadian cities, historically seen as provincial, a chance to showcase themselves as cities 'come of age through recent economic development' (Hiller, 1989: 119; see also Ley & Olds, 1988 on Vancouver). In Australia, likewise, the America's Cup and Expo '88 offered Perth and Brisbane, respectively, opportunities to 'put the local on show for the global' in cities that international tourists and investors had seldom visited (Fry & Willis, 1988). For these newly wealthy regional cities in both countries, moreover, these events provided opportunities to reposition themselves nationally – to stake claims to being more dynamic, in other words, than the older metropolitan centres of their respective nations (Montreal, Toronto, Sydney, Melbourne).

In Canada, it is useful to understand that Montreal and Toronto have historically been Canada's cultural and economic capitals. Certainly they continue to be Canada's largest cities and, until recently, they were the major centres where new immigrants have settled. Since the 1970s, however, the economy of Western Canada has boomed. Oil has fuelled spectacular growth in Alberta, especially visible in the cities of Calgary and Edmonton. In British Columbia, although natural resources were important (in this case, forest products and mining), the boom was also fuelled by migration (especially from Asia, but also from other parts of Canada). All three cities have undergone transformations that reflect the growth of more diverse and educated populations, including affluent business and professional classes. Incomes and housing prices rose dramatically, and country clubs sprouted, along with opportunities for cosmopolitan dining. Interest in the performing arts spurred the construction of high quality venues, while major new facilities were also built for professional sport.

The latter, in particular, conferred the status of 'major league' on what used to be seen as hinterland cities, not unlike the way that major league sports franchises brought new national attention to American cities like Dallas, Atlanta, Denver, and Phoenix. This, however, was not quite the same as the 'world class' status enjoyed by truly global cities, and coveted by aspiring cities that are not quite there. Thus, just as civic boosters in Atlanta believed that hosting the Olympics would bring their city international recognition and respect (Whitelegg, 2000), so too have leaders in Calgary and Vancouver hoped that hosting mega-events (the 1988 Winter Olympics in Calgary, and Expo '86 and the 2010 Winter Olympics in Vancouver) would draw the world's attention to their attractions. In Vancouver, a city already known for its climate and physical setting, and for the lifestyle opportunities afforded by its proximity to mountain and ocean-based recreation, the provincial government hoped that Expo would showcase a more urbane version of Vancouver. Visitors, it was hoped, would remember the city for its arts and architecture, its 'world class' dining and shopping, and its immigrant energy. In Calgary, the objective was to demonstrate that 'in spite of its reputation, Calgary is not a cowboy town' (Wamsley & Heine, 1996). Trying to shake off the stereotype of 'Stampede City', local leaders saw the Olympics as their chance to show that 'We are a vibrant, modern city eagerly awaiting the opportunity to be introduced to the world' (Wamsley & Heine, 1996).

It is important to appreciate that in western Canada, the discourses of identity that were circulated before and during these events were directed as much at locals as they were at visitors and external audiences. Before the Olympics, for example, civic discourse in Calgary invoked ideas like the quest for excellence, and (especially) competitiveness. These are ideas that are rendered 'natural' in popular understandings of sport, and Calgary citizens were exhorted to take them on as a new kind of collective identity. Calgarians (and Calgary companies) were further invited to 'think big', to look beyond their traditional regional horizons, to make themselves into national, even global leaders. For the Premier of Alberta at that time, Peter Lougheed, the most important legacy of the Olympics was that it demonstrated to Albertans they could shine on a global stage, and got them thinking about what they could accomplish in the future, in other fields of endeavour. Next door in BC, likewise, political leaders in the 1980s articulated the theme of British Columbians 'achieving great things together'. Literature encouraged people, especially young people, to identify with the 'spirit of achievement' through which Vancouver would assume its new destiny as a 'Pacific Rim' city (Ley & Olds, 1988). Since then, a new discourse of achievement, in which civic identity is articulated in terms of global competitiveness, is being recycled as Vancouver prepares to host the 2010 Olympics. A special supplement in the *Globe & Mail*, Canada's national newspaper, on March 31, 2004, for example, included stories entitled 'Businesses ponder how to reap benefits', and 'Corporate Canada keen to be involved'. A full-page advertisement identified the 'Spirit of 2010' as 'the spirit of discovery, enterprise, and opportunity', and went on to emphasize that 'BC leads the nation' in categories like lowest tax rates, and highest job growth.

What lessons can be drawn from these accounts of the place promotion aspirations of three Canadian cities? First, it can be suggested that today, in what Lash & Urry (1994) have called global 'economies of signs and space', investment in civic image is believed to be crucially important in attracting capital and people 'of the right sort' (see also Harvey, 1989). Cities have become imaged commodities whose 'sign values' are crucial to the values that can be realized from a host of other commodities sold there: from T-shirts and gifts to hotel rooms and restaurant meals, and, of course, property itself. As global culture makes the world a smaller place, moreover, and 'entrepreneurial cities' are forced to compete for increasingly mobile consumers and investors, the attraction of outside money is believed to depend increasingly upon civic image. Moreover, when impressive facilities are built on time, and Games are staged successfully (as in Calgary), this is widely regarded as a political and organizational accomplishment, indicating both an ambitious corporate sector and an effective and business-oriented political leadership. Important signals are sent to outside investors about wealth and organizational competence, and about governments that work effectively with the private sector.

Furthermore, it is useful to think about the practices and discourses through which provincial identities are 'modernized'. Fry & Willis (1988) have proposed that for 'places on the margin' (see also Shields, 1991), international Games and Expositions are occasions for self-representation, signalling the arrival of once marginal communities into membership in the dominant world order. Their example is Brisbane, where the 1982 Commonwealth Games and Expo '88 are presented as strategic steps in the 'recoding' of a city once widely regarded as an 'overgrown country town'. The most important audience, however, for discourse about Brisbane's new identity was not visitors from abroad, who in the end didn't come to either event in sufficient numbers to matter very much. It was the people of Brisbane themselves who were the primary targets of messages about the kind of city they could become. The chairman of the Expo Authority proclaimed, for example, 'Brisbane will never be the same after Expo – shopping hours, outdoor eating, the greening of the city, attitudes to hospitality . . . all these things will permanently transform our city' (Bennett, 1991: 46). Expo was thus envisaged, Bennett suggests, as an instrument in the 'cosmopolitanization' of Brisbane, an event through which Brisbane citizens would be initiated into new codes and habits of consumption, and (not unlike Calgary) a more ambitious perspective on their place in the world.

What is going on here, we propose, is that the growth that local elites anxiously hope will result from the re-imaging of their cities does not follow from outside investment alone. What is also necessary is that a regional population who have traditionally been thought as provincial – *and have thought of themselves as provincial* – are encouraged to become more ambitious and outward-looking in their aspirations. As producers, Calgary or Vancouver companies must no longer be satisfied with being the best in western Canada; they must seek to produce value-added products that will find markets around the world. As consumers, meanwhile, individuals' higher knowledge-industry incomes and new tastes for 'world class' products will create value-added opportunities for local retailers, as well as sustained growth in the local real estate and construction sectors. A mega-event, therefore, is not only about showing the city off to the world; it is also about putting the global on show for the locals, and inviting them to take on new identities as citizens of the world – identities that will henceforth be lived in the production and consumption of global products. It is through such self-representations, Bennett suggests, that locals are invited, 'to practise what we must become if progress is to progress, and if we are to keep up with it' (1991: 34). And it is through such new practices and habits of mind that the transformation of 'cities on the margin' is effected, as well as signalled.

Who do Olympics benefit? Opportunity costs

This brings us, finally, to political questions concerning who benefits most from the expenditure of public resources on an Olympics, and whether there are others who lose out when resources that could have been deployed elsewhere are used for these purposes. Certainly the most direct beneficiaries – in both Canada and Japan – are those identified above: construction companies and suppliers, engineers and architects, local security firms, media outlets, and anyone professionally involved in the promotional economy that now surrounds any Olympics (advertising, marketing, public relations). To this list should be added those in the land development and real estate businesses, and indeed anyone else well positioned to benefit from rising property markets. At first glance, this may appear to encompass a wide range of interests.

It is important to understand, however, that there are many lower-income citizens (and, indeed, others) who will not benefit in any direct way from Olympic-related business, and who may actually be hurt by rising property markets, when affordable housing is converted by landlords to more lucrative uses. Moreover, there are others whose quality of life depends upon well-functioning public services, and is diminished when these services are cut back in order to pay for Olympic infrastructure. Sometimes, there seems little alternative, as was the case when Montreal's debt load became so large that many public services in Montreal suffered from underfunding throughout much of the 1980s, with the deterioration in facilities and services that one would expect. Sometimes, though, cuts to public services are made with apparent zeal, as was the case in British Columbia in the 1980s, when the same provincial government that spared no expense in its efforts to make Vancouver's Expo '88 a success imposed an 'austerity program' on provincial public services (Ley & Olds, 1988). This hit hardest at Vancouver's poor and at people in the rural hinterland – the people least likely to benefit from Expo in any way. Our point here is simply that when public funds are pre-empted in order to build facilities for mega-events or to subsidize 'world class' sports venues, this inevitably divides an urban or regional population 'into those who consume world class entertainment and benefit in other ways from its presence, and those who cannot' (Wilson, 1996: 608).

In British Columbia, today, moreover, we are living through a reprise of the 1980s, with another neo-liberal government firmly committed to investing in the Olympics while simultaneously slashing taxes and 'rationalizing' public services. It is important to appreciate, in addition, that Olympic infrastructure (and hence Olympic investment) will be concentrated in what is already the wealthiest corner of the province – Vancouver and the ski resort of Whistler – while schools and hospitals and courthouses are being closed in rural communities in the Interior. It is thus not surprising that, just like in Japan, the biggest boosters of Vancouver's Olympic bid have been the Vancouver corporate sector – precisely the group that stands to get most of the public money that will be spent on construction and promotion, as well as benefit personally from the rises in property values that are already enriching homeowners in Whistler and West Vancouver. For these people and their allies in the government of Premier Gordon Campbell, it may not be going too far to say that the Vancouver Olympics are envisaged as a celebration of a decade of neo-liberalism, just as in 1984 the 'free enterprise' Olympics in Los Angeles were celebrated by US conservatives as confirming the values of the Reagan years. Their boosterism needs to be challenged, however, by critical analysis of the distribution of costs and benefits, and by public debate about 'opportunity costs' that will inevitably fall most heavily on poorer people in the city and the province (Klein, 2003).[2]

For Sassen (1996) and other critics of neo-liberalism, one of the significant developments of the 1980s was the coalescence of two different kinds of claims (and claimants) on public resources. In one camp, local elites aligned themselves with transnational businesses and investors in arguing for major capital expenditures on mega-events and on venues for 'world class' sports and shopping, in order to create post-modern entertainment districts that will attract money back downtown (see Hannigan, 1998). Against these are pitted the claims of neighbourhood and environmental groups, and advocates for poor people and other disadvantaged constituencies, all making claims for *their* needs for labour intensive public services and for 'community-use' facilities of a sort that affluent citizens and tourists almost never use. Advocates for capital spending on developments aimed primarily at the 'visitor class' (Eisinger, 2000) typically claim that the projects they propose will benefit the city as a whole, by increasing tourism and contributing to economic growth. As Bauman (2000) has proposed, however, the 'socio-cultural bubble' in which many affluent people now live has insulated them from any real awareness of how people on wages – let alone social assistance – actually live, and hence of the impacts of neo-liberal social policies on their lives.

These different kinds of claims were illustrated in the unsuccessful Olympic bid of Toronto, which lost the 1996 Olympics to Atlanta. The Toronto bid was initially inspired by the commercial success and the corporate model of Los Angeles '84. The Toronto Ontario Olympic Committee (TOOC) was formed on a corporate model, and included some of Toronto's major construction and real estate interests. Although TOOC had to seek political approval to bid on Toronto's behalf, and pursue agreements to build facilities on land owned by the federal government, they sought to avoid detailed public discussion of their plans. They were challenged, however, by a group of social activists, calling themselves 'Bread Not Circuses', who encouraged public opposition to the spending of public funds on Olympic facilities at a time when both Ontario and Toronto were cutting back on social services. At a minimum, Bread Not

Circuses wanted any Olympic plans to include environmental and social impact assessments, to provide for social housing, and to guarantee jobs to women and minorities (Kidd, 1992).

In this context, a core of social democratic Toronto Councillors worked with city officials to develop what came to be called the 'Toronto Olympic Commitment', a document that committed Toronto to fulfilling a number of social objectives, in the event that the city was awarded the Games. Only the provisions for social housing stood to cost the private sector any real money; however, TOOC leader Paul Henderson (a former Olympic yachtsman) and some of his corporate allies railed against 'political interference', insisting that 'social issues are not sport issues'. Yet, as another Torontonian and former Olympian, Bruce Kidd, has argued, 'Mega-projects like the Olympic Games require a tremendous investment of human and physical resources from the communities that stage them. . . . They play a decisive role in the character and pace of a region's development, often reshaping the pattern of land use . . . and the infrastructure of the localities where they take place.' They are, as a result, very properly the subject of public debate, not least because they 'illuminate competing notions of the public good' (Kidd, 1992: 154–167).

Concluding remarks

In summing up, we have highlighted a number of parallel developments in the pursuit of hosting major international sports events in Canada and Japan. In both countries, Olympic hosting has been the project of political and corporate elites, and in both countries large claims were made for the economic and social benefits that would follow from hosting Olympics and other mega-events (in Japan, such as the football World Cup). The outcomes, however, have been that public and private investments in the 'infrastructure of play' have created expensive sporting infrastructure and other consumer spaces, but with few social benefits for those unable (or dis-inclined) to present themselves as consumers. Hosting sports mega-events was also intended to signal the emergence of once 'peripheral' cities as major players in the national and global economies, and to attract international tourism. Once again, however, the historical experience suggests that these efforts at 'place promotion' have impacts that are fleeting, at best, and as the years pass it becomes difficult to isolate the impacts of the mega-event on the fortunes and stature of a city from those of other economic triggers or from larger cycles of growth and recession.

Flyvbjerg, Bruzelius & Rothengatter (2003: 60) suggest that, with respect to the impacts of megaprojects, 'Rarely is there a simple truth . . . What is presented as reality by one set of experts is often a social construct that can be deconstructed and reconstructed by other experts'. Nonetheless, our reading of the success of these projects is on balance a sceptical one. In Canada, in the case of Montreal, the evidence is overwhelming that hosting the Olympics was an economic disaster, with negative effects on the city's ability to fund social services and infrastructure that lasted for more than twenty years. For Calgary and Vancouver, their timing was/is much more fortuitous. Since 1984, enhanced television revenues as well as the IOC's new strategies for raising both television and sponsorship revenues and sharing these with the host city mean that no Olympic host should incur the deficits and debts that Montreal did (though reports suggest that Athens now faces very similar burdens). Calgary made a profit, and other Olympic cities should, too.

In Japan, too, investments in sport facilities and sport events have captured a central position in consumption-based, economic development, politics. As in other late capitalist societies, municipal governments have faced increasing competition for private investments in the local infrastructure and amenities in order to attract business investors, jobs, and residents for the ultimate purpose of generating new revenue streams. Yet hosting the Winter Olympic Games (1998) and the football World Cup (2002) did not produce the outcomes predicted in advance of the events (Manzenreiter & Horne, 2005).

What must be understood, in any case, is that the calculation of sports mega-event profits and losses is seldom transparent, and always complicated by what 'other' costs (let alone opportunity costs) are included in the accounting. It is worth noting, moreover, that even though Olympic cities today get far more financial support from the IOC than they did in the 1970s, cities that win the right to host Olympics do so only by promising to provide facilities and services that still require large investments by host governments. This was true in Calgary, as it was in Athens, and will undoubtedly be so in Beijing and Vancouver. Income from television and sponsorship is intended to offset these costs, but much of this is absorbed in providing security and state-of-the-art telecommunications infrastructure. A full and transparent account of an Olympics will still show a loss on the public account, most unbiased evidence suggests, so the questions become whether the event and the facilities will lead to other desirable outcomes. Are the facilities of a sort that will be valuable to the city afterwards, following Baade & Matheson (2002), or are they, as we observed was the case in Nagano, not well suited to the city's needs? As Chernushenko (1994: 28) notes, 'The challenge for any host city . . . is 'to make the Olympics fit the city' and not the city fit the Olympics'. What this points to, in the end, is that environmental and social impact assessments, as well as full public consultation *before* submitting bids, are necessary if major sports events are ever to become democratically accountable (Flyvbjerg, Bruzelius & Rothengatter, 2003).

Notes

1 It should be noted that this was not always the case. In the aftermath of Montreal's deficit and the 1980 Moscow boycott, Los Angeles was (after the withdrawal of Teheran) the only serious bidder for the 1984 Summer Games.
2 Another suggestion that the road to the 2010 Winter Olympics will not be without its obstacles is that, at the time of completing the writing of this chapter in February 2006, the organisers, the

Vancouver 2010 Organizing Committee (VANOC), were reported to be seeking an additional Ca\$110 million to cover rising construction costs (http://www.theglobeandmail.com/servlet/ArticleNews/TPStory/LAC/20060204/BCOLYMPICS04/TPNational/). For some of us it is not surprising.

References

Baade, R. & Matheson, V. (2002) 'Bidding for the Olympics: Fool's gold?', in C. Barros, M. Ibrahimo & S. Szymanski (eds) *Transatlantic Sport*. London: Edward Elgar, 127–151.

Bauman, Z. (2000) *Community*. Cambridge: Polity.

Bennett, T. (1991) 'The shaping of things to come: Expo '88', *Cultural Studies* 5 (2): 32–46.

Chernushenko, D. (1994) *Greening our Games: Running Sports Events and Facilities that won't Cost the Earth*. Ottawa: Centurion.

Crompton, J. (2001) 'Public subsidies to professional team sport facilities in the USA', in C. Gratton & I. Henry (eds) *Sport in the city*. London: Routledge, 15–34.

Eisinger, P. (2000) 'The politics of bread and circuses: building the city for the visitor class', *Urban Affairs Review* 35: 316–333.

Flyvbjerg, B., Bruzelius, N. & Rothengatter, W. (2003) *Megaprojects and Risk*. Cambridge: Cambridge University Press.

Fry, T. & Willis, A. (1988) 'Expo '88: backwoods into the future', *Cultural Studies* 2 (1): 127–138.

Gratton, C. & Henry, I. (eds) *Sport in the City*. London: Routledge.

Hall, C.M. (2001) 'Imaging, tourism and sports event fever: the Sydney Olympics and the need for a social charter for mega-events', in C. Gratton & I. Henry (eds) *Sport in the City*. London: Routledge, 166–183.

Hannigan, J. (1998) *Fantasy City*. London: Routledge.

Harada, M. (2005) 'Hosting mega-sports events and its impact upon city development in Japan'. Unpublished paper presented at an international workshop entitled 'Hosting Major International Sports Events: Comparing Asia and Europe', the University of Edinburgh, 10–11 March.

Harvey, D. (1989) *The Condition of Postmodernity*. Oxford: Blackwell.

Hiller, H. (1989) 'Impact and image: the convergence of urban factors in preparing for the 1988 Calgary Winter Olympics', in G. Syme *et al.* (eds) *The Planning and Evaluation of Hallmark Events*. Aldershot: Avebury Press, 119–131.

Horne, J. (2004) 'The global game of football, the 2002 World Cup and regional development in Japan', *Third World Quarterly* 25: 1233–1244.

Horne, J. & Manzenreiter, W. (2004) 'Accounting for mega-events: forecast and actual impacts of the 2002 Football World Cup finals on the host countries Japan and Korea', *International Review for the Sociology of Sport* 39 (2): 187–203.

Jessop, B. (2002) *The Future of the Capitalist State*. Cambridge: Polity.

Judd, D. (ed.) (2003) *The Infrastructure of Play: Building the Tourist City*. London & New York: M.E. Sharpe.

Kidd, B. (1992) 'The Toronto Olympic Commitment: towards a social contract for the Olympic Games', *Olympika: International Journal of Olympic Studies* 1: 154–167.

Klein, N. (2003) 'An Olympic land grab', *The Guardian* 22 July, 21.

Lash, S. & Urry, J. (1994) *Economies of Signs and Space*. London: Sage.

Levine, M. (1999) 'Tourism, urban development, and the "world-class" city: the cases of Baltimore and Montreal', in C. Andrew, P. Armstrong & A. Lapiere (eds) *World Class Cities: Can Canada Play?* Ottawa: University of Ottawa Press, 421–450.

Ley, D. & Olds, K. (1988) 'Landscape as spectacle: World's Fairs and the culture of heroic consumption', *Society and Space* 6: 191–212.

Manzenreiter, W. & Horne, J. (2002) 'Global governance in world sport and the 2002 World Cup Korea/Japan', in J. Horne & W. Manzenreiter (eds) *Japan, Korea and the 2002 World Cup*, London: Routledge, 1–25.

Manzenreiter, W. & Horne, J. (eds) (2004) *Football Goes East: Business, Culture and the 'People's Game' in China, Japan and Korea*. London: Routledge.

Manzenreiter, W. & Horne, J. (2005) 'Public policy, sports investments and regional development initiatives in contemporary Japan', in J. Nauright, & K. Schimmel (eds) *The Political Economy of Sport*. London: Palgrave, 152–182.

McCormack, G. (2002) 'Breaking the Iron Triangle', *New Left Review* (2nd Ser.) 13: 5–23.

Morin, G. (1998) *La cathédrale inachevée*. Montreal: XYZ editeur.

Mount, J. & Leroux, C. (1994) 'Assessing the effects of a mega-event: a retrospective study of the impact of the Olympic Games in the Calgary business sector', *Festival Management and Event Tourism* 2: 15–23.

Noll, R. & Zimbalist, A. (1997) *Sports, Jobs, and Taxes: Economic Impacts of Professional Sports Teams and Stadiums*. Washington: Brookings Institution.

Ritchie, B. & Smith, J. (1991) 'The impact of a mega event on host region awareness: a longitudinal study', *Journal of Travel Research* 30: 3–10.

Roberts, K. (2004) *The Leisure Industries*. London: Palgrave.

Roche, M. (2000) *Mega-Events and Modernity*. London: Routledge.

Sassen, S. (1996) 'Whose city is it? Globalization and the formation of new claims', *Public Culture* 8: 205–223.

Seki, H. (1997) *Sengo Nihon no supotsu seisaku. Sono kozo to tenkai* [Sport policy in post war Japan]. Tokyo: Taishokan Shoten.

Shields, R. (1991) *Places on the Margin: Alternative Geographies of Modernity*. London: Routledge.

Shoval, N. (2002) 'A new phase in the competition for the Olympic gold: the London and New York bids for the 2012 Games', *Journal of Urban Affairs* 24 (5): 583–599.

UK Sport (1999) *Measuring Success*. London: UK Sport.

UK Sport (2004) *Measuring Success 2: The economic impact of major sports events*. London: UK Sport.

Vigor, A., Mean, M. & Tims, C. (eds) (2004) *After the Gold Rush*. London: Institute for Public Policy Research.

Wall, S. (1995) *Nagano Story: The Hidden Costs of Hosting the Winter Olympics in Japan*, film directed by S. Wall, London: London Guildhall University.

Wamsley, K. & Heine, M. (1996) 'Tradition, modernity and the construction of civic identity: the Calgary Olympics', *Olympika: International Journal of Olympic Studies* 5: 81–90.

Whitelegg, D. (2000) 'Going for gold: Atlanta's bid for fame', *International Journal for Urban and Regional Research* 24 (4): 801–817.

Whitson, D. (1998) 'Circuits of promotion: media, marketing, and the globalization of sport', in L. Wenner (ed.) *MediaSport*. London: Routledge, 57–72.

Wilson, H. (1996) 'What is an Olympic city? Visions of Sydney 2000', *Media, Culture & Society* 18 (3): 603–618.

Modernizing China in the Olympic spotlight: China's national identity and the 2008 Beijing Olympiad

*Xin Xu**

Introduction

The XXIX Olympiad is coming to Beijing at a critical juncture of the world history of globalization and the Chinese history of grand socioeconomic transformation. Following in the footsteps of its two East Asian neighbours, Japan and South Korea, who respectively hosted the Tokyo Olympiad in 1964 and the Seoul Olympiad in 1988, the People's Republic of China (PRC) is determined to turn this sporting mega-event into the celebration of a Chinese renaissance and the harmonization of world civilizations under the theme slogan 'One World, One Dream'. In the making is a new history – as the low politics of sport is conspicuously connected with the high politics of national identities and international relations in the spotlight of the upcoming Beijing Olympics in 2008.

The significance of sport for nation-states has been increasingly acknowledged in recent years (Brownell, 1995; Maguire, 1999; Roche, 2000). Yet, its specific socio-political meanings for countries at different stages of socioeconomic development and with different political and strategic objectives remain understudied in the social sciences (Roche, 2000). The core – periphery dichotomy in international sport (Horne and Manzenreiter, 2004) that coincides with the 'West – Rest' fault line in the world political-economic system has only recently gained sparse attention from international relations scholars (Huntington, 1996). A detailed analysis of the relationship between nation building and sport policy in terms of modernity (pre-modern, modernizing, and postmodern) may reveal different patterns of state-sport relations in the community of nations. By the same token, an examination of the political dynamics of international sport may also enrich our knowledge about contemporary international relations. To the extent that sporting mega-events such as the Olympic Games and the World Football Cup have become central stages on which elite athletes represent their nations to compete for physical excellence and primacy, they have provided nation-states with a universally legitimate way to present and promote their national identities and cultures; this is especially true for host countries.

This chapter looks at China's tortuous paths toward the Olympics in the context of China's identity politics and international relations from a socio-political perspective. The intriguing notion that China cannot claim to be a great power unless it becomes a 'great nation of physical culture and sport' (*tiyu daguo*) serves as a departure point for a political analysis of the 2008 Beijing Olympiad. My main argument is that the Beijing Olympiad marks a watershed in China's continued long march toward a modernized, unified, and interna-tionalised nation in the global community of nations. While the award to host the Olympiad has certainly set the new impetus for China's modernization drive and international integration, it has also compelled China to carefully handle some intractable contradictions in the process of modernization, particularly with regard to the complex identity politics across the Taiwan Strait. The vision of staging 'the best ever Olympic Games' will be subject to a great test hinging upon China's balancing act in dealing with several major contradictions – between utilizing the state-centric sport administrative system for 'elitist, com-petitive sport' (*jingji tiyu*) and developing societal-level modern physical culture and sport (*quanmin tiyu*), between encouraging nationalist pride to enhance internal cohesion and fostering the harmonization of different civilizations for the purpose of external resonance, and between containing the Taiwan inde-pendence movement and promoting greater national reconciliation across the Taiwan Strait. What 'unique legacy' the Beijing Olympiad will leave to the nation and the Olympic Movement will depend not only upon whether Beijing will stage the 2008 Games as an extravagant festival of great sport in the Olympic spotlight but also, more importantly, upon how well China will conduct a bal-ancing act in these areas in the socio-political background.

The discussion that follows consists of three main sections. The first section will provide a historical review of China's sports policy in terms of its role in modern nation building and international integration. The second section will focus on staging the Beijing Olympics as a mega-event for presenting China's international image and promoting the harmonization of East-West civiliza-tions. The final section will examine the daunting problem of emerging diver-gent nation building across the Taiwan Strait in the context of the Beijing Olympiad. In conclusion, the chapter will try to shed light on the implications of the Beijing Olympiad for China's continued modernization drive beyond the 2008 Games.

Sport as the continuation of politics by other means

It is almost a truism that contemporary sport is embedded in the global politi-cal economy, as well as in the development of the modern international state system. Sport is conceptualized as practices, institutions, and ideologies that have evolved and migrated across national boundaries under globalization's transformative pressures (LaFeber, 1999). Historically, the development of modern sport in Europe was inseparable from the rise of modern nationalism after the French Revolution (Brownell, 1995: 46, citing Eichberg). In East Asia, modern sport was imported from the West alongside western imperialist expansion during the 19th century (Horne, 2004: 1235). For China, physical culture in general and sport in particular developed alongside efforts to turn a dynastic realm into a modern nation-state according to the political ideas of the times (Brownell, 1995: 46).

In the history of the PRC, sport can be best understood as the continuation of politics by other means. Sport features prominently in the Communist-led social transformation and has played a unique role in bridging a gap between the state and society. Revolutionary leader Mao Zedong once favoured 'mass sport' as opposed to 'elitist, competitive sport'. In the first few years after the founding of the PRC, people's sports activities and events were officially encouraged and staged across the country. Driven by the revolutionary ideal of building an egalitarian society, Communist body culture played a part in the PRC's early socialist transformation. It did not take long for the state to realize that another equally significant political implication could be inferred from state sports policy for new China's nation building and international prestige – namely, representation of a nation through sports competition in the international arena. China's rushed participation at the Helsinki Olympic Games in 1952 served as a departure point when the frustrated Chinese athletic delegation was shocked and amazed by the outstanding performance of Soviet and East European athletes in the Games (Li and Su, 2004). As a result, the government decided to establish a centralized sports system in 1955 after the Soviet model, thus endowing sport with a greater international political meaning. Vice Premier He Long, one of the People's Liberation Army's (PLA) ten marshals, was appointed as the first chairman of the State Sports Commission. Sport has been ever since implicitly or explicitly defined as another frontier, apart from military and diplomacy, of New China's struggle for its international legitimacy and prestige. Chinese athletes, like PLA soldiers, were expected to fight for the glory of New China in the international sports arena. Indeed they were organized, disciplined, and trained very much like soldiers according to militaristic spirits. In the process of new nation building, they were endowed with a nationalist mission to transform the 'sick man of East Asia' (*Dong Ya bingfu*) into a strong and modern nation respected by the world. The link between sport, the military, and national salvation has persisted even until today (Brownell, 1995: 22; Li and Su, 2004).

The severing of ties with the IOC in 1958 due to the 'two Chinas' problem, however, functionally blocked Chinese athletes' participation in almost all international sports events. Not until the 1970s, when China took the new initiative in promoting its 'Third World diplomacy', did Chinese athletes begin to get actively involved in the state-sanctioned 'cultural diplomacy', serving as China's cultural envoys to visit many foreign countries. Under these circumstances, Chinese athletes enjoyed the privileges and convenience to go abroad for sports exchanges without much restriction and for an extended period (Li and Su, 2004). The mission they were instructed to carry on was 'friendship first, contest second' (*youyi diyi, bisai dier*) which politically defined their role more as a vehicle of the state's diplomacy than as athletes in competitive matches. This happened against the background of China's enhanced assistances to Third World countries with many of its aid projects being construction of stadiums and gymnasiums in those beneficiary countries.

Thus it is no accident that the famous 'ping pong diplomacy' that helped break the ice in China-US relations also took place in this period. Sport, as a form of state soft power, was deliberately employed by political leaders to fulfil subtle and seemingly impossible diplomatic tasks at a certain critical moment. When US President Nixon at last came to Beijing to hold a summit meeting with Mao in 1972, 'the small ball' (ping pong) eventually moved the 'big ball' (the globe).

The 1970s constituted a turning point in China's participation and integration in the international community. Starting with the PRC's entry into the UN in 1971 and concluding with the normalization of PRC-US diplomatic relations in 1979, China emerged on the world stage as a rising great power. Underscoring China's international integration was its 'second revolution', as demonstrated in the shift of its developmental course from Maoist 'continuous revolutions' to Dengist 'four modernizations' through reform and opening-up. China's sports policy in general and its relations with the Olympic Movement in particular were part of this transformative process. The change of national development paths and reformulation of national identity along reformist modernizing lines coincided with China's re-entry into the Olympic Movement in 1979. As Brownell (1995: 110) observes, the Olympic 'Games gave the overall impression of an attempt to symbolically link economic modernization, Chinese nationalism, and Communist Party legitimacy into a meaningful and even moving totality'. The slogan 'break out of Asia and advance on the world' (*chongchu Yazhou, zouxiang shijie*) was a manifestation of the Chinese nation's aspiration for the status of a great power revitalized by the Dengist 'new long march' toward a modern and strong nation in the family of nation states.

Ironically, persistent efforts to engineer structural reforms through decentralization and 'marketization' in many realms contrast starkly with continued and even greater reliance on the Soviet-style centralized administrative system in the field of sport as an effective mechanism for fulfilling the 'great power dream' (*qiangguo meng*) (Zhao, 1988; Brownell, 1995; Li and Su, 2004). The party-state has found itself in the challenging situation in which it has had to rely more on patriotism for reinforcing its legitimacy, which has been weakened by de-ideologization and the market-oriented modernization drive. Sport, again, appears to be a powerful instrument for state legitimization and national cohesion. In many ways, Chinese athletes are expected to be agents of representing China's reformed national identity on the world stage, both symbolically and physically. Projecting the image of a strong sports nation in the international arena has become an essential component of China's rise on the world stage.

Under these circumstances, the notion of 'elitist, competitive sport' has replaced the concept of 'friendship first, contest second' as a new organizing principle of state sports policy. In particular, hosting sporting mega-events has gained an even greater political and national meaning for the state and for the nation as a whole. This is the backdrop against which China began its bid for an Olympic Games built on the momentum of its staging a successful Asian Games in 1990. It was Deng Xiaoping who first challenged Chinese sports officials with the mission to bid for the Olympic Games (Chinese Olympic Committee, 2004; Lianhe Zhaobao, 2001b).

Despite growing strained relations between the state and society, it is here in sport, and in China's bid for the Olympic Games in particular, that the state interest and public aspiration converge. Although Beijing's first bid for the 2000 Olympic Games ended with failure and frustration, the nation remained enthusiastically behind its second attempt for the 2008 Games. The Beijing Olympic Bid Committee claimed 94.9 per cent public support in Beijing (Tang, 2001: 13), whereas the IOC poll showed 96 per cent support in Beijing and other urban areas (IOC, 2001: 60). This may well represent people's great enthusiasm for the first ever China-held Games nationwide. The IOC Evaluation Commission concluded that 'There is significant public support for the prospect of organising the Olympic Games and a feeling that a successful bid would bring recognition to the nation' (IOC, 2001: 75).

Because of the growing importance of promoting national unity through active participation in international sports activities, the Soviet-style system leaning on competitive sport not only remains unchanged, but also has even reached its peak of development in recent years (Li and Su, 2004). Here arises a critical question: how far can China go in its committed drive for great nationhood, of which a great sports nation is an essential part, by relying on the state-centric, highly politicised sports system?

As early as in the 1980s, some within the PRC already criticized the state sports system and took issue with the idea of using sport to fulfil the 'great power dream' (Zhao, 1988). The signs of change have also appeared from within the state sports system. Since the mid 1980s, thanks to the overall relaxing political atmosphere, more space for individual freedom, and new incentives created by market-oriented reform, many Chinese elite athletes have gone abroad on their own to play or coach in national teams of other countries. In the Chinese press, they are described as the 'overseas corps' (*haiwai bingtuan*) who directly challenge the prominence of China in some sport fields, of which table tennis and diving are most conspicuous. On the other hand, Chinese soccer teams, national and local alike, have invited foreign coaches to help train their players in order to meet Chinese fans' ever higher yet often frustrated expectations. More recently, the Chinese basketball player, Yao Ming, joined the Houston Rockets in America's National Basketball Association (NBA) and has become a sports star in China as well as in the United States. These are signs of a gradual transition in the background, which will come to the fore on a much larger scale sooner or later.

According to Yuan Weimin, who oversaw China's sports administration and held the presidency of the Chinese Olympic Committee until after the 2004 Athens Olympiad, China cannot boast itself as a great power in terms of physical culture. A strong sports nation, in Yuan's view, would encompass many aspects, including citizens' moral and physical qualities, sport and recreation facilities, people's consciousness of physical culture and participation in it, individual investments in sports activities, as well as sports industry and the level of competitive sport (Li and Su, 2004). Yuan's sober observation is an invaluable reminder of an even greater challenge ahead. Although it will be unrealistic to expect that anything could be done to address this challenge in the lead up to the Beijing Games, as public expectations concentrate on winning the first place in terms of medals and projecting the image of the nation (Li and Su, 2004), it is hoped that the Beijing Games will constitute a new turning point in China's continuous grand transformation in sport and beyond.

East meets West

The Olympic Games, due to its great public exposure, means that 'the stakes have been higher and the need for circumspection correspondingly greater than in other sports organizations' (Hill, 1992: 31). The Games 'increasingly serve as an arena for debate about modern nationhood and international relations' (Brownell, 1995: 313). According to MacAloon (1991: 42) 'To be a nation recognized by others and realistic to themselves, a people must march in the Olympic Games Opening Ceremonies procession'. As to the IOC, in Brownell's (1995: 31) words, 'In its scope, it is perhaps rivalled only by the United Nations and the Roman Catholic Church.'

Until 1979 the Cold War and the 'two Chinas' issue had dominated the IOC politics when it came to the question of representation of China in the Olympic Movement. The PRC severed all contacts with the IOC in 1958 in protest at Taiwan's continuing membership in the IOC under the title of the 'Chinese Olympic Committee'. Since 1979, however, China's participation in the Olympic Movement has been part of its increasingly widening and deepening integration into world affairs, as well as its continuous modernization through a grand strategy of reform and opening-up.

Based on its successful hosting of the 1990 Asian Games, Beijing started its first bid for the Olympic Games. That Beijing lost its bid for the 2000 Olympic Games to Sydney by a margin of only two votes in the last round after it led the vote counts in the previous three rounds was not lost on political scientist Samuel Huntington, who put forth a provocative thesis of the 'clash of civilizations' as a new paradigm for post-Cold War global politics (Huntington, 1993). For Huntington, the dramatic results of the votes provided ammunition to his combative argument that the new fault line in world politics falls between the West and the 'Rest' (Huntington, 1996).

Arguably, there has always been an inherent tension between Baron Pierre de Coubertin's notion of internationalism, by which he meant respect for each person's country, based on an appreciation of the differences between countries, and the tendency of homogenizing world culture through the worldwide spread of the Olympic Movement (de Coubertin, 1967: 20; Brownell, 1995: 32). Also as has been noted before, the core-periphery barrier in international sport as a manifestation of the evolution of the world capitalist system remains to be overcome. In so far as China is the largest developing country striving to move upward from the peripheral status to one of the core, bidding and hosting an Olympic Games certainly has an enormous implication for itself and global politics. In fact, in its bids for both the 2000 and 2008 Olympic Games, China put an emphasis on the argument that a truly international Olympic Movement would have to encompass the non-Western world. In his letter to the IOC in 2000, then China's President Jiang Zemin wrote:

> It will be of extremely great significance to promoting and carrying out the Olympic spirit in China and across the world and to facilitating the *cultural exchanges and convergence between East and West* if the Games of the XXIX Olympiad are held in China, a rapidly developing country with a long-standing civilization and 22 percent of the world's population (Jiang, 2000; Italics added).

On 13 July 2001 at the 112th IOC Session in Moscow, Beijing was elected the Host City for the Games of the XXIX Olympiad in 2008. The vote followed in line with 'the Commission's belief that a Beijing Games would leave a unique legacy to China and to sports. The Commission is confident that Beijing could organize an excellent Games (IOC, 2001: 95).' During his visit to the Beijing Organising Committee for the 2008 Olympics (BOCOG) in February 2003, Ottavio Cinquanta, member of the IOC executive board, stated:

> You have a great opportunity to use the Games through television to present China in the modern concept to the entire world. But more importantly, it's for China. The 2008 Olympics will be so important that it becomes a special event in Chinese history (*People's Daily*, 2003).

Aiming at the objective of 'New Beijing, Great Olympics' (*xin Beijing, xin Aoyun*)[1], the BOCOG has defined the 'Green Olympics, High-tech Olympics, and Humanistic Olympics' (*luse Aoyun, keji Aoyun, renwen Aoyun*)[2] as the three major themes of the Beijing Games. Liu Qi, in his capacity as the chairman of the BOCOG, further elaborated on the characteristics of the Beijing Olympic Games as 'Chinese style', 'cultural attractions', 'spirit of the times', and 'public participation' (BOCOG News, 2005a).

Susan Brownell (1995: 314) suggests that 'The Olympic Games have become the world's largest single event for the production of national culture for international consumption'. According to Jin Yuanpu, director of China's Remin University's Humanistic Olympics Studies Center, the concept of 'Humanistic Olympics' represents a creative idea of unique value, which is at the heart of the spirit of the Beijing Olympics. Efforts to 'rediscover' humanism as a core

Chinese cultural legacy have been made in recent years in order to reconstruct a moral order as opposed to the materialistic tendencies in China's drastic modernization. By preparing for and hosting the Olympic Games according to humanism, Jin argues, China will greatly promote the development of the 'three major civilizations'. First, 'Humanistic Olympics' provides China with an opportunity of reconstructing the value system of Chinese civilization and re-projecting the image of cultural China so as to reshape China's international environment into one of enduring harmony. Second, it presents to China also an opportunity of putting the 'scientific notion of development' into practice, adjusting China's development strategy in a well-balanced, well-coordinated, and more comprehensive way. Third, it constitutes an opportunity to promote democratization by emphasising human wellbeing and realisation of full human potential as the ultimate goal of development (Jin, 2005).

Underscoring this discourse is the party-state's new emphasis on the notion of 'development for people' (*yi min wei ben*) in its modernization strategy. Since 2003, President Hu Jintao and Premier Wen Jiabao have articulated a new vision for building a 'harmonious socialist society' through the 'scientific and sustainable pursuit' of China's development. The resonance of the Beijing Olympics' themes with the renewed state policy highlights the efforts to redefine China's political identity in line with traditional and universal values of greater appeal.

A good illustration of the main themes of the Beijing Olympics is the message embodied in the official emblem of 'Chinese Seal, Dancing Beijing,' which cleverly combines the Chinese seal and the art of calligraphy with sporting features, transforming the elements into a human figure running forward and embracing triumph. As a unique Chinese cultural product the Chinese seal in particular represents the identity and credibility of China that is attached and committed to the 2008 Olympics (BOCOG, 2003). Another highlight of the Beijing Games will be its opening and closing ceremonies. As the 1990 Asian Games hosted in Beijing showed, opening and closing ceremonies can prominently represent the Chinese nation to the outside world, and reflect a shift from the National Games that functioned as a representation of the nation unto itself. The 1990 Asian Games made use of symbols that evoked positive emotions among the majority of Chinese people as the ceremonies expressed much popular nationalism (Brownell, 1995: 315–317). But the 2008 Beijing Olympiad will be different from the 1990 Asian Games both in its historical context and in terms of its global audience. The ocean-themed opening ceremony of the 2000 Sydney Olympic Games and the one inspired by the ancient Greek mythology of the 2004 Athens Games also compel Beijing to be creative and competitive in impressing the world with grand ceremonies that will present China both as an ancient civilization and as a modernizing nation (BOCOG, 2005b; on opening and closing ceremonies see Tomlinson, 1996). Underpinning the new thinking about the Beijing Games is a growing consciousness of turning the momentum of hosting the Games into an enduring opportunity of cultural rejuvenation – the Chinese renaissance – and China's deepening integration into the international community.

In the past four years, Beijingers have become used to regarding their city as a 'grand construction site', consisting of about 2,000 new construction projects each year. The lifespan of a Beijing map has been reduced from three years in the 1980s to about a month due to the lightening speed of change in the landscape of the city. Nowadays even old Beijingers can get lost very easily! Beijing's rate of development is so massive that building for the 2008 Olympics actually represents only about 10 per cent of the city's construction plans spread over the next seven years.

Much of the ongoing construction work has cultural content. As the IOC notes, 'China's ancient civilization features prominently in the cultural programme. There will be a prolonged cultural build up to the 2008 Games involving communications, educational programs, cultural events and ceremonies, with different themes in different years' (IOC, 2001: 73). The Beijing municipal government has planned to invest 7 billion Yuan (US$854 million) in renovating cultural relics and building museums, ie, allocating 120 million Yuan (about US$14 million) annually. This means not only renovating big cultural relics, such as the Ming city walls, but also bringing a reprieve for hundreds of old-fashioned alleys (*hutong*) and quadrangles (*siheyuan*), where ordinary people live, which would otherwise have been demolished. Beijing now has 118 museums, and by 2008 it will have about 130. Each year, over 200 permanent exhibitions and 400 touring ones are held in Beijing museums, which attract 30 million visitors, according to figures from Beijing's Cultural Relics Bureau (Xinhua, 2003).

The 'renaissance' has also appeared to penetrate at the community level. New style community building is under way. For example, in the Andingmen District, communities have established an academy of Chinese learning (*guoxue guan*), providing pre-school children with a systematic education in traditional culture. The notion of the 'book fragrant community' (*shu xiang shequ*) has become a motif of 'spiritual civilization' programmes at the community level, aiming at the objective of 'everyone reads, everyone succeeds' and 'book fragrant Beijing, humanistic Olympics'. In July 2003, the first Olympic community was established in Beijing (China Sports News, 2004).

Olympic fever has also manifested itself in Beijingers' enthusiasm about learning English. For taxi drivers, public servants, and workers in the service sector, learning English has become the order of the day. Since Beijing won the bid to host the Games in 2001 the Imperial Ancestral Temple in the centre of Beijing has turned, during the holiday 'golden' week in May each year, into a mass gathering for and celebration of foreign language learning, attracting tens of thousands of people annually (China Sports News, 2004).

Despite all these efforts, Beijing's Mayor Wang Qishan has openly expressed his 'biggest concern' about the 2008 Games – the demeanour of Beijingers (*Beijingren de suzhi* – literally, the quality of Beijingers) as both host and audience. As early as when Beijing won the bid, the Beijing municipal government's Office of Spiritual Civilization issued a declaration challenging Beijingers to remould their manners by eliminating twelve 'little diseases' (*xiao maobing*), such as spitting, queue- jumping, paying no attention to traffic rules while cross-ing a street, smiling too little, and being too talkative. While many Beijingers may feel embarrassed and ashamed about explicitly exposing their bad manners in such a way, how much progress they can make remains to be seen. In August 2004, when Japan defeated China to win the Asian Football Confederation Championships, thousands of Chinese fans 'displayed what could mildly be termed a 'lack of sportsmanship' by burning Japanese national flags, shouting anti-Japanese slogans, clashing with police . . . Much of the media outside the PRC saw the Chinese soccer fans as uncivilized and immature and their demon-stration of nationalism as little less than virulent' (Global News Wire, 2004). While underscoring this incident is the Chinese nationalistic sentiments against Japan that were evoked by their memory of Japanese atrocities before and during World War Two and provoked by some recent incidents such as Japan's Prime Minister Koizumi's repeated visit to the Yasukuni Shrine, the burst of radical popular nationalism against foreign countries attests to Mayor Wang's concern in the worst possible way. More importantly, it has posed a big chal-lenge to the party-state to channel the expression of popular nationalism in a civilized way at the time when its legitimacy is so attached to nationalism but the goal of its hosting policy is to promote harmonization between China and the rest of the world. Apart from building up policing at sports events, as the Shangdong provincial government did for a recent football match between a Chinese and Japanese team, it seems uncertain at this point what else the gov-ernment will do to contain any future expressions of popular nationalism.

Across the Taiwan Strait, 'no Olympic break'?

In April 2001, a mock vote by students of City Sports College in Taipei showed that for the 2008 Olympic Games, Beijing 'won' the vote by a large margin, with 83 out of 200 votes against Osaka, 32, Toronto, 30, Paris, 28, and Istanbul, 12. The organizer of this mock vote was Wu Ching-guo, a member of the IOC from Chinese Taipei. As the only Chinese member sitting on the IOC who was eligi-ble to vote for both the 2000 and 2008 Olympiads, Wu cast his vote on both occasions in favour of Beijing. The reason he gave was simple: 'I am an indi-vidual member of both the Chinese nation and the IOC; for the consideration of both the interest of the Chinese nation and international Olympics, I am assured of myself that Beijing ought to be awarded the right to host [the Olympic Games]' (BBC, 2001).

Shortly before the IOC's decision about a host city for the 2008 Olympic Games, Yuan Weimin, head of China's State General Administration of Sport, said after returning from a visit to Taiwan, 'If Beijing wins the bid, it is possi-ble that Beijing might host the 2008 Olympic Games with Taiwan under the principle of One China' (China Daily, 2001). On the part of Taiwan, among political leaders, Taipei Mayor Ma Ying-joung was in favour of co-hosting some events in Taiwan. He urged the Taiwan government to explore such a possibility and expressed his full support of such an effort (Lai, 2001). The Chinese Taipei Olympic Committee (CTOC) also expressed a positive view of a Beijing Games. As Kevin Kou-i Chen, secretary-general of the CTOC, said, if Beijing won the Olympic bid it would greatly benefit Taiwan, because the Games would increase business, sports, and political exchanges across the Strait (Lianhe Zhaobao, 2001a).

It might be well conceivable that Beijing would love to take advantage of hosting the Olympic Games to promote national reconciliation across the Taiwan Strait. The fact that the BOCOG has reached an agreement with the IOC and the International Equestrian Federation to allow Hong Kong to host equestrian events of the 2008 Games attests to the wisdom of promoting the Chinese national identity transcending the two systems in one nation. Most recently, the agreement reached between North and South Korea to compete as a single nation at the 2006 Asian Games and the 2008 Olympic Games (Choe, 2005) also indicates that the Olympics can play a constructive part in facilitating national reconciliation in a divided nation.

However, the situation in the Taiwan Strait appears quite different from the Korean Peninsula. The 'greater China mentality', manifest in Wu's remarks and implicit in Ma's gesture, is highly contested in contemporary Taiwanese society and squarely resisted by the ruling party and other pro-independence politicians. Over the past 15 years Taiwan has witnessed fast-track democratization and indigenization that gave rise to a stronger sense of 'Taiwanese identity' as opposed to 'Chinese identity'. The political landscape has been restructured along the dividing line between the 'pan-green' camp of independence and the 'pan-blue' camp of unification. In 2000, the historical 'regime change' took place in Taiwan when the green Democratic Progressive Party (DPP) defeated the blue Kuomingtang (KMT) in the presidential election. In 2004, the DPP's Chen Shuibian won his second term in a much controversial election. Coming from a different political and ideological background, the DPP government under Chen seeks to move toward new Taiwanese nation building, thereby bidding a final farewell to the identity of 'greater China' (*da Zhongguo*). This has significantly strained cross-Strait relations as the mainland regards reunification with Taiwan as a sacred national mission.

Against this backdrop, the Beijing Olympiad is linked with identity politics over the status of Taiwan in a complex way. When Beijing won the bid in July 2001, Taiwan's reactions were at best mixed. While many Taiwanese shared the joy of having the first Olympic Games in China, the official reaction was a 'guarded welcome' (CNN, 2001). In a written statement, the cabinet spokesman of the pro-independence Democratic Progressive Party (DPP) government expressed 'sincere congratulations', while also hoping the mainland to carry out the Olympic spirit in cross-Strait relations, and to abandon the use of force in cross-Strait disputes (Lianhe Zaobao, 2001b). Tsai In-wen, chairperson of the cabinet-level Mainland Affairs Council, was concerned that Beijing's success might have an adverse impact as it could deepen nationalistic sentiments thus hindering democratic development in China (CNN, 2001). Outspoken vice president Annette Lu warned that 'Beijing's hosting of the 2008 Olympic Games will greatly challenge the ethnic and national identification of the Taiwanese people' (Central News Agency, 2002). For others, represented by Lee Teng-hui, former president and spiritual leader of the independence-fundamentalist Taiwan Solidarity Union ('greenest' on the political spectrum), awarding Beijing the right to host the Olympiad amounted to granting Taiwan a window of opportunity to realize its dream of building a new Taiwanese nation formally independent of 'One China'.

Clearly, as the Beijing Olympiad appears to have created fertile political opportunities for both unification and secessionists, 'peace' in the Taiwan Strait has become increasingly contested. The difference between a peace that means a reinforced dynamic for 'peaceful reunification' and one that means a window of opportunity for 'peaceful independence' is so stark that managing conflicts of peace in the Taiwan Strait has become a major challenge to a successful Olympic Games in 2008.

Having acknowledged that the mainland has a vested interest in presenting China's new, modern, and peace-loving face to the world, Taiwan independence proponents did not wait long before exploiting the 'window of opportunity' by launching a new independence offensive (Peterson, 2004). In July 2002, Lee proposed that Taiwan write a new constitution by 2006 and put it into practice by 2008, and urged the DPP government to take decisive actions toward independence before the Beijing Games, arguing that post-Olympics Chinese nationalism would smash any glimpse of hope for building separate statehood and that Taiwan's 'separate voices will be submerged' (Cheong, 2002; Hsien, 2002). In September 2003, amidst the presidential elections, Chen Shui-bian endorsed such an idea by announcing a timeline for drafting a new constitution by 2006 and implementing it by the summer of 2008 (Pomfred, 2003).

The rhetoric and actions of Taiwanese secessionists to seize a rare historical opportunity to materialize independence drew Beijing's close attention and swift reaction. In January 2003, the PRC's Taiwan Affairs Office warned the Taiwan authorities not to declare independence before 2008, stating that the Olympics is not one of China's three major tasks – namely, economic development, national reunification, and world peace – but 'reunification is' (Harmsen, 2003). In December, an interview with military-background scholars, which was carried in major official newspapers, warned that had Taiwan secessionists dared to take a decisive move toward independence, the mainland would rather sacrifice many of its national interests, including the 2008 Olympiad, in order to preserve its sovereignty and territorial integrity (Huang and Yang, 2003). Beijing blamed those leading pro-independence figures for being immoral and sinister and as having a 'gambler's mentality' and 'playing with fire' in their attempt to hijack the Beijing Olympiad for the sake of their secessionist agenda (Xinhua, 2004). To make the Olympic Games successful, the official line goes, is an international interest not merely a national interest. Anyone who adventures to sabotage this international event by hijacking it with its selfish political scheme, therefore, shall be condemned internationally. Xu Bodong, the mainland's leading Taiwan affairs scholar, put it bluntly, 'There will be no Olympic breaks. . . . The timetable for Taiwan independence is in fact the timetable for the mainland to be compelled to adopt non-peaceful means. . . . The Olympics will be a grand gathering of all humanity. Seeking Taiwan independence at that time would be a challenge to entire humanity' (Agence France Presse, 2003).

The dispute between Beijing and Taipei is more about their growing divergent nation building than about the Olympics. But it does raise questions about the political meaning and implications of the Olympics for nation-states. Two questions are particularly pertinent here for the purpose of this discussion. First, does hosting an Olympic Games exert any restraining effects on a host country in terms of its domestic and international policies? Second, in terms of the Beijing Olympiad, which side, Beijing or Taipei, has an advantage to push forward its own political agenda?

In general, a host state would be very sensitive to international perceptions of and reactions to its behaviour in the context of hosting a sports mega-event such as the Olympics. It may even make extraordinary efforts to tackle some daunting problems such as those of human rights, ethnic minority representation, and environmental degradation before the global audience. Yet, to expect that hosting the Olympics will tie a host state down with regard to issues of sovereignty and territorial integrity may be wishful thinking. Past experience is bound to demonstrate little or no restraining effects on host nations when it comes to important issues that concern their vital national interests.

To the extent that China defines the Taiwan question as its 'foremost core and vital national interest', it would be naïve to expect, let alone take advantage of, the so-called window of opportunity to proceed with Taiwanese independence in drastic fashion without jeopardizing regional stability. Like it or not, as one international relations scholar puts it, Beijing's capability and credibility are both high in so far as it will resort to whatever actions to defeat Taiwan's decisive move toward *de jure* independence (Ross, 2004). In March 2005, China's National People's Congress passed the Anti-Secession Law which authorizes the state to employ all necessary means, including non-peaceful ones, to protect China's sovereignty and territorial integrity should Taiwanese secessionists act to 'cause the fact of Taiwan's secession from China' (China Daily, 2005). This development has further demonstrated the state's resolve to prevent Taiwan from declaring independence.

As to the second question, given that the focus of the political game between Beijing and Taipei is the contested legitimacy of the status quo across the Taiwan Strait centred on the norm of 'One China', which Beijing defends and Taipei challenges, Beijing should have an easier task than Taipei does because the 'One China' norm has been legally and extensively embedded in China's international relations since the 1970s. The so-called 'Olympic formula' that the IOC managed to create, long before Taiwan started its new course of nation building, to finally settle the 'two-China problem' in 1980 is a case in point. According to this formula, the People's Republic of China represents China to participate in international Olympics under the name of the Chinese Olympic Committee, while Taiwan remains in international Olympics under the name of the Chinese Taipei Olympic Committee (Chan, 1985). Against the background of the PRC's entry into the UN in place of the 'Republic of China' (ROC; the official name of Taiwan) to represent China a decade earlier, this arrangement was no surprise. But that the IOC tried to save a seat for Taiwan within the legal and normative framework of 'One China' attests to the Olympic wisdom of creative inclusiveness. Apparently, the final deal is a compromise solution to the 'two Chinas problem'. It is politically and legally favourable to Beijing but acceptable to Taipei, however reluctantly. This compromise was possible because both Beijing and Taipei, particularly the latter, showed a great degree of flexibility, and more importantly because the then KMT government in Taiwan remained committed to the 'One China' norm.

As identity politics intensifies in Taiwan, however, the 'Olympic formula' seems to become one of many liabilities for Taipei that the DPP government attempts to redress. By the same token, Beijing happens to rediscover much of the value in such a formula, which serves its national interest as an asset to contain the Taiwan independence movement internationally. It is thus only natural that the political contests between Beijing and Taipei will intensify within the context of international Olympics, far beyond their sports competitions, particularly given that the DPP government has recently launched a new campaign of 'rectification' (*Taiwan zhengming yundong*) aiming to rename Taiwan's organizations, companies, and the like after 'Taiwan' in the place of 'China' at home and abroad. Under these circumstances, the name of 'Chinese Taipei' sounds less and less politically correct. In his recent interviews in Taipei, Douglas Shelton found that both CTOC officials and international relations scholars tended to believe that any attempt to challenge the 'Olympic formula' may not be in Taiwan's interest, but they did express concerns about politicians' unwise manipulation of this issue before and during the Beijing Games (Shelton, 2005). He Zhengliang, former member of the IOC from the PRC, warned against any attempt to change the name of 'Chinese Taipei' by Taiwan authorities as an act that would only endanger its membership in the IOC (China News Agency, 2004).

Not long ago, many people were still hopeful that the Beijing Olympics would help ameliorate tensions in areas of high politics involving Beijing and Taipei. There indeed have been efforts by people from both sides to seek reconciliation through exchange of sports activities such as jointly sponsored marathon races. The idea of including Taiwanese athletes in the upcoming torch relay has already been proposed by the BOCOG to the IOC. Even the possibility of offering Taiwan to host certain events has from time to time come to the fore. More recently, Yu Muming, head of Taiwan's pro-unification New Party, even brought up this idea to the Chinese leaders during his visit to Beijing in the summer of 2005. But 'unforeseen circumstances may derail any good intentions to foster closer ties via the Olympics' (Chan, 2002: 148). As a torch relay including

Taiwan may imply that Taiwan is part of China, which Beijing so insists and Taipei so resists, it raises a serious doubt that this may happen at all. Thus, in so far as China is compelled to prioritize deterring Taiwanese secessionists from hijacking the Beijing Games, the intensity of the high politics of national identity has been only highlighted, rather than ameliorated, in the Olympic spotlight.

Conclusions

Achieving the right to host the 2008 Olympic Games has brought international recognition to China as a great ancient civilization and a rapidly developing society. It marks a watershed in China's deepening integration into the international community. China as a modernizing nation yearning for great power status attaches great political importance to the Beijing Olympics in terms of constructing national identity and pursuing international primacy. As East meets West in Beijing, China has a great opportunity to turn the 2008 Olympiad into the celebration of a Chinese renaissance and the harmonization of western and non-western civilizations in an age of globalization. Its commitment to staging a great Olympic Games under the themes of 'Green Olympics, High-tech Olympics, and People's Olympics' coincides with its redefined national grand strategy based on the notion of scientific, sustainable, and pro-people development, and aiming at building a harmonious socialist society. The Beijing Olympiad is bound to set a new impetus for China's continued modernization drive.

The Olympic spotlight, however, also discloses some fundamental paradoxes that confront China. First, instead of reforming the old-fashioned state-centric sports administrative system, it has to rely on such a system to meet the Chinese people's ever increasing expectation about achieving sporting triumph in the Beijing Games. Second, while people's patriotism stimulated by the Beijing Olympiad may be good for national unity, the party-state must also carefully channel hyper-nationalistic sentiments into a good manner of sportsmanship. And third, before it can reach out across the Taiwan Strait to engage Taiwanese people in the process of jointly promoting the Chinese renaissance, Beijing must first effectively contain the Taiwan independence movement through peaceful means in the build-up to the Beijing Olympic Games. All of these issues pose great challenges to the Chinese state, whose legitimacy is at stake in successfully hosting the 2008 Games. As the priority of the hosting policy is to ensure that Chinese athletes will perform well and that the Games will be a successful sports event, the state appears to strengthen the authoritarian elements of its governance in the lead up to the 2008 Games; yet, so far as the interests between the state and society are significantly converging on staging the 'best ever Olympic Games', it is also possible to speculate that a greater and bolder effort to transform the Chinese polity as a whole will be forthcoming following on from the Beijing Games.

Notes

* I would like to thank John Horne, Yi Jiandong, Wolfram Manzenreiter, and Salomé Marivoet for their comments on an earlier version of this chapter, which was presented at a European Alliance for Asian Studies/Asia-Europe Foundation funded Workshop on 'Hosting Major International Sports Events: Comparing Asia and Europe', held at The University of Edinburgh, in March 2005 and Douglas Sheldon for his assistance during the research.
1 *'Xin Beijing, Xin Aoyun'* literally means 'New Beijing, New Olympics'. The difference in its Chinese and English versions is puzzling.
2 *Renwen Aoyun* also has two renditions in English translation, 'Humanistic Olympics' and 'People's Olympics'.

References

Agence France Presses (2003) 'Chinese scholars warn against Taiwan independence bid during 2008', November 21, 2003.
BBC (Chinese) (2001) 'Olympics links both sides of the Taiwan Strait', May 14, 2001. Available at http://news.bbc.co.uk/chinese/simp/hi/newsid_1320000/newsid_1329600/1329674.stm. Accessed December 22, 2004.
BOCOG (2003) *The Emblem of Beijing 2008 Olympic Games and Its Cultural Connotation.* http://en.beijing-2008.org/13/59/article211615913.shtml. Accessed December 12, 2004.
BOCOG News (2005a) 'Liu Qi elaborates on characteristics of Beijing Olympic Games', January 27, 2005. Available at http://en1.beijing-2008.org/07/37/article211643707.shtml. Accessed January 28, 2005.
BOCOG News (2005b) 'BOCOG in search of proposals for grand ceremonies', March 1, 2005. Available at http://en.beijing-2008.org/27/50/article211645027.shtml. Accessed March 2, 2005.
Brownell, S. (1995) *Training the Body for China: Sports in the Moral Order of the People's Republic.* Chicago, IL: The University of Chicago Press.
Central News Agency (2002) 'Taiwan vice president urges reconciliation among political parties', May 21, 2002.
Chan, G. (1985) 'The "Two-China" problem and the Olympic formula', *Pacific Affairs* 58 (3): 473–490.
Chan, G. (2002) 'From the "Olympic Formula" to the Beijing Games: Towards greater integration across the Taiwan Strait?', *Cambridge Review of International Affairs* 15 (1): 141–148.
Cheong, C. (2002) 'Statehood for Taiwan by 2008: Teng-hui', *Straits Times*, July 25, 2002.
China Daily (2001) 'Taiwan Supports Beijing's 2008 Effort', May 17, 2001. Available at http://www.china.org.cn/e-shenao/modern/01-05-22.htm. Accessed December 15, 2004.
China Daily (2005) 'Anti-secession law adopted by NPC (full text)', March 14, 2005. Available at http://taiwansecurity.org/News/2005/CD-140305.htm. Accessed December 20, 2005.
China News Agency (2004) 'He Zhenliang: The Chinese Taipei Olympic Committee would be expelled by the IOC if it changed its name', *Voice of Strait* website, November 28, 2004. Available at http://www.vos.com.cn/2004/11/18_40664.htm. Accessed December 18, 2004.
China Sports News (2004) 'Aoyun gaibian le Beijing shenme?' [What has been changed in Beijing by the Olympics], October 21, 2004. Available at http://www.sport.org.cn/olympic/2008/2004-10-21/358303.html. Accessed December 15, 2004.
Chinese Olympic Committee (2004) China and the Olympic Movement, Available at http://en.olympic.cn/china_oly/index.html. Accessed 20 December 2005.
Choe, S. (2005) 'Two Koreas to compete as single nation at Olympics', *International Herald Tribune*, November 1, 2005. Available at http://www.nytimes.com/2005/11/01/international/asia/01cnd-korea.html?pagewanted=print. Accessed November 2, 2005.
Coubertin, P., de (1967) *The Olympic Idea: Discourses and Essays.* Schorndorf: Karl Hoffman.

CNN (2001) '2008 Olympic in Beijing: Mixed response from Taiwan', July 14, 2001. Available at http://taiwansecurity.org/News/2001/CNN-071401.htm. Accessed December 2, 2005.

Global News Wire (2004) 'Chinese nationalism is risk to Beijing as well Taiwan', August 10, 2004. Available at http://www.nexis.com/research/search/documentDisplay?_document. Accessed August 15, 2004.

Harmsen, P. (2003) 'China warns 2008 not a good year to declare independence', *Agence France Presse*, January 27, 2003.

Hill, C.R. (1992) *Olympic Politics*. Manchester, UK: Manchester University Press.

Horne, J. (2004) 'The global game of football: The 2002 World Cup and regional development in Japan', *Third World Quarterly* 25 (7): 1233–1244.

Horne, J. and Manzenreiter, W. (2004) 'Accounting for mega-events: forecast and actual impacts of the 2002 Football World Cup finals on the host countries Japan/Korea', *International Review for the Sociology of Sport* 39 (2): 187–203.

Huang H. and Yang L. (2003) 'Junshi zhuanjia tan fan 'Taidu': Liutiao diaijia zhanfan bicheng' [Military experts talk about anti-Taiwan independence: Six prices, war criminals must be punished], *Liaowang Xinwen Zhoukan*, December 3, 2003. Available at http://tw.people.com.cn/GB/14810/14858/2224550.html. Accessed December 6, 2004.

Hsien, D. (2002) 'China analysts play down risk of war with Taiwan', *Straits Times*, August 10, 2002.

Huntington, S. (1993) 'The clash of civilizations?', *Foreign Affairs* 72 (3): 22–49.

Huntington, S. (1996) *The Clash of Civilizations and the Remaking of World Order*. New York, NY: Simon & Schuster.

IOC (2001) *Report of the IOC Evaluation Commission for the Games of the XXIX Olympiad in 2008*. Lausanne, Switzerland: IOC.

Jiang, Z. (2000) 'Letter of Support', *Candidature Files* Vol. 1, Preface. Available at http://en.beijing2008.com/65/68/column211716865.shtml. Accessed July 20, 2004.

Jin, Y. (2005) 'Hexie shi renwen Aoyun de linghun' [Harmony as the soul of humanistic Olympics], *Renwen News*, January 11, 2005. Available at http://www.c2008.org/rendanews/knowledge_detail.asp?id=1276. Accessed January 20, 2005.

LaFeber, W. (1999) *Michael Jordan and the New Global Capitalism*. New York: W.W. Norton & Co.

Lai, V. (2001) 'Taiwan should seek to co-sponsor Olympic events: Taipei mayor', *Central News Agency*, July 13, 2001.

Li, L. and Su, Y. (2004) 'Zhongguo tiyujie huibie "Yuan Weimin shidai"' [The Chinese sportsworld bids farewell to the 'Yuan Weimin era'], *The Southern Weekend*, December 16, 2004. Available at http://www.nanfangdaily.com.cn/zm/20041216/xw/szxw1/200412160006.asp. Accessed December 17, 2004.

Lianhe Zhaobao (2001a) 'Ma Yingjiu Zhi Taiwan Ying Zhengqu Heban Saixiang' [Ma Ying-joung Favours Taiwan's Co-hosting Events], July 13, 2001. Available at http://www.zaobao.com/special/realtime/2001/07/130701_39.html. Accessed January 4, 2005.

Lianhe Zhaobao (2001b) 'Deng Xiaoping zuizao tichu ban Aoyun' [Deng Xiaoping first proposed for an Olympic bid], July 14, 2001. Available at http://www.zaobao.com/games/olympics/bid2008/pages/bid140701.html. Accessed January 4, 2005.

MacAloon, J.J. (1991) 'The turn of two centuries: Sports and the politics of international relations', in F. Landry, M. Landry and M. Yerles (eds.) *Sport . . . The Third Millennium: Proceedings of the International Symposium* (Sainte-Foy: Les Presses de l'Universite Laval), 31–44.

Maguire, J. (1999) *Global Sport: Identities, Societies, and Civilizations*. Cambridge, UK: Polity Press.

People's Daily (2003) 'IOC official hopes 2008 Olympics leave unique legacy for China', February 14, 2003. Available at http://english.people.com.cn/200302/14/eng20030214_111664.shtml. Accessed December 16, 2004.

Peterson, A. (2004) 'Dangerous games across the Taiwan Strait', *Washington Quarterly* 27 (2): 23–41.

Pomfret, J. (2003) 'Taiwan's top agitator aims to create a country', *Washington Post*, October 14, 2003: D16.

Roche, M. (2000) *Mega-Events and Modernity*. London: Routledge.

Ross, R. (2004) 'East Asia's response to China's rise: Accommodation, balancing, and the emerging balance of power'. Unpublished manuscript, Olin Institute of Strategic Studies, Harvard University.

Shelton, D. (2005) *Cross-Strait relations and the 2008 Beijing Olympic Games: Opportunities and vulnerabilities*. Unpublished master's thesis, Ritsumeikan Asia Pacific University.

Tang, Y. (2001) 'Beijing creates history', *Beijing Review*, August 2, 2001, 12–16.

Tomlinson, A. (1996) 'Olympic spectacle: opening ceremonies and some paradoxes of globalization', *Media, Culture and Society* 18: 583–602.

Xinhua (2003) 'Beijing to invest 7 billion Yuan on museums', February 26, 2003. Available at http://news.xinhuanet.com/english/2003-02/26/content_746906.htm. Accessed December 16, 2004.

Xinhua (2004) 'Chinese scholars warn Taiwan against raising stakes during 2008 Olympics', May 18, 2004.

Zhao, Y. (1988) 'Qiangguo meng' [Great power dream], *Dandai*, February: 163–198.

The 2010 Football World Cup as a political construct: the challenge of making good on an African promise

Scarlett Cornelissen and Kamilla Swart

Introduction

It is today widely understood that sport mega-events are complex affairs which originate from specific sets of economic objectives but which have political and social corollaries that usually extend far beyond the event itself. Sport mega-events are generally initiated and driven by cadres of societal (ie, political and corporate) elites and are aimed at satisfying development goals or ambitions around projection, competitiveness or growth targets. In the planning, implementation and execution of events, however, cultural, social and other imprints are left that can have enduring impacts on the society. Further, the economy of sport mega-events has developed to such an extent internationally, that events have gained a self-perpetuating dynamic of their own, characterized by distinct coagulations of interests and the predominance of certain corporate actors. The gains that are widely thought to be made from participation in this mega-events 'market' prompt states continually to seek involvement: noticeably, once a country is able to break into the international arena of hosting mega-events, this stimulates the desire to attract more and often larger mega-events. Once on the mega-event circuit, there is an aspiration to host more of them (Hiller, 1998), often without proper attention to the economic and social counter-costs of events.

These aspects are highly visible in post-apartheid South Africa's engagement with sport mega-events. Slightly more than a decade into the new democratic dispensation, sport mega-events have seemingly come to play an important socio-political role. Prompted by the successful hosting and victory of the 1995 Rugby World Cup, a more or less sustained campaign has been undertaken by political and other elites to make bids, with varying degrees of success, for the hosting of some of the most important events on the world sports tournament calendar. Underpinning this, at least from the government's perspective, is an attempt to utilize sport mega-events as key social and political instruments: on the one hand events are regarded as one mechanism to support the government's nation-building project, while on the other, they are viewed as economic and development catalysts. Rhetorically, bid processes or events themselves have been used to communicate key messages to the South African populace and the wider international community, partly with the purpose of shaping a new South African society, and partly with the aim of bolstering the so-called African Renaissance. In addition, in a society that remains nominally racially polarized, it has been sought to use major sport events as an instrument of reconciliation. The fact that a country's ability to succeed in the arena of hosting mega-events signals international recognition, in terms of economic, social and political capacity, has also fuelled the South African government's growing enthusiasm to invest the resources in often costly campaigns.

Winning the rights to host the FIFA Football World Cup Finals in 2010 has presented South Africa with both the opportunity to provide momentum to its mega-events campaign, driven as it is by specific socio-economic and political objectives, and the challenge of delivering – not only in the form of a successful tournament but also on the political and social promises on which South Africa's bid campaigns have thus far been based. This seems a daunting task, no less for the fact that, despite the numerous attempts to host mega-events, only a slim foundation has been laid upon which South Africa could design goals and plans. In addition, in a developing context such as South Africa, the difficulty of balancing the initial investment of resources (which can be extensive), with the vast socio-economic exigencies of the country, is great. The debate on how resources should be spent most judiciously to benefit the South African society is one that pertinently colours the wider politics surrounding the planning towards the 2010 World Cup. In addition, the way in which South Africa manages the event, its successes and failures in this regard is widely regarded as an important test case, not only for the African continent, but developing countries more broadly.

This chapter assesses the prospects for the 2010 Finals as it is shaped by currently emerging political, economic and social processes. The thrust of this investigation is to explore the extent to which the ambitions and premises of the 2010 Finals – particularly claims towards using the event to support social and economic development, and the revival of the wider African continent – could be realized. This is done against the backdrop of assessments both of South Africa's encounter with major events over the past twelve years and of the lessons to be learned from the hosting of mega-events by other countries. The first part of the chapter explores the main themes that characterize developed and developing countries' experience with mega-events. The second part reviews the primary features of post-apartheid South Africa's engagement with mega-events, highlighting some of the challenges and inconsistencies to the country's approach. The concluding part discusses the implications of these features, and prospects for the 2010 World Cup. Progress with respect to planning and preparation has thus far been mixed. Important tasks remain in order for the country to deliver fully on the projections for the FIFA Finals.

Mega-events as mega-projects: promises and snares

The growth in the scale, visibility and significance of sport mega-events over the past few decades has been accompanied by increased scrutiny of the particular elements of which mega-events are composed and the factors that could lead to success or failure. 'Booster' campaigns typically over-emphasize the economic potential of sport mega-events, and their ability to attract foreign direct investment, bolster tourism growth and contribute to regeneration and broader developmental goals. A burgeoning body of research (eg, Coates & Humphreys, 1999; Eisinger, 2000; Ley & Olds, 1992; Owen, 2002) has, however, indicated that the drawbacks – not only economic but also political – to mega-events can efface most gains to be made from events in the first instance.

As far as the economic facets of mega-events are concerned, it is most commonly noted that there is a very fine balance between the benefits and costs associated with these events, and that there are fewer examples of success than there are of costly initiatives that have incurred great debt for hosts (eg, Teigland, 1999). Further, while mega-events may stimulate investments and developments in the broader economy of an aspiring or current host, gains from these may be offset by the way in which mega-events are organized, and the particular set of corporate interests tied to an event. This, along with other non-economic factors, may translate into much of the anticipated spin-offs from mega-events not materializing. For instance, analyses of the 2002 FIFA World Cup, jointly hosted by South Korea and Japan, illustrate the complexity of forecasting financial and tourism impacts in the face of manifold exogenous factors. Costly undertakings for both states – South Korea built ten new stadia at a cost of nearly US $2 bn, while Japan constructed seven new stadia and refurbished three others at a cost of US $4 bn (Horne & Manzenreiter, 2004) – the tournament notoriously under-delivered on the expectations of the respective organizers. Replacement spending and a 'crowding out effect', where tourists replace other visitors who would normally visit the host venues, were apparent (Matheson & Baade, 2003; Horne & Manzenreiter, 2004). Indeed, Lee and Taylor (2005) suggest that the actual tourist arrivals to Korea may have fallen more than one-third short of predictions, and been much lower than tourist arrivals in the same month of the previous year.

Aside from the economic outcomes, sport mega-events can leave several other legacies that can persist long beyond bidding campaigns and tournaments have come to an end. These include the development of infrastructure both before and after events either to enhance a bidder's prospects of hosting an event (in the case of bid campaigns), or to maximize the investment impetus that usually characterizes the build-up to events. Cape Town's bid for the 2004 Olympic Games (discussed in some greater detail below) is exemplary of the former, where as part of the developmental philosophy that underlay the bid, and in anticipation of the momentum even a failed bid would give to the city's economic sector (largely from increased publicity), several urban and sports infrastructure projects were initiated up to one year before the announcement of the host was made by the International Olympic Committee (Hiller, 2000; Swart & Bob, 2004). While these projects still mark the landscape of the city, few have contributed substantially to subsequent development programmes, or have been incorporated into the planning related to other mega-events in which the city has been involved.

Another legacy that is often overlooked, but may be more significant and lasting in its impacts, is the political counter-effects that the rhetorical arguments used in support of bid campaigns, or even during events themselves, can evoke. Generally, developing countries tend to use sports mega-events in ways highly distinct from developed countries. A growing body of research (eg, Nauright & Schimmel, 2005; Black & van der Westhuizen, 2004) suggests that, partly because developing countries face conditions that do not extend to their more developed counterparts, and partly because developing states are circumscribed by an unequal global arena in their competition to host events, they often seek to use mega-events to meet specific political or foreign policy goals: as a way of signalling particular messages to the international community; as a means of engaging in international activities far beyond what objective measures of their international capacity would enable (ie, 'punching above their weight'); and as a mechanism to compensate for the lack of sources of power and influence in the international sphere. In this way recent activism around sport mega-events by Malaysia (eg, Van der Westhuizen, 2001), the People's Republic of China (Haugen, 2003), and South Africa (Cornelissen, 2004b) can be understood as attempts by these states to attain certain foreign policy goals, such as image enhancement and profiling, along with gaining economic advantage from mega-events. As will be illustrated below, a distinctive and persistent feature of South Africa's bid and event campaigns has been the country's use of particular symbolic arguments based on its status as an African country. Such rhetoric was geared to maximizing support from both domestic and international constituencies. As effective as political and other rhetoric may be in certain instances, however, it could also rebound dangerously and jeopardize the campaigns driven by developing countries (Black & Van der Westhuizen, 2004).

Overall, sport mega-events can evolve or transpire in very singular fashions in developing countries, shaped by unique sets of factors resulting from a colonial past, or societal complexities. Nonetheless, there is an overarching political economy to mega-events that commonly affect developing and developed states. This includes the corporate coalitions that emerge in all bidding and event hosting processes. Such coalitions could have major imprints on events, for example in the way that sponsorship and publicity arrangements can determine the form and overall character that events can take (see Nauright & Schimmel, 2005 in this regard). Further, first-order events such as the FIFA World Cup, by sheer global reach (through media coverage), scale of spectatorship and yields through the sale of memorabilia, have immense revenue potential. As such the World Cup is a profit-driven endeavour in the first instance, and FIFA seeks to maintain taut control of all Finals. This involves strict regulation of the number and quality of stadia that are used by hosts – broadly, given the manner in which Finals are organized, FIFA generally requires the availability of ten stadia of high standard, spread across the entire country, that are able to accommodate 32 teams and 64 matches – but can extend to the publicity material and promotional campaigns tied to a Finals (through pre-established FIFA sponsorship agreements) and even the unique 'brand' that is developed for each Finals.[1] As is discussed more extensively below, the circumscription that FIFA maintains on all Finals, including the 2010 Finals in South Africa, have from an early stage had a significant impact on the political wrangling that arose shortly after the event was awarded to South Africa in mid-2004. More importantly, FIFA's regulation on how the event is organized may have repercussions on the South African government's objectives with respect to using the Finals for developmental and nation-building purposes. This only increases the challenges of delivering on the promises made by the South African campaign.

Other factors that play a role in how preparation for the 2010 World Cup unfolds, and how the event in itself may transpire, arise from the very specific manner in which South Africa has sought to use events instrumentally, to accomplish specific political goals, and have accordingly tailored bid campaigns and other hosted, major events. The next section briefly outlines the main features of the politics of South Africa's mega-events activism and how this sets the context for the country's hosting of the 2010 Finals.

Rhetoric and rationale: the features of South Africa's mega-events drive

South Africa's successful hosting of the 1995 Rugby World Cup set in motion an activism around sport mega-events that was cumulative in its ambitions and objectives. This was partly driven by a demonstration effect that led to growing confidence that the country had the requisite capacity to host international events of a particular scale and significance, and partly drew from the unexpected non-material benefits that the Rugby World Cup had brought. Occurring at the cusp of South Africa's democratization and attempts by the post-apartheid government to forge a new society, victory of the Rugby World Cup seemingly united the highly divided and racialised society (Black & Nauright, 1998). This provided the impetus for a clear political (ie, nation-building) objective around sport mega-events that were to continue beyond the Rugby World Cup (Grundlingh, 1998).

Buoyed by an ostensible demonstration effect, South Africa disposed itself to become more extensively involved in the mega-events circuit. In 1996 it hosted and won the African Cup of Nations, the two-yearly continental football competition that is held under the auspices of the Confederation Africaine de Football (CAF), the African football governing body. In the early 1990s Cape Town launched its bid to host the 2004 Olympic Games; from 1998 onwards South Africa made a failed bid attempt to host the 2006 FIFA Finals, which was successfully re-launched a few years later; and in 2003 the country hosted a fruitful, if politically marred Cricket World Cup. In 2003 South Africa also successfully hosted the President's Cup, a prestigious international golf tournament. This event had one important spin-off, in that South Africa hosted the international Women's Golf Cup in 2004. In an attempt to draw from the legacy of success of the 1995 Rugby World Cup, the South African Rugby Football Association (SARFU) made a failed bid for the 2011 Finals (which eventually were awarded to New Zealand). It is noteworthy that this campaign, and the reception of the eventual outcome, was decidedly more muted than some of the other popular sport events campaigns described below. In part, this may reflect the racial division that still characterizes sport in South Africa, with (despite the emotional success of the 1995 Rugby World Cup) football or soccer still being the sport of preference and identity association for the majority of South Africa's population (see for instance Alegi, 2004).

South Africa seemingly therefore, has embraced the ideology of the 'sport-media-tourism' complex (Nauright, 2004) and like many other developing countries is seeking to promote an event-driven economy. This has not occurred without evoking extensive dispute over the desirability and feasibility of the South African government's strategy. Opponents of South Africa's numerous bid attempts argue that the resources spent during the bidding process can be better used for social and economic development programmes aimed at alleviating poverty (Hiller, 2000). Eisinger (2000) adds that while these ventures enable some people to benefit economically, they do little to change the position and plight of the majority of people who are marginalized. On the other hand, proponents of bidding in South Africa assert that the hosting of mega-events will result in economic and other benefits – such as job creation, destination marketing, and the development of national pride – that far exceed initial investments.

Two features predominate in South Africa's bidding and overall mega-events activism. The first is a strong developmental thrust to the country's bidding campaigns and a characteristic attempt, through the use of specific rhetoric and lobbying, to infuse political discourse and common understanding of mega-events with a developmental philosophy. First utilized to a substantial degree in Cape Town's failed bid for the 2004 Olympic Games, the developmental argument has been a recurring feature of subsequent bids. A second, related feature, has been the promotion of a particular conception of the African continent, and an overall tailoring of bid campaigns or even hosted events around arguments of the need for Africa's revival – and axiomatically the obligation on the international community to reward all efforts towards this end, including South Africa's goals of furthering the so-called African Renaissance through political programmes. Notably, these two features have often accounted for outright failures of South Africa's bid campaigns or have threatened to jeopardize the course that hosted events have followed.

The Cape Town Olympic bid

The processes around Cape Town's Olympic Bid (CTOB) are reflective of the sabotaging effects that the developmental argument, along with internal political strife, had on the city's prospects of being awarded the event. Moreover, many of these miscalculations or errors have continually appeared in subsequent event campaigns.

The Cape Town bid saw a lengthy period of gestation. Raymond Ackerman, a leading businessperson, initiated it in 1990. South Africa underwent a national bidding process and the National Olympic Committee of South Africa (NOCSA) selected Cape Town as the candidate city in 1994. The Ackerman bid, however, was not wholly supported by NOCSA who wanted to wait until the 1994 inaugural democratic elections, to gain the support of national government, and chose not to be aligned with the Ackerman bid (De Lange, 1998). In 1995, the Ackerman group was ousted and a new bid company was instituted under the leadership of Chris Ball, a prominent former banker. Hiller (2000) contends that at this stage the bid became more visibly a partnership between the public and private sectors as well as an instrument of national government policy.

The national cabinet committed to underwriting the costs of the Olympic Games (a requirement of the International Olympic Committee (IOC)) in 1996, and this was supported by guarantees signed by provincial, metropolitan and local levels of government. In addition, Fuller (personal communication, 2004) notes that the government had agreed to directly fund the Organizing Committee of the Olympic Games (OCOG) with R3 305 million (approximately US$ 905 million). It is important to note that support for the bid went beyond these groupings, as all political parties and labour unions, as well as the Cape Town community generally supported the bid. It could be argued that without the developmental underpinnings of the bid, it may have not have garnered the widespread support it did achieve.

Cape Town competed against ten other cities in the race to host the 2004 Games. It was also the first time that there were so many developing cities that participated in the bid, namely Buenos Aires, Cape Town, Istanbul and Rio de Janeiro. At the IOC session at which the Olympic host city was selected in September 1997, the IOC members voted by secret ballot, and by a simple majority the host city – Athens – was determined.

Importantly, the Cape Town bid presented a first opportunity for South Africa to engage in both place promotion and identity construction. At the time, a strongly promoted idea in South Africa was that since the Olympic Movement was the first to expel South Africa from international sport, it should be the first to welcome it back by awarding the 2004 Games. Cape Town purposely made an appeal to the symbolism of giving the Games to Africa. Hosting the Games in South Africa could be seen as playing a role in the rejuvenation of the continent (Olympic Assessment Team, 1997).

114

The developmental nature of the bid was evident in the location and nature of the proposed development of infrastructure and in the entire ethos that underlay the bid book. The building of facilities required by the hosting of major events is often legitimated on the grounds of the benefits of the infrastructure to the local community and the consequent sports development that this will promote (Standeven & De Knop, 2000). Whitson and Macintosh (1996) note that since these facilities are required for elite sport, the facilities are often too large and too sophisticated for general community use. To counter this argument in favour of civic investment, the CTOB focused on the development of training venues throughout the various communities within the province of the Western Cape (of which Cape Town is the capital). The location of these venues was decided upon after consultation with various local sport federations. They were located in areas of assumed potential sport growth. They were also designed in a way that would lend itself to multipurpose use, for maximum utilization by the respective communities. Overall, long-term community requirements were given as much priority as the technical requirements for the hosting of the Games as set out by the IOC.

Cape Town went beyond the use of major event facilities for local sports development, as the underlying philosophy of the bid was 'developmental.' The principle of 'human development' distinguished Cape Town's bid from its competitors. Moreover, it was the first bid in the history of the Games which sought to promote the ideal of human development as the fourth pillar of Olympism, the others being sport, culture and the environment. Its aim was to use the Olympic Games as a platform to improve the lives of all its citizens, especially those who were disadvantaged by apartheid, as well as to redesign the structure of the apartheid city (Olympic Assessment Team, 1997). Thus it is evident that the Olympic Games became an apparent instrument of government policy related to the development of a 'new' South Africa[2].

Comparing Cape Town's bid to that of the other bid cities, De Lange (1998) reported a number of weaknesses. Most significantly, strategic faults were displayed by NOCSA. The ousting of the original bidding committee led to the loss of services of experienced international consultants and left the new team with little time to prepare. One of the major criticisms levelled against the bid pertained to the high level of crime in South Africa, an issue that was not adequately dealt with by the Bid Committee, whilst the problem of visitors' safety was a constant worry for IOC decision-makers. It is worth underscoring, however, that a significant aspect of the issue of crime in South Africa is linked to perceptions and the way in which the international media portrays criminal activities and rates. The problems pertaining to dealing with perceptions remain widespread for developing countries competing in a markedly unequal global system.

Relatedly, as South Africa had only recently returned to the arena of international sport, it did not have the experience other cities had in being able to host major sporting events, particularly Olympic sports. Ingerson and Westerbeek (2000) argue that the experience and knowledge of the bid team structure plays a critical role in bidding success. This experience is built up over time and provides the opportunity to build relationships with the event promoters. In the case of the Cape Town bid, discussions with key African sport leaders and African IOC members occurred too late. Bearing in mind that it was an African bid, key figures in Africa's sporting movement should have been consulted in the initial phases of the bid. Further, the overarching developmental argument and the strong use of symbolism, seemingly served to alienate, rather than ingratiate IOC evaluators. Athens's success with its bid, for instance, has been attributed to bid campaigners emphasizing less the role of the city as the birthplace of the modern Olympics (as was the case in the city's failed bid for the 1996 Games), but rather the city's experience in hosting major international sporting events, the availability of high-technology sports complexes and plans to construct new stadia (Pappas, 1997).

The FIFA bid processes and the Cricket World Cup

The CTOB provided an opportunity for South Africa to present a new image to the world, signalling the beginning of the post-apartheid era and re-entry on to the global stage. Yet it also laid the foundation for much miscalculation and misdirected strategies that were replicated in some of the major bids and events that were to follow. Most significant of these were the processes and outcomes of the bids for the FIFA 2006 and 2010 World Cups and the 2003 Cricket World Cup. Although the bids for the FIFA and the Cricket World Cup were multifaceted and distinctive in their nature and outflows, it is possible to highlight a few common and important features (see Cornelissen, 2004a and 2004b for extensive reviews). The first is the directed way in which all three were designed around and driven by a keen desire to promote South Africa's status as an African country, and the manner in which key arguments around Africa's revitalization were used to gain support from domestic and international constituencies. This was most conspicuous in the slogan upon which the 2006 bid was initially based, that is, 'It's Africa's Turn!' In all instances, there was a marked attempt by the South African government to use bid and event campaigns to shore up wider foreign policy goals with respect to the African continent. As such, the international relations between the South African government and national sports management figures, and officials of FIFA and the International Cricket Council (ICC), had an overriding purpose: mutually to increase the global statesmanship of the other through the common support of the 'African cause.' In this way, for instance, the ICC saw an opportunity to globalize the sports discipline by awarding the event to an African state, while at the same time raising its own moral stature.

A second feature is that despite well-intentioned pan-African campaigns, the rhetorical and political utilization of 'Africa' had rebounded several times: in the case of the 2006 FIFA bid an under-sophisticated campaign did little justice to the pan-African drive of the bid (this was later addressed in the bid for the 2010 Finals); while in the case of the Cricket World Cup exogenous factors – which included political controversy surrounding Zimbabwe and fears of terror attacks in Kenya – disrupted the distributionist goals of the event.

A strong pan-African element still underlies the 2010 Finals. Although this does not take the form of a multi-country tournament as with the Cricket World Cup – while some Southern African countries will be drawn in to provide training venues, all competition venues will be located in South Africa – there is a robust, public discourse that places emphasis on gaining as much out of the event for the African continent, particularly with respect to changing international perceptions of existing capacity. Nonetheless, boosterist campaigns during the bid process have created a highly expectant domestic population, who are in anticipation of sustained economic and tourism growth and employment opportunities. Aside from this, planning processes have been marred by political dispute and other controversies from an early stage. These and other factors provide the parameters by which build-up to the event, and its eventual characteristics, take shape. It is to a discussion of the contexts and major influencing factors that will determine the prospects for the 2010 Finals that the chapter now turns.

Making good on an African promise: controversies, claims and prospects

Much criticism against mega-events as a catalyst to tourism and economic development is focused on the extent and costs of bidding processes (Jones, 2001). Gamage and Higgs (1997) note that the public costs associated with bidding are generally not subject to public debate and accountability. Slack (1998) further notes that the commercialization of sport has reduced benefits for host economies in favour of commercial sponsors. This has important implications for the economic justification of these events. Events also have significant social impacts, and since events are usually controlled and organized by international sport federations outside of the region, local authorities are unwilling or unable to mitigate (Hiller, 1998). All of these factors are relevant to the possibilities and restrictions that surround the 2010 FIFA Finals. Added to this, political factors and internal strife have emerged as important constraints in the early planning phases of the event.

On 27 October 2004, the South African government and FIFA signed the Organization Association Agreement to formalise the country's hosting of the 2010 World Cup (SA 2010 Bid Company, n.d.a). While Joseph Blatter, the FIFA president and a long-standing supporter of South Africa's bid noted that, 'South Africa needs a perfect organization to show the world it is possible to do it here' (SA 2010 Bid Company, n.d.b), two early events cast a shadow on the initial enthusiasm surrounding the awarding of the event to South Africa. The first was when, shortly after the announcement of South Africa's winning bid in June

2004, the South African Football Association (SAFA), the national football management body and the institution responsible for overseeing the organization of the event, became mired in controversy over its finances (the body had been close to bankruptcy for many years prior). Second, at the end of 2004 a highly public dispute broke out within SAFA over the constitution of the Local Organizing Committee (LOC), the panel of people responsible for implementing, in collaboration with FIFA, all arrangements. Mainly, the contention centred on whether Danny Jordaan, who had led both South African bids for 2006 and 2010, or higher-ranked officials within SAFA (such as the president of the body) should be the chairperson of the LOC. Due to personality clashes, a fairly strong constituency existed within SAFA (in stark contrast to popular social sentiment) that favoured Jordaan to be sidelined. The matter was resolved when Blatter intervened and indicated his preference for Jordaan. Media and public assessments of the dispute were largely negative; the affair was seen as an embarrassment (*Business Day*, 13 January 2005). Later in 2005 the LOC and the progress made in planning towards the major event, was dismissively assessed by the media, when it was reported that, at a comparable stage, the German organizers of the 2006 Finals had accomplished much more (*Mail and Guardian*, 25 April, 2005).

More recently, evaluations of the manner in which the LOC is carrying out its tasks, have been shaped by the politics around the selection of match venues. The debate on the infrastructural and economic legacies, the distribution of these, and access to opportunities, has also started to intensify. The South African 2010 bid revised some of its 2006 proposals, notably extending the number of stadia from nine to thirteen. Of these, seven were stated to require minor upgrading, three major upgrading and three were to be newly constructed (SA 2010 Bid Company, n.d.b). As with the Cape Town 2004 Olympic Bid, the upgrading of training venues formed a significant part of the developmental bid, as illustrated in the following statement: 'The training ground upgrade programme forms a crucial part of the overall strategy to leave a lasting legacy. SAFA is firmly resolved to provide facilities that meet every FIFA requirement and, when the tournament is over, continue to have a positive, relevant impact on local communities for decades to come.' (South Africa 2010 Bid Book, 2003, p. 10). By 2005, however, under the encouragement of FIFA, the LOC had announced its decision to reduce the number of stadia participating in the event once again to ten.

Given that much of the support for the 2006 and 2010 bid campaigns were secured on promises to spread the potential outflows as far as possible – and thus by including as many sites or cities as possible venues (Cornelissen, 2004b) – the reduction of the number of stadia was not well received by urban authorities, who had already mobilised and established boosterist partnerships. Although contracts are due to be concluded with host cities by March 2006, lobbying and conflict around the final selection of stadia is likely to continue for a while longer, since the final FIFA inspection will only take place in June 2008 (Claasen, 2004).

Several major infrastructure development (or mega-) projects have also been tied to the event. Notably, these mega-projects have already become politically controversial affairs. Some of these developmental projects that will be fast-tracked as a result of the bid include a large initiative to establish a train commuter linkage between Johannesburg and Pretoria, the two major urban centres in Gauteng (South Africa's most densely populated and economically significant province), and the establishment of a new international airport at Durban, one of the country's major cities (Philip & Donaldson, 2004).

Nationally, planning and preparation have been initiated by agencies such as the South African Industrial Development Corporation (IDC), which has secured a R50 million loan from the African Development Bank to start upgrading South Africa's infrastructure ahead of 2010. In addition, the IDC together with the Development Bank of Southern Africa has created a business unit, 2010! SWC Business Funding, to assess infrastructural requirements and how this can be sustained with maximum utility value (Pillay, 2005). The 2010! SWC Business Funding unit will aim to provide various types of funding to medium and large businesses for all opportunities related to the event beyond that of construction (Venter, 2004). The focus will be on transactions that will deliver key developmental imperatives such as job creation, black economic empowerment, and assisting in the regeneration of historically black townships (Venter, 2004).

It is clear that early organization and preparation are focused on upgrading South Africa's underdeveloped public transport system, as well as addressing the economic and spatial legacies of apartheid. Event-specific requirements (such as the availability of sufficiently sized stadia and the ability to bring spectators to events) dictate that infrastructural requirements related to accommodation and transport become even more pressing. Initial desires to capture as much support as possible in the bidding stages, however, may have enduring impacts as far as the selection and capacity of venues is concerned. Further, as Jones (2001) indicates, negotiations between host authorities and world organizing bodies often have major implications for the success and impact of an event, but are rarely in the public domain. Infrastructural developments, which serve as a legacy for the host region, are also used as a justification for these types of events. These facilities, however, generally do not serve the purposes of the local community and are often under-utilized (Higham, 1999). The approach of using designated training venues to serve community purposes better (as was the case in the 2004 Cape Town Olympic Bid) is evident in some of the initiatives that the City of Cape Town has for instance undertaken. Improved community facilities will in all likelihood increase community participation in sport, and consequently enhance the quality of life. The question remains, however: 'At what costs?'

The organizers of the 2010 World Cup Finals will need to ensure that the expenditure impact is not restricted in its geographical and temporal spread, so that critical potential additional spending within the regions is not lost. For example, as tourism distribution in South Africa is unevenly spread (Visser,

2004; Cornelissen, 2005), to what extent do the 2010 plans redress or enhance these inequities? South Africa, and some regions in particular, such as the Western Cape province, should maximize opportunities for additional visitor spend as this event will be taking place outside the normal tourism season, thus reducing the usual impact of seasonality. A critical question remains as to the extent to which local companies would be able to benefit from marketing, licensing and hospitality attached to the games, as these key revenue streams for FIFA are tightly controlled. For the 2006 FIFA Football World Cup, to be held in Germany, expenditure-related issues tend to be most contested between FIFA, the LOC, the host cities and regional governments (Walters, 2005: 20). Walters (2005) adds that in order to deal with developmental and economic aspects of sponsorship, it is critical for negotiations to take place with the LOC prior to the signing of host city contracts, to enable local suppliers and sponsors to offset government costs. The equivalent in South Africa would lead to the creation of a marketing platform that would provide impetus to the 'Proudly South African' campaign, which encourages the purchases of South African goods and services. Managing the high expectations of local businesses, however, will perhaps be one of the most significant challenges.

It would also be necessary for South Africa in general, and the LOC in particular, to ensure that its organizational capability is not questioned so that South Africa is portrayed positively in the media and that 'Africa can deliver' in the global arena of mega-events. South Africa should also ensure that its strategy of hosting major sport events serves to build institutional capacity across different related sectors, such as tourism, trade and investment. Education and awareness of how to leverage the associated benefits will be critical. Chalip (2004: 228) notes that since events are legitimized on economic grounds, event organizers, destination marketers and the political elite have an obligation to deliver the best economic impact. In order for mega-events to have a sustainable positive impact on local communities, understanding how these events work, and how to leverage the associated opportunities, is critical. Leveraging refers to the processes through which the benefits of investments are maximized. Chalip (2004: 228) notes that immediate event leveraging includes activities intended to maximize visitor spending, use local supply chains and build new markets. In contrast, he asserts that long-term leveraging seeks to use events to build the host destination's image in order to enhance the quality of its brand or its market position (Chalip, 2004). As foreign investment is critical to local economic development, place marketing via 2010 can play an important role in mobilising local stakeholders and attracting investment (Wyatt, 2004).

Finally, it is critical that the theme of an 'African' World Cup is woven into all aspects of the Games and that key African stakeholders are involved from the beginning. An important lesson learned from the CTOB bid was that it is imperative to include African leaders within the federation in all phases of the Games, particularly in the initial stages. At this stage it is uncertain how many non-ticket holders, particularly from the rest of Africa will travel to be part of the event. According to the Department of Transport's World Cup Project Team (2005), if South Africa sees the promise of delivery on an African World Cup as significant, the implications of greater involvement of African citizens creates a greater demand for travel. With a population and national economy as unstable and vulnerable as that of South Africa's, it is imperative that the country should be aware of the pitfalls of World Cup boosterism, and that the government be as transparent as possible (Wyatt, 2004). In addition, government spending should be carefully monitored as critical expenditures could be cut pre- and post-2010.

Conclusion

As a relative newcomer to, and an African participant in, the global sports mega-events 'circuit', South Africa has experienced marked success with bidding campaigns and with the events the country has hosted. To date, preparation towards the 2010 World Cup has been of a varied nature, with some early planning triumphs and some, significant, miscalculations. The developmental and wider political objectives tied to the hosting of the World Cup constitute significantly self-imposed parameters to South Africa's efforts. These, along with the overall success of the tournament would be the most important indicators by which South Africa's role as a host would in future be measured. In all, despite the clear advantages tied to sports mega-events, they can also place excessive fiscal, management and social burdens on a country. For South Africa, the principal challenge lies not only in garnering the requisite economic and material resources, but also in effectively managing these. Long-term and broad-based development goals that reach beyond the event itself, however, should constitute the primary bases upon which planning and organization take place.

Notes

1 For instance, the sports manufacturer, Adidas, owns the right to produce the footballs used in all FIFA and UEFA (the European football association affiliated to FIFA) Finals. For each competition, new footballs are manufactured by the firm. Adidas also undertakes a marketing campaign whereby it develops a 'name' for the event football, which usually takes on an idiosyncratic characteristic of the host country. For example, the name given to the matchballs for the 1998 World Cup, held in France, was 'Tricolore', while that for the 2002 finals hosted by Japan and South Korea, was 'Fevernova.' The ball manufactured for the 2004 European finals, held in Portugal, was 'Roteiro.'

2 Hiller (2000) notes the main ways in which the bid was 'developmental': it would act as a transformational catalyst accelerating change; contribute to the construction of facilities in disadvantaged areas; promote the development of quality sport facilities supporting community sport programmes; serve as a human resource opportunity; contribute to the stock of affordable housing; generate greater support for small business; and add to urban integration of the transport system.

References

Alegi, P. (2004) *Laduma! Soccer, Politics and Society in South Africa*. Scottsville: University of Kwa-Zulu Natal Press.

Black, D.R. & Nauright, J. (1998) *Rugby and the South African Nation: Sport, Cultures, Politics and Power in the Old and New South Africas*. Manchester: Manchester University Press.

Black, D.R. & Van der Westhuizen, J. (2004) 'The allure of global games for "semi-peripheral" polities and spaces: a research agenda', *Third World Quarterly* 25 (7): 1195–1214.

Business Day (2005) 'Blatter reads the riot act to SA soccer chiefs on 2010', 13 January 2005.

Chalip, L. (2004) 'Beyond impact: a general model for sport event leverage' in B.W. Ritchie & D. Adair (eds) *Sport Tourism: Interrelationships, Impacts and Issues*. Cleveland, UK: Channel View, 226–252.

Claasen, L. (2004) 'Not only does SA's reputation depend on it, Fifa's future is tied up it in as well – Getting the tactics right for 2010', *Business Day*, September 30. [On-line], 01 February 2005. Available: http://www.brain.org.za/2010/articles/bday300904.html.

Coates, D. & Humphreys, B. (1999) 'The growth effects of sport franchises, stadia and arenas', *Journal of Policy Analysis and Management* 16: 601–624.

Cornelissen, S. (2005) 'Tourism impact, distribution and development: the spatial structure of tourism in the Western Cape province of South Africa', *Development Southern Africa* 22 (2): 163–186.

Cornelissen, S. (2004a) 'Sport mega-events in Africa: Processes, impacts and prospects', *Tourism and Hospitality Planning and Development* 1 (1): 39–55.

Cornelissen, S. (2004b) 'It's Africa's turn! The narratives and legitimations surrounding the Moroccan and South Africa bids for the 2006 and 2010 FIFA finals', *Third World Quarterly* 25 (7): 1293–1310.

De Lange, P. (1998) *The Games Cities Play*. Monument Park, South Africa: C.P. de Lange.

Eisinger, P.K. (2000) 'The politics of bread and circuses: building the city for the visitor class', *Urban Affairs Review* 35 (3): 316–333.

Gamage, A. & Higgs, B. (1997) 'Economic of venue selection for special sporting events: with special reference to the 1996 Melbourne Grand Prix', *Asia Pacific Journal of Tourism Research* 1 (2): 15–25.

Grundlingh, A. (1998) 'From redemption to recidivism? Rugby and change in South Africa during the 1995 Rugby World Cup and its aftermath', *Sporting Traditions* 14 (2): 67–86.

Haugen, H. (2003) *The construction of Beijing as an Olympic City*. Unpublished dissertation, Oslo: University of Oslo.

Higham, J. (1999) 'Commentary – sport as an avenue of tourism development: an analysis of the positive and negative impacts of sport tourism', *Current Issues in Tourism* 2 (1): 82–90.

Hiller, H. (1998) 'Assessing the impact of mega-events: a linkage model', *Current Issues in Tourism* 1 (1): 47–57.

Hiller, H. (2000) 'Mega-events, urban boosterism and growth strategies: an analysis of the objectives and legitimations of the Cape Town 2004 Olympic Bid', *International Journal of Urban and Regional Research* 24 (2): 439–458.

Horne, J.D. & Manzenreiter, W. (2004) 'Accounting for mega-events: forecasts and actual impacts of the 2002 Football World Cup Finals on the host countries Japan/Korea', *International Review for the Sociology of Sport* 39 (2): 187–203.

Ingerson, L. & Westerbeek, H.M. (2000) 'Determining key success criteria for attracting hallmark sporting events', *Pacific Tourism Review* 3 (4): 239–253.

Jones, C. (2001) 'Mega-events and host-region impacts: determining the true worth of the 1999 Rugby World Cup', *International Journal of Tourism Research* 3: 241–251.

Lee, C. & Taylor, T. (2005) 'Critical reflections on the economic impact assessment of a mega-event: the case of 2002 FIFA World Cup', *Tourism Management* 26: 295–603.

Ley, D. & Olds, K. (1992) 'World's Fairs and culture of consumption in the contemporary city', in K. Anderson & F. Gale (eds) *Inventing places*. Melbourne: Longman Cheshire, 178–193.

Mail and Guardian (2005) 'World Cup: "We started earlier than the Germans"', 25 April 2005.

Matheson, V.A. & Baade, R.A. (2003) *Mega-sporting events in developing nations: playing the way to prosperity?* [On-line], 20 January 2005. Available: http://www.williams.edu/Economics/neudc/papers/matheson.pdf.

Nauright, J. (2004) 'Global games: culture, political economy and sport in the globalized world of the 21 century', *Third World Quarterly* 25 (7): 1325–1336.

Nauright, J. & Schimmel, K. (eds) (2005) *The Political Economy of Sport*. Houndmills: Basingstoke: Palgrave.

Olympic Assessment Team (1997) *Strategic Environmental Assessment of the Cape Town 2004 Olympic Bid.* [On-line], 05 August 2005. Available: http://users.iafrica.com/s/sh/shandler/exec4.htm.

Owen, K. (2002) 'The Sydney 2000 Olympics and urban entrepreneurialism: local variations in urban governance', *Australian Geographical Studies* 40 (3): 563–600.

Pappas, I. (1997) 'Athens win 2004 Olympic Games', *Hellenet – An Online Look into the Future*, October 17. Available: http://hellenet.com/10-17-97.htm.

Philip, R. & Donaldson, A. (2004) 'Economic cup will overflow – soccer event will create jobs and fast-track some of the country's biggest projects', *Sunday Times*, May 16. [On-line], 01 February 2005. Available: http://www.suntimes.co.za/2004/05/16/news/news04.asp.

Pillay, U. (2005) 'Golden chance for SA's cities to score from 2010', *Business Day*, January 28. [On-line], 01 February 2005. Available: http://allafrica.com/stories/printable/200501280073.html

SA 2010 Bid Company (2003) *South Africa 2010 Bid Book*. Johannesburg: SA 2010 Bid Company, 10/16.

SA 2010 Bid Company (n.d.a) *Fifa, SA complete 2010 agreement.* [On-line], 01 February 2005. Available: http://www.sa2010bid.co.za/default.asp?aId=129681.

SA 2010 Bid Company (n.d.b) *Blatter: Rally behind SA.* [On-line], 20 February 2005. Available: http://www.sa2010bid.co.za/default.asp?aId=135517.

Slack, T. (1998) 'Studying the commercialisation of sport: the need for critical analysis', *Sociology of Sport Online 1*. Available: http://brunel.ac.uk/depts/sps/sosol/.

South Africa, Department of Transport (2005) Initial travel demand projections for the FIFA 2010 World Cup in South Africa – Draft for circulation and discussion. Pretoria: Department of Transport.

Standeven, J. & De Knop, P. (2000) *Sport Tourism*, Champaign, IL: Human Kinetics.

Swart, K. & Bob, U. (2004) 'The seductive discourse of development: the Cape Town 2004 Olympic bid', *Third World Quarterly* 25 (7): 1311–1324.

Teigland, J. (1999) 'Mega-events and impacts on tourism: the predictions and realities of the Lillehammer Olympics', *Impact Assessment and Project Appraisal* 17 (4): 305–317.

Van der Westhuizen, J. (2001) 'Marketing the "Rainbow Nation": The power of the South African music, film and sport industry', in K.C. Dunn and T.M. Shaw (eds) *Africa's Challenge to International Relations Theory*. New York: Palgrave, 64–81.

Venter, I. (2004) 'New soccer World Cup business unit at IDC', *Creamer Media's Engineering News:* October, 22. [On-line], 01 February 2005. Available: http://www.emgineeringnews.co.za/eng/uitlities/search/?show=58187.

Visser, G. (2004) 'South African Tourism and its role in the perpetuation of an uneven tourism space economy', in C.M. Rogerson & G. Visser (eds) *Tourism and Development: Issues in Contemporary South Africa*. Pretoria: Africa Institute of South Africa, 268–289.

Walters, B. (2005) 2010 World Cup: Report on visit to Germany, July-August 2005. Unpublished report.

Whitson, D. & Macintosh, D. (1996) 'The global circus: international sport, tourism and the marketing of cities', *Journal of Sport and Social Issues* 20 (3): 278–295.

Wyatt, A. (2004) *Managing Events: International Social Development*. Unpublished MA dissertation, Falmer, England: University of Sussex.

Part 3
Sports Mega-Events, Power, Spectacle and the City

UEFA Euro 2004™ Portugal: The social construction of a sports mega-event and spectacle

Salomé Marivoet

Major international sporting competitions are complex phenomena in which the political and economic interests of nation states, sporting organizations, the media and multinationals interact. While many aspects of these events today may be perceived as part of a general trend in modern sport (such as the representational nature of national teams, the urge for national affirmation and the need to transmit sociocultural identities), there have also been important changes that need to be explored further.

As globalization intensifies, sport is increasingly being used as a vehicle for the affirmation of territorial or cultural identities on regional, national and continental scales. This becomes all the more obvious in the case of major sporting events, given the enormous media attention that they attract (Friedman, 1994; Roche, 2000; Miller *et al.*, 2001). Analysing the 2002 World Cup in Korea and Japan, John Horne and Wolfram Manzenreiter conclude that major sporting events today are 'simultaneously driven by globalization and promote it', at the same time as they present 'an opportunity to construct or promote identities, not only top-down from the state but also bottom-up from publics' (2004: 200, 192).

In this context, it appears that there has been a diversification of the opportunities offered by modern sport for the affirmation of national identity. Throughout the 20th century, nation states acquired visibility chiefly through the results they achieved in sports contests; since the 1990s, however, the hosting of these events and the mass mobilization of populations for the collective assertion of their respective identities have become new resources. When various opportunities for national affirmation arise at the same time, such as occurs when host countries' national teams emerge victorious, a space for new large-scale identity phenomena is created. This is what happened at the European Football Championship in Portugal in 2004, and also in the 1998 World Cup in France.

Hugh Dauncey & Geoff Hare have analysed the French case, perceiving it as a metaphor of national self-esteem and as a way of affirming new and traditional values, 'particularly regarding questions of ethnic and cultural integration' (2000: 344). Although the question of integration through recognition of ethnic diversity was pertinent for France in 1998, as Patrick Mignon (1999) and John Marks (1999) have pointed out with regards to the role of the Algerian player Zinedine Zidane as national symbol alongside the French coach Aimé Jacquet, Portugal in 2004 had no such equivalent.

There are certainly specific issues associated with the manifestations of nationalism occurring at major sporting events, despite the general consensus in current academic debate that these constitute not only unprecedented opportunities for the affirmation of nation states as cultural realities on the global stage, but also space-times for the redefinition of meanings, values and symbols of affiliation. In this context, major sporting events seem to accurately express the reflexive tendency of the current phase of late modernity, as has been pointed out by various authors (eg, Smart, 1999; Beck, Giddens & Lash, 2000; Wagner, 2001).

To understand the sociological complexity of major sporting events in the present context of late modernity, however, especially given the intensification of globalization, it is important to know what social processes are operating in its production. Thus, Pierre Bourdieu's suggestion (1994) about the social impact of the Olympic Games is revealing, particularly when he argues that research aimed at identifying the mechanisms regulating the practices of the agents involved in the social construction of the event is the only way of ensuring collective comprehension of its effects.

In our analysis of the 2004 European Football Championship as a case study of a major sporting event, we intend to discover to what extent the social construction of the event made it a media phenomenon in Portuguese society (by producing 'witnesses' that could legitimize a differential identity and by constituting a space-time for the reassessment and re-dimensioning of national symbols, such as occurred with the creation of the 'brand' Portugal within the broad or global framework).

As presuppositions underlying this research, we assumed that the manifestations of identity citizenship in the tournament were powerfully affected by the political, ideological and ethical dimensions surrounding the involvement of public bodies, the commercial and media aspects involved in the promotion of the event, and also the results obtained by the Portuguese team in the championship. We also considered that the kind of (relatively infrequent) violent behaviour displayed by fans resulted from the radicalization of the opportunities offered by major sporting events for the expression of differential identities on the global stage.

Different data-gathering techniques were used, including observation during the tournament (18 of the 31 matches were studied from inside the stadia, while fan behaviour on the eve and day of the match was observed in the respective city centres); documentary sources (Portuguese newspapers, police reports, legislation and international recommendations), and also informal interviews of fan workers from the fan 'embassies'. Fieldwork mostly involved participant observation with informal note taking and the use of protocols for the description of contexts and forms of violence. The fact that our presence was accepted amongst fans from the *hooligan/casual* culture gained certain relevance in the light of complementary sources of information.

The research was carried out under the auspices of the Centre for Sociological Research of Coimbra University, with the support of Euro 2004, SA, which issued accreditations to enable us to gain access to the stadia and surrounding precincts, and granted our team-members the status of volunteer-observers. The Institute for Police Science and Domestic Security (Portuguese Public Security Police) also provided assistance.

Public commitments and investments

Portugal's application to host the Euro 2004 represented from the outset a serious commitment between the government in power and the Portuguese Football Federation. The public authorities (both central and local government) shouldered most of the expenses necessary for the construction or remodelling of the infrastructure. Public investment in the construction of seven new stadia and the remodelling of another three accounted for around 75 per cent of the total costs[1]. In a report on the *Assessment of the Economic Impact of the 2004 European Championship*, published by Portugal 2004, SA, in February 2005, the total cost of the construction or remodelling of infrastructures for the championship was one billion Euro, of which 21 per cent was contributed by the government (205 million Euros). According to this study, around 47% of this public investment was recovered by 31st December, considering only direct taxes. The cost of mounting an enormous security and safety operation, involving around 20,000 national police officers (with the usual international cooperation) also came from the public treasury.

Never before had Portugal organized anything on such a scale. It required an unprecedented effort, not only economically but also on the organizational level; for although Portugal had already had the experience of organising Expo'98, even this could scarcely compare to the demands of Euro 2004. As Dauncey & Hare (2000) pointed out in relation to France, Portugal also witnessed the definition of policies by public authorities that aimed to use the European Championship to transmit an image of a 'modernized' Portugal, particularly through the provision of high quality facilities and services.

This indicates how the hosting of a major sporting event provokes a certain reflection on the subject of national identity, providing the opportunity for a reassessment of self-image with a view to re-branding the country on the global market. In this sense, we seem to be faced with a re-dimensioning of the logic governing the internal production of national self-representation, according to which factors intrinsic to each society (peculiarities, special traits, internal social dynamics, periods for the assessment of national policy, etc) are apparently weakened by expectations from the global framework. This is one of the ways in which sporting events promote globalization, as Horne and Manzenreiter (2004) argue, particularly as regards the hegemony of western values or of the more industrialized societies in the ordering of nations on the global stage.

The commitments assumed by nation states when applying to host major events and the policies resulting from them suggest a dimension to the social construct that we may call ideological-political. The facts show that public policies aim not merely to comply with the minimum requirements of hosting as regards infrastructure and security, but rather to produce a 'brand image' of the country, even if this involves having to deal with critical debate and internal opposition from sectors of the public or other agents of opinion formation. Opposition to public policy concerning the hosting of the 2004 European Championship was manifested early on in Portuguese society, mostly taking the form of arguments that the country was being taken over by football mania to the detriment of primary sectors, such as education and healthcare, which still had poor infrastructures. In Portugal, however, the level of opposition did not rise as far as the organization of pressure groups or the intention to boycott, as happened in France (Dauncey & Hare, 1999).

For example, the decision to rebuild completely three of the largest stadia (those belonging to FC Porto, Benfica and Sporting) and demolish the old ones aroused great controversy in Portuguese society, despite the fact that the clubs that owned them promised to contribute to the investment. The demolition of the old stadia, however, acquired important symbolic overtones, since they had been built during a dark period of Portugal's history, a period marked by backwardness and closure to the democratic world when football was used for propaganda purposes by the fascist regime. By constructing its new stadia in an elegant architectural style, with comfortable safe infrastructures, commercial and leisure areas, and cutting-edge security technology, Portugal was creating an image of itself as a creative, efficient country, equipped with the most modern technology.

Alongside public investment in the building of great works as 'witnesses' to the infrastructural development of the country, there was also the construction of an institutional discourse designed to validate the country's commitment to the tournament (as also happened in other countries that had hosted similar events). The expenses were presented by public authorities as an investment that would yield returns, not only during the event itself with the attraction of foreign fans, teams and media, but also by promoting the country as a tourist destination throughout the world, which would of course have effects in the medium term.

A hundred days before the start of the championship, when it was predicted that the event would attract around half a million foreign fans, the Secretary of State for Youth and Sports insisted that the Government fully believed the returns would compensate the investment (*Newsletter UEFA EURO 2004^TM* of March 2004). A few days before the start, however, when it seemed that the immediate income from tourism would fall short of expectations, a government spokesman (who at that point was responsible for the tournament) publicly claimed that the investment had not been undertaken with a view to reaping immediate returns, but with a somewhat less tangible purpose. 'I prefer to see the European Championship as the positive affirmation of a modern united country', he stated in the *Diário de Notícias* (12th June)[2]. Asked if Portugal would make money with the organization of the championship, he replied in an interview with that newspaper:

> I did not see things in that way. We should remember that we have here 8,500 foreign journalists. They have already broadcast many images of our country to the world at large. It has been predicted that 9 billion people will watch the championship on television. That is the best way to promote a country. And there is a climate of confidence that helps to unify the Portuguese people, with their national flag as a symbol of that confidence.

Alongside institutional discourse designed to sensitize the public to the importance of the event for the promotion of the country in the world, there were also carefully planned marketing strategies aimed at arousing an emotional response amongst the Portuguese people.

The marketing of the event

The human logo presented when the Portuguese applied to host the event in 1999 was from the outset innovative and even earned an entry in the *Guinness Book of Records*. 34,309 people were gathered together on the pitch of the national stadium in Lisbon to form the stylized shape of a player with the ball and the words 'Euro 2004 Portugal' on a background of red and green, representing the colours of the Portuguese flag. The slogan on the first promotional poster, '*Portugal loves football*', also appealed to the public to get involved, evoking the strong tradition of football in Portuguese society.

All the organizational aspects, including national and international promotion, were given top-class marketing treatment, where once more the brand image evoked style and efficiency. For example, the iconography of the official poster promoting the Euro 2004 in Portugal, which was diffused throughout the world by the international press, made use of traditional historical symbols updated to bring them into line with contemporary tastes. This poster showed the most magnificent square in Lisbon, the Terreiro do Paço or Praça do Comércio (built in the elegant style of the palace of Versailles after the violent earthquake of 1755 that destroyed part of the city) covered in grass like a football pitch, with the hill of the castle (which had been reconquered from the Moors in the 12th century after the formation of Portugal) in one corner; opposite it was the slogan:

> *In Portugal, the extra time*
> *is always the best part of the game*

The ways in which the event was promoted clearly illustrate what Horne and Manzenreiter call the 'beatification of business' (2004: 201). Behind the appeals to the heart (the official logo of the *UEFA Euro 2004^{TM} Portugal* was presented in such a way as to involve a football, with stylized images of the cock of Barcelos, one of the traditional symbols of Portuguese identity) was the hard logic of commerce, the use of psychological resources that would be scarcely perceptible to most consumers.

This emotional appeal was also visible in the Portuguese slogan that was associated with the official logo during the event (*'Vive o 2004!^{TM}*[3]) as well as in the choreographed displays during the opening and closing ceremonies. These evoked historical facts and deeds, indicating that this was not the first time that Portugal had opened itself up to the world. In the opening ceremony, a 16th century caravel, reminding us of the golden period of the Portuguese discoveries, slid across the grass, which was now transformed into an ocean; at the end, spectators were invited to create a panel with the traditional Portuguese cobbles, while the Canadian pop singer, Nelly Furtado, who is of Portuguese descent, in some way evoked the historical experience of Portuguese emigration during the 20th century, singing from a stage that was now a futuristic caravel.

As we can see, these ceremonial displays, like the iconography of the promotional posters and the official discourse of public personalities in the various debates that took place in Portugal about the Euro 2004, were highly symbolic, involving a reworking and an updating of national and historical emblems. The aim was ultimately to transmit the notion of 'modernization' and 'progress' in the light of dominant world values.

Thus the historical period when Portugal had been an important power was now glorified in a space-time where it was once again able to claim a place at the centre of the world stage through the hosting of a major sporting event. As we have seen, this cannot be dissociated from the various manifestations of national pride that occurred during the tournament. With Euro 2004, history was reintroduced onto the national agenda, with certain facts highlighted and others effectively extinguished; and the symbolic power of the iconography, choreography and stylistic and rhetorical resources used functioned as stimuli for the reassessment of Portuguese self-representation in the world.

Euro 2004, SA also invested in the Internet as a resource for the promotion of the event on the world scale. With the creation of the site 'euro2004.com', it became possible for the games to be watched live, with audio commentaries in eight different languages, thus overcoming to some extent the obstacles raised by the different time zones. As regards merchandising, which was considered by the event organizers to be the best ever, the products marketed were grouped into six different categories: *National Pride, Street, Fashion, Event, Photographic* and *Kinas Character*[4]. As mentioned in the last issue of the *UEFA Euro 2004^{TM}* newsletter, which circulated from March 2004, all were 'designed with a view to bring fans closer to the event in a spirit of celebration of football', an invitation aimed at the world market, once more made possible by the internet:

The next step is to penetrate foreign markets from March onwards, particularly in Europe – Spain, France, England, Italy and Germany – and Asia, especially Japan, Korea and Thailand. By the end of March, products may be acquired online at the site www.store.euro2004.com. In April, advertising of the official EURO 2004 articles will be stepped up with the launch of a campaign using different media – television, newspapers, billboards and point-of-purchase promotion.

With the marketing of products associated with the event, Euro 2004, SA not only reaped huge profits (all the more so given the quality and diversity of the merchandise and the 'new creative and daring' designs), but also certainly helped to stimulate and involve the public in Portugal, Europe and the rest of the world, and secure their loyalty. The marketing of *UEFA Euro 2004™* clearly shows the dimension of seduction used to urge the public to get involved, which was of course an essential factor in ensuring the profitability of the event.

The results seem to have lived up to expectations, since more fans attended Euro 2004 than Euro 2000, organized by Belgium and Holland[5]. As well as the profits resulting from ticket sales, the event organizers also made a lot of money out of television broadcasting rights, which hit record levels, and of course from sponsorship from the large multinationals[6].

As we can see, the innovative and sophisticated commercial dimension of the social construction of the event, which created an association between the tournament and the carefully reworked iconography of the Portuguese identity, thus launching the product onto the global market (as was clearly visible in the registered trademark '*UEFA Euro 2004™* Portugal'), was ultimately the final stage of a European football championship involving sixteen national teams, which took place between 12th June and 4th July 2004 in ten stadia based in eight Portuguese cities. As Horne and Manzenreiter (2004) pointed out ever since the 1994 World Cup Finals in the USA, there has been increased commercial exploitation of great football events, as well as the Olympic Games[7].

National unity and hospitality

Hosting a major sporting event is an enormous organizational challenge for the countries concerned. As well as the logistics involved in providing accommodation, transport and catering for large numbers of fans, there is also the question of security of fans, teams and visiting personalities, an issue which has become all the more pertinent with the threat of terrorism in the present international political context. In the case of Euro 2004, there were also additional risks from the violence associated with football fan subcultures.

From the 1990s, public authorities and sporting bodies began clamping down on violence and xenophobia in international football events, mainly through the institution of *fan projects*, which encouraged attitudes of hospitality towards visiting fans, the dynamisation of cultural spaces and the creation of *fan embassies* (Comeron *et al.*, 2002; Schneider & Gabriel, 2004). Although Portuguese institutions had not themselves organized these types of action, exchanges were established on the local level within the ambit of the project 'Good Hosting, Fewer Problems', financed by the Deputy General of Justice and Interior Affairs of the European Commission, which brought together *fan coaching* organizations from Germany, the United Kingdom, Czech Republic, Italy and Holland[8].

The message of good hospitality was also given a high profile by the official authorities connected to the event, with the construction of a discourse that appealed to all Portuguese to collaborate in welcoming the foreign fans, as if this were some kind of national mission. Public and sporting bodies involved in the event persistently emphasised Portugal's commitment in hosting the event, as can be seen in the words that the director of Euro 2004, SA, addressed to the 4,000 volunteers that directly collaborated in the organization of the event[9]:

> Dear Friends,
> Portugal is, as you know, the host of a major sporting event in Europe, which will take place between 12th June and 4th July 2004, in which once again the competence of the Portuguese, which has already proved itself in matters of reception and management will be put to the test before you and the eyes of the world. (. . .) It is not only the capacity of the Portuguese to achieve their aims which is in question. It is, above all, the image of Portugal in the world.

This sense of patriotic duty was extremely important in influencing the attitude of the various Portuguese institutions, particularly in their quest for information about similar events and experiences. For example, the *low profile* adopted by the Public Security Police, who were responsible for policing most of the stadia and host cities, was extremely important for the prevention of any escalation of violence in high-risk games, although other strategies had also been adopted on the part of the militarized Portuguese security force (GNR), which got involved in serious confrontations with English fans in the tourist region of the Algarve[10].

The various cultural events organized by local authorities in the designated 'Fan Zones' were another way of encouraging hospitality, in addition to the exchange with the foreign fan embassies. Moreover, the fact that the Portuguese Football Federation had encouraged the constitution of a *claque* (or group of supporters) to support the national team, and had even made contact with some groups of *ultras* from the biggest national clubs, inviting their members to join in, revealed the spirit of national mission assumed by the event organizers.

An example of this appeal to good hospitality as a way of preventing violent disturbances was the open letter sent in May to all Portuguese citizens by mail, from the then deputy Prime Minister, responsible for Euro 2004:

> *Dear Portuguese citizens*
> We are a few days away from the beginning of the final phase of the European Football Championship, Euro 2004, which constitutes the third biggest sporting event at an international level. (. . .)
> Nevertheless, it is natural that an event of this scale could cause some disruption to the daily life of the city and to the individuals that live there (. . .)

But we should take any possible disruptions as the consequences of a very special festive occasion that the country is about to experience.

It is important that we take full advantage of this event and demonstrate our innate cordial hospitality to those who visit us. I am certain that together we will ensure that this moment will be a great success, given the effort of the Portuguese people to rise to the occasion in a determined fashion.

We are all invited – Portugal is ready and counts on you!

The spirit of national mission that was continuously impressed upon the public by the event organizers and the top level organs of sovereignty (especially in the person of the President of the Republic) in order to encourage national cohesion, self-esteem and tolerance towards the visitors, suggest the existence of an ethical dimension to the social construction of these events. It is possible, however, that this dimension may take on different forms in different contexts, given the specific nature of each society, or may not even be manifested at all.

In the case of Portugal, large swathes of the population cooperated in helping to promote a spirit of national cohesion and hospitality, as could be seen by the intermingling between local people and foreign fans that took place in the cities hosting the matches, and also by the great celebrations of Portugal's victories that took place in the main squares of the cities throughout the tournament, sprinkling the landscape with the green and red of the national colours, through the unprecedented and surprising appropriation of the national flag as symbol of identity[11].

The facts suggest that this deliberate reinforcement of national unity, together with the promotion of tolerance towards visiting fans, particularly by appealing to the Portuguese tradition of good hospitality, played a big part in creating an atmosphere of good will between citizens of different European nations, thus allowing the Euro 2004 to become a stage for the peaceful expression of cultural diversity. This aspect was highly praised by international commentators, particularly by the heads of UEFA.

The effects of the mediatization of the football mega-event/media spectacle

The high level of interest and involvement generated at European football championships far transcends the sporting nature of those events, as we have seen. In addition to the economic dimension, there are also powerful motivations at work on the part of the teams, which are presented as representatives of their country (players, technical teams and sporting bodies), the public in general, and football fans in particular, who actively get involved in support of their national colours (Dunning, 1999; Giulianotti, 1999; Finn & Giulianotti, 2000).

In addition to the thousands of Portuguese who came out into the streets to participate in the great party of European football, around a million spectators watched the games in the stadia, half of whom were foreign fans, while almost

200 television stations and hundreds of journalists and photographers transmitted news and pictures of the Euro 2004 to the four corners of the earth, where they were followed by millions of viewers and readers during the 23 days of the championship (cf note 6). There was, thus, a global media dimension to the social construction of the event; the media agenda not only helped to promote the event but also stimulated its own business. As Jean-Marie Brohm (1992) has noted, a sporting performance is meaningless without the knowledge of the public at large, and so it is difficult, if not impossible, to dissociate the sporting aspect from the media aspect.

In a major sporting event, everything is therefore hyped up, and given massive media coverage, from the main actors (players, coaches, referees and directors of sporting bodies) to the matches, and the public, who recreate performances *ad hoc* in the stadia and squares of the cities or simply affirm their identities in ritualized fashion in the intervals between the organized cultural events. The time-space of the event therefore becomes the platform for the staging of a mega-spectacle on the global scale.

The top players, whose achievements deservedly bring them to the attention of the media, are a reminder of the meritocratic values of democratic societies, as a number of authors have pointed out (Bromberger, Hayot & Mariottini, 1995; Holt, Mangan & Lanfranchi, 1996). They become almost apotheosised, elevated into national heroes, as happened to the charismatic Eusebio in the 1960s. Patrick Mignon (1999), amongst other authors, refers to the case of Zidane in France; while in Portugal in 2004 there was Luís Figo and the rising new talent, Cristiano Ronaldo.

While the media strove to inform the world of everything that was happening in and around the championship, the way in which this was done involved a certain amount of re-creation of the real, as a number of authors have pointed out[12]. In the case of the Portuguese press, the effect produced upon large sectors of the population was very visible. Amongst the events highlighted by the national press during the Euro 2004, many focused upon forms of interaction set in motion by the media. Historical rivalries were re-enacted by the Portuguese public, for example, as they celebrated the achievements of their national team; while highly charged symbolic language was used for their collective stimulation.

The Portuguese example is therefore not so dissimilar to what happened in France during the 1998 FIFA World Cup. As Lucy McKeever (1999) concluded, the media, far from being a passive means of communication, both influenced and were influenced by the society that they portrayed, operating as a mirror of French society. In fact, the dimension of identity-citizenship expressed in major football championships cannot be detached from the media portrayal of the event and from the national symbols transmitted by it, including the national teams and the highly mediatized manifestations of exultation and national pride.

It seems, therefore, that the media and sporting dimensions of the social construction of such events not only interact in the manifestations of citizenship that take place there, but also affect future responses; thus, team victories acquire the potential to involve much broader sectors of the population. In this context, the expression of national identities, as powerfully transmitted by the media during championships, is an example of what Maurice Roche (2000) calls 'mediatized citizenship'.

The 'theatre' of European citizenships

During the UEFA Euro 2004, fans from the sixteen European teams that had made it into the final phase of the European Championship came together in Portugal, appropriating the squares and other symbolic sites in the host cities in different ways. The common denominator throughout was the spectacular display of different national flags, affirming once more the theatricality involved in the affirmation of national identity in a multicultural Europe.

In this *mise en scène*, a relationship could be established with the historical backgrounds of the different societies. For example, in the case of England, there was a clear sense of territorial appropriation of space in the affirmation of identity, visible in the concentration of fans in the main squares of the host cities in which their matches were played, where central monuments and statues were symbolically covered with enormous English flags. Although fans of other nationalities also glorified their countries, in some cases setting up great swathes of their national colour, the sense of identity assertion was manifested more in a carnival atmosphere, with amusing performances that often alluded to traditional symbols or historical facts, as in the case of the Danish, Swedes, Swiss and Dutch (the last of whom would parade into the stadia).

Support was also manifested in a variety of ways in the stadia, revealing the differences in the traditional terrace culture of each society. Particularly worthy of attention was the seriousness and effusiveness of the English, Czechs, Croatians and Greeks, the last three of whom reproduced a mixture of the Italian *ultra* style with what Gary Armstrong & Malcolm Young (2000: 205) call the English 'traditional macho football supporter'. The *ultra* influence upon the stadium culture was most visible amongst the Italians, Portuguese, Spanish and French, and also amongst some groups of Germans, although this seemed to be more of a question of imitation of style rather than a similar mentality, since members of this subculture did not mobilize in large numbers to support their teams. The presence of Russians, Lithuanians and Bulgarians was less visible inside and outside the stadia, due to their smaller numbers.

Although the Portuguese had got involved in the 1996 UEFA European Championship in England, the support manifested at that time had been more subdued. There was a great increase in interest in subsequent tournaments, as a result of team success; but there had never before been such fervent manifestations of national pride and rejoicing as took place during the 2004 European Championship. The crowds of Portuguese that surged out onto the streets to celebrate the victories of the national team had only ever been paralleled by the jubilation expressed at the fall of the fascist regime on 25th April 1974.

Unlike in Portugal, France and Greece, where the large-scale manifestation of support for the national team is a relatively recent phenomenon, some countries of northern Europe have a long tradition of fan participation during European Championships and World Cups (Murphy, Williams & Dunning, 1990; Williams, 1997; Mignon, 1999). This is evident in the large numbers of fans that travel from these countries to support their teams, and amongst whom manifestations of identity citizenship acquire a powerful symbolic dimension.

In the case of Portugal, large sectors of the public were stimulated to get involved in a variety of different ways. The media played an important role, as we have seen, both directly, through its appeals or by giving voice to figures of recognized merit in this area, and indirectly, by using the iconography taken from the symbolism of national identity. This stimulation, experienced as an invitation to get involved in the collective manifestations of identity and group affirmation, had a disinhibiting effect on many Portuguese, who gave in to emotional outbursts, while the media coverage of this public expression had the effect of amplifying and spreading the involvement.

When this was experienced live, however (in the stadia and on the streets of the host cities), it was easy to understand the transcendent or religious nature of the process of collective identity affirmation and the celebration of nation, as various authors have pointed out (Durkheim [1912], 1968; Maffesoli, 1988; Gellner, 1994; Llobera, 2000). It is difficult, if not impossible, to remain detached or indifferent in such circumstances. As Michel Maffesoli tried to show in *Le Temps des Tribus*, the 'social divine' emerges out of the experience of 'going beyond oneself', of transcending the notion of 'the self' and 'the other' by merging with the group in a shared passion. It operates through the religious sentiment of *'re-ligare'* (meaning to 're-connect') with physical and symbolic territories seen as spaces for the creation of identities (Maffesoli, 1988: 84).

The celebration of nationhood experienced by large sectors of the Portuguese population – not only those resident in the country but also amongst communities resident abroad (as also happened with the Greeks, whose team won the Final of the 2004 European Championships playing against the Portuguese) – despite being circumscribed by the virtual space-time of the event, will remain in the collective imagination as scarcely perceptible resources from which new self-representations of national identity may be formed. Moreover, when a particular population experiences this deep and widespread urge to manifest its identity in this way, there will inevitably be an attenuation of the internal tensions resulting from sociocultural and ideological differences, giving way to collective experiences involving cross-sections of society. Although these are located in space and time, they permit experimentation with new patterns of interaction between the groups involved.

The processes of identity affirmation that are set in motion by great sporting events appear to be based on feelings of unitedness; for as Maffesoli mentions, although these are experienced in a local or ephemeral way, they operate as a kind of 'social cement' (*'ciment sociétal'*), constituting the *ethos* of the cohesion necessary for any society to survive (Maffesoli, 1988: 84). Dauncey and Hare (1999: 2) also read the situation in this way, when they claim that the collective experiences of national integration on the occasion of the 1998 World Cup marked the 'collective psyche' of the French.

Similarly, fan subcultures, which invest enormous amounts of emotional energy in football and typically cultivate the 'us versus them' mentality in their behaviour by treating adversaries as the enemy, reveal the radicalization of sport's potential for reproducing and affirming differentiated sociocultural identities. In the research carried out, we can identify specific features within football fan subcultures, particularly in the forms of violence used; the famous distinction of course is between the *hooligan/casual* of English origin, most common in the countries of northern Europe, and the *ultra* of Italian origin, which is strongly implanted in the South. Unfortunately it is not possible to undertake a complete analysis of this here[13].

Final considerations

Great football events have become excellent stages upon which different societies display themselves for the rest of the world. They also act as vehicles of institutional policy by means of which nation states affirm themselves, alongside the various manifestations of citizenship. In this context, they are indicative of the present stage of globalization, characterized not only by standardization as regards markets, cultures and lifestyles, but also by a resurgence of the local and national within the global.

In no other sport is this as widespread as in football, nor has any other sport achieved the same levels of commercialization, presenting its spectacles as one of the most important products on the market of cultural consumption. We have tried to show throughout this chapter, however, that the sociological reality surrounding major football events will not be properly understood without an analysis of the social construction that produces them.

Taking as a case-study the UEFA Euro 2004™ Football Championship held in Portugal, we aimed to examine further the underlying social construction, particularly the interaction established between the various agents involved, in order better to understand the nature of its impact. In the ensuing analysis, we identified a series of dimensions underlying the social construction of the event, which we have called ideological-political, ethical, commercial, mediatic, sporting and identity citizenship or differential identity.

Public investment in the creation of a 'brand image' for the country, and a spirit of national mission and hospitality, allied to the commercial dimension involved in the promotion of the event on the global market, were stimulated by the widespread mediatization of the mega-spectacle, which offered multiple opportunities for the manifestation of cultural identity, not only in the sporting performances of the various national teams that got through to the final phase of the tournament, but also in the presence of the fans.

The facts have suggested that the social construction of major sporting events, and football championships in particular, have become phenomena for the mediatization of societies, since they produce 'witnesses' that legitimize national identities, as transmitted by the media. In the case of Portugal, as host country of the 2004 European Championship, the space-time of the event (including the preparation stage) was perceived as the perfect opportunity for a reassessment and redimensioning of the symbols and self-representations of national identity, in which the past was transformed into a modernized present in the production of a brand image to be circulated throughout the world.

The widespread involvement of the Portuguese people in shows of rejoicing at their team's victories suggests that the celebration of national identity that tends to occur at great football spectacles is not merely reflected by the media coverage, marketing strategies and institutional discourse but also actively influenced by them. The collective experience of celebrating the achievements of the national team, with the strong emotional charge that this involves, seems to be based on the religious desire for union and sharing (*'re-ligare'*), which, in promoting social cohesion, effectively reinforces its affirmation. In the case of the countries hosting these events, the reassessment and redimensioning of their image on the global stage also contributes to this identity affirmation.

Although these experiences are limited to the space-time of the events, they would appear to be possible resources for future self-representations of national identities. Only further research, however, will allow us properly to assess their true impact. We should nevertheless consider that, amongst possible consequences, we may find not only factors stimulating cohesion and national self-esteem, but also frustration at the lack of fit between the everyday reality and the self-representations created during these sporting events (since these are designed for foreign rather than domestic consumption).

The research carried out into the social construction of the 2004 European Championship has led us to conclude that large-scale football events are today complex phenomena that reveal the potential of sport in late modernity for the reassessment and redimensioning of national identities, through the introduction of space-times in which these can be played out and the revalidation of the importance of the symbolic in the existential expression of societies on the global scene.

Notes

1 Two public limited companies were set up for the organization of Euro 2004: *Euro 2004, SA* (responsible for the organization, promotion and marketing of the event), whose capital was divided between the UEFA (54.8%), the Portuguese Football Federation (40.2%) and the Portuguese state (5%); and *Portugal 2004, SA* (responsible for the construction or remodelling of the stadia and access roads), whose capital was divided between the Portuguese state (95%), and the Portuguese Football Federation (5%). Both companies entered into total liquidation after 31st December 2004.

2 According to declarations made by the president of the Association of Hoteliers and Tourism Entrepreneurs of the Algarve (the most touristic region of the country), the high expectations of the 2004 European Championship organizers as regards the influx of tourists during the event had the effect of driving away the usual public from the region in the holiday period, either because they anticipated excessive crowds and inflated prices, or for security fears (*O Jogo*, 16ᵗʰ June). However, in the final balance, only the Algarve registered a drop in numbers (−13%), while other resorts showed increases of over 25% compared to the same period in 2003 (*Visão*, No. 592, 8ᵗʰ to 14ᵗʰ July).

3 The message means literally 'enjoy Euro 2004'.

4 This is pronounced the same as '*quinas*', the name of the five shields on the Portuguese flag, representing the arms of Portugal.

5 The total number of spectators that passed through the stadia during the 2004 European Championships was 1,165,192, averaging 37,587 per match (62,865 in the Final). This figure exceeded that of the 2000 European Championship organized by Belgium and Holland (where there was a total of 1,126,443 spectators with an average of 36,337 per match), although it was less than achieved by the 1996 European Championship in England, calculated at 1,276,171 (41,167 per match) (*Público*, 6ᵗʰ July).

6 According to a study carried out by the international agency *Initiative* in 52 countries (Europe, USA and Latin America, Africa, Asia and Australia), the 2004 European Championship attracted a total of 2.5 billion television viewers, with an average of 80 million per match (between 130 and 150 million for the Final). This represented an increase of 20% in relation to the 2000 European Championships. According to UEFA's director of communications, the France-England match attracted the greatest number of viewers in those countries. In France the estimated audience was 13.3 million, a higher figure than recorded for the French team's games in the 2002 FIFA World Cup in Korea and Japan, while in England, 20.7 million spectators followed the game on television. As regards Portuguese viewers, it was estimated that from the quarter-finals, there was an average of approximately 3.7 million television viewers per match (*Público*, 17ᵗʰ June).

7 For example, in an economic study into sport Wladimir Andreff & Jean-François Nys (2001) suggest that in the Olympic Games, there was an increase from US$1.2 million dollars involved in 1960 (Rome) to US$907 million in 1996 (Atlanta). Since 1980, the organizing committees have shouldered all the costs of the Games and have nevertheless made a surplus.

8 The exchange of experiences and the increased cooperation between the different organizations permitted, as the elaboration of the methodological guide clearly elucidates, the establishment of a conceptual base of reference for future events, with respect to measures of socio-prevention in the framework of football supporters, as will be the case for the 2006 FIFA World Cup in Germany, and the UEFA Euro 2008 Championship to be held in Austria and Switzerland (Schneider and Gabriel, 2004).

9 A total of 4,000 volunteers and 17,000 private stewards were involved in Euro 2004.

10 Altogether, there were four incidents of violence in the space of a week, resulting in injuries (around twenty) and 55 fans (96% English) receiving expulsion orders. It appears that some *hooligans/casuals* had attempted to involve English fans that were angry at the police response to the early incidents, leading to an escalation of premeditated violence aimed at retaliation.

11 The idea seems to have come from a young man, who called for the Portuguese flag to be flown from each house as a manifestation of pride in being Portuguese, an appeal that was broadcast by a commentator on one of the television channels at the end of May. From this moment onwards, Portugal from north to south was 'sprinkled with green and red', which led to new appeals, particularly from the national coach Luiz Felipe Scolari. The phenomenon even received a comment from the President of the Republic, who publicly expressed his appreciation and the wish that the democratic appropriation of the national flag would not come to an end with the Euro 2004.

12 For example Bourdieu (1999); McKeever (1999); Roche (2000); Porro & Russo (2000); Coelho (2001) and Horne & Manzenreiter (2004).

13 As we have argued in previous studies, the use – deep-rooted in academic and other institutions
– of the term *hooliganism*, as a synonym for violence caused by football fans, is an inaccurate
generalization of the reality within a multicultural European framework. The term is not very
precise, especially since violent behaviour at football matches is not limited to members of the
two European sub-cultures, *hooligan/casual* and *ultra*; indeed, much of the violence is caused by
traditional fans of various societies and also by players and other figures involved in the process,
as several authors have pointed out (Bromberger, 1997; Lassalle, 1997; Podaliri & Balestri, 1998;
Roumestan, 1998; Marivoet, 2002a, 2002b).

References

Andreff, W. & Nys, J.-F. (2001) *Économie du Sport* (4). Paris: PUF.
Armstrong, G. and Young, M. (2000) 'Fanatical football chants: creating and controlling the carnival', in G. Finn and R. Giulianotti (eds) *Football Culture. Local Contests, Global Visions*. London: Frank Cass, 173–211.
Beck, U., Giddens, A. Lash, S. (2000) *Modernização Reflexiva. Política, Tradição e Estética no Mundo Moderno*. Oeiras: Celta Editora.
Bourdieu, P. (1994) Les jeux olympiques. Programme pour une analyse, *Actes de la Recherche en sciences sociales* 103: 102–103.
Bourdieu, P. (1999) 'The state, economics and sport', in H. Dauncey and G. Hare (eds) *France and the 1998 World Cup: The National Impact of a World Sporting Event*. London: Frank Cass, 15–21.
Brohm, J.-M. (1992) *Sociologie Politique du Sport*. Nancy: PUN.
Bromberger, C. (1997) 'Le football et son public: cadre historique et sociologique' in M. Comeron (ed.) *Quels Supporters pour l'An 2000? Sport, Foot et Violence. Comment Gérer le Phénomène?* Bruxelles: Éditions Labor, 17–31.
Bromberger, C., Hayot, A. & Mariottini J.-M. (1995) *Le Match de Football: Ethnologie d'une Passion Partisane à Marseille, Naples et Turin*. Paris: Maison des Sciences de l'Homme.
Coelho, J.N. (2001) *Portugal A Equipa de Todos Nós. Nacionalismo, Futebol e Media*. Porto: Edições Afrontamento.
Comeron, M. (eds) (1997) *Quels Supporters pour l'An 2000 ? Sport, Foot et Violence. Comment Gérer le Phénomène?* Bruxelles: Éditions Labor.
Dauncey, H. & Hare, G. (eds) (1999) *France and the 1998 World Cup: The National Impact of a World Sporting Event*. London: Frank Cass.
Dauncey, H. & Hare, G. (2000) 'World Cup France'98. Metaphors, meaning and values', *International Review for the Sociology of Sport* 35 (3): 331–347.
Dunning, E. (1999) *Sport Matters. Sociological Studies of Sport, Violence and Civilization*. London: Routledge.
Durkheim, É. ([1912] 1968) *Les Formes Élémentaires de la Vie Religieuse. Le Système Totémique en Australie*. Paris: Presses Universitaires de France.
Finn, G. & R. Giulianotti, R. (eds) (2000) *Football Culture. Local Contests, Global Visions*. London: Frank Cass.
Friedman, J. (1994) *Cultural Identity & Global Process*. London: Sage Publication.
Gellner, E. (1994) *Pós-Modernismo Razão e Religião*. Lisboa: Instituto Piaget.
Giulianotti, R. (1999) *Football. A Sociology of the Global Game*. Cambridge: Blackwell Publishers.
Holt, R., Mangan, J.A. & Lanfranchi, P. (eds) (1996) *European Heroes. Myth, Identity, Sport*. London: Frank Cass.
Horne, J. & Manzenreiter, W. (2004) 'Accounting for mega-events. Forecast and actual impacts of the 2002 Football World Cup finals on the host countries Japan/Korea', *International Review for the Sociology of Sport* 39 (2): 187–203.
Lassale, J.-Y. (1997) *La Violence dans le Sport*. Paris: PUF.
Llobera, J.R. (2000) *O Deus da Modernidade. O Desenvolvimento do Nacionalismo na Europa Ocidental*. Oeiras: Celta Editora.

Maffesoli, M. (1988) *Le Temps des Tribus. Le Déclin de l'Individualisme dans les Sociétés Postmodernes.* Paris: La Table Ronde.

Marivoet, S. (2002a) 'The public at football stadia', in M. Comeron & P. Vanbellingen (coord.) *Prevention of Violence in Football Stadia in Europe.* Liège: Eurofan, 24–30.

Marivoet, S. (2002b) 'Violent disturbances in Portuguese football', in E. Dunning *et al.* (eds) *Fighting Fans. Football Hooliganism as a World Phenomenon.* Dublin: University College Dublin Press, 158–173.

Marks, J. (1999) 'The French national team and French national identity: 'cette France d'un 'bleu métis''', in H. Dauncey & G. Hare (eds) *France and the 1998 World Cup: The National Impact of a World Sporting Event.* London: Frank Cass, 41–57.

McKeever, L. (1999) 'Reporting the World Cup: old and new media', in H. Dauncey & G. Hare (eds) *France and the 1998 World Cup: The National Impact of a World Sporting Event.* London: Frank Cass, 161–183.

Mignon, P. (1999) 'Fans and heroes', in H. Dauncey & G. Hare (eds) *France and the 1998 World Cup: The National Impact of a World Sporting Event.* London: Frank Cass, 79–97.

Miller, T. *et al.* (2001) *Globalization and Sport.* London: Sage Publications.

Murphy, P., Williams, J. & Dunning, E. (1990) *Football on Trial. Spectator Violence and Development in the Football World.* London: Routledge.

Podaliri, C. & Balestri, C. (1998) 'The ultràs, racism and football culture in Italy', in A. Brown (ed.) *Fanatics! Power, Identity and Fandom in Football.* London: Routledge, 88–100.

Porro, N. & Russo, P. (2000) 'The production of a media epic: Germany v. Italy football matches', in G. Finn and R. Giulianotti (eds) *Football Culture. Local Contests, Global Visions.* London: Frank Cass, 155–172.

Roche, M. (2000) *Mega-Events and Modernity. Olympics and Expos in the Growth of Global Culture.* London: Routledge.

Rousmestan, N. (1998) *Les Supporters de Football.* Paris: Anthropos.

Schneider, T. & Gabriel, M. (2004) 'Football supporter coaching programs in the framework of international tournaments', *Good hosting, Fewer Problems. A Methodological Guide on Concepts and Measures of Socio2000? Sport, Foot et Violence. Comment Gérer le Phénomène?* Bruxelles: Éditions Labor, 44–74.

Smart, B. (1999) *Facing Modernity. Ambivalence, Reflexivity and Morality.* London: Sage Publications.

Wagner, P. (2001) *Theorizing Modernity. Inescapability and Attainability in Social Theory.* London: Sage Publications.

Williams, J. (1997) 'Grand-Bretagne et hooligans un couple infernal?' in M. Comeron (ed.) *Quels Supporters pour l'An 2000? Sport, Foot et Violence. Comment Gérer le Phénomène?* Bruxelles: Éditions Labor, 44–74.

143

Sport spectacles, uniformities and the search for identity in late modern Japan[1]

Wolfram Manzenreiter

Opening

The public display of team colours as an expression of loyalty has become a characteristic trait of sport fandom all over the world. Replica shirts, which had been initially conceived of (and marketed) as kids' stuff, spilled over from the football pitch into the grandstands in the early 1980s. A decade later, they were turning into an 'essential part of the lingua franca of football supporters' (Fawbert, 2004:134). Since the spectacularization of sport seems to have originated in North American sport culture (Kutcher, 1983), it is hardly surprising that face painting, stylish masquerades and the variegated prop stock of a burgeoning sport paraphernalia industry have also changed the way football is followed and supported at international tournaments around the world since the United States hosted the World Cup in 1994. When Japan and Korea co-hosted football's mega-event in 2002, spectators in the stadia as well as television audiences worldwide could observe entire grandstands soaked in blue and red, the colours of the respective hosts' national teams. Samba drums and marching bands in Japanese stadia, bare-chested youngsters intoning the Korean supporters song based on the melody of 'Go West', and carefully planned and rehearsed presentations from the stands in the fashion of Italian ultras, suggested to the observer the successful appropriation, or even domestication, of a transnational football fan culture. The 'Blue Heaven', as one creative genius from Ultra Nippon, the core organization of fans of the national team, named the stadia filled with Japan's supporters, and perhaps, even more, the 'Sea of Red' that flooded the streets of most major South Korean cities, remained in the public memory as two lasting impressions of the 'Hollywood World Cup' (Hirose, 2002).

The ubiquitous and unconstrained mass display of the *hinomaru*, Japan's long-time contested national flag, and the *taegeukgi*, Korea's 'national flag of emotion' (Whang, 2004:158) in stadia and streets, on bodies and buildings were spectacular aspects, albeit more visible than any others, that differentiated the 2002 World Cup from previous sports mega-events hosted in these countries.

Both Japan and Korea had already enjoyed the experience of staging the Olympics and used that opportunity for the purpose of bringing the country to the global television screen.

Tokyo 1964 was the first Olympic Games to have employed satellite technology for overseas live broadcasting, while Seoul 1988 was riding high on the lucrative wave of deregulating national media markets and the inroad of big sponsorship money into television sports. As urban planning initiatives, these Asian Summer Olympics spurred construction projects that impacted deeply upon the face of the host cities. As showcase events for international consumption, they laid proof to the level of socio-economic development and the political reliability of their hosts; at the same time, holding up a mirror reflecting the tangible merits of labour, thrift and dutifulness to their local audiences, the Games were also a politically motivated event, meant to reconcile the former antagonistic blocs within their own populations. But these prototypes of modern mega-events were staged back in the 20th century at a time when both countries had undergone a process of state-monitored economic growth, rapid industrial maturation and integration into both the world market and political order under US hegemony. In the new 21st century, Fordist values were no longer in vogue or even functional, international alliances were formed, and sports mega-events were at the service of new masters.

Striving for excellence was the common goal that united workers and athletes in Fordist capitalist society. The rising importance attached to consumerist values such as individualism, creativity and self-expression opened up doors for the play-like attitude in which young Japanese and Koreans alike used the secular symbols of state power in a fashion which had been unthinkable under the former regime. Largely due to repercussions of a glorious or a ghostly past, the mass display of national symbolisms was met with very different reactions in both societies. While social critics in South Korea immediately discussed the mass phenomenon from a wide array of perspectives (Hong, 2004; Jeon and Yoon, 2004), it hardly aroused any responses among Japanese intellectuals (Ueno, 2004). While this difference is not merely a question of quantity, there were also striking qualitative differences. Public discourse in South Korea benevolently embraced the patriotic attitude of the young generation, particularly since the national sentiments that the national flag aroused among older generations were rooted in emotionally moving memories of a tragic past (Whang, 2004). To a certain extent, the positive response was also predictable because of the leading role of influential Korean corporations in preparing the ground for the patriotic outburst. Before and during the tournament, televised commercials from telecommunication giant SK Telecom presented members from the 'Red Devils', the official fan club of the Korean national team, as supporting actors for popular celebrities that taught 'Learn the Reds' and encouraged 'Do the Reds' to the rest of the nation, to support the national squad. In contrast, public opinion in Japan oscillated between two mutually opposed positions that either mildly criticized the careless or vilifying display of the sacred symbols of state, nation and imperial reign (the first line of the national anthem 'Kimigayo' addresses the imperial lineage of the tenno, or emperor), while a rather diverse assemblage of voices reluctantly or avidly welcomed the event for giving birth to a 'new Japan' and new collective identities. Only the very extreme left bluntly rejected the World Cup as a promoter of mass mobilization, nationalist ideology and xenophobic chauvinism.

All those positions are better understood as approximations than appropriate models to assess a rather complex phenomenon. The following discussion of uniforms, uniformities and sports spectacles will show that the mass display of national symbols does not necessarily equate with nationalist attitudes. Nor does the visual impression of a uniform mass or a mass in uniforms allow the simple inference of the existence of a unified collective. Rather it is a consequence of the particular cultural form of the 'spectacle' that gives birth both to the emergence of phenomena of uniformity and the codes to read or misread them.

I argue that the spectacular within sports mega-events changes in line with its historic constellations and its participants. Rendering the World Cup as sports spectacle thus demands paying attention equally to the political economy *and* the performative nature of the sports mega-event. Uniforms and uniformity are well suited to illustrate this duality because the specific cultural phenomenon revealing the unitary appearance attaches special meaning to the body, which, being both a signifier of things beyond imagination and a consciously employed medium of communication, is located at the interface of social structures and the individual's desire for identity. These reflections about the body in uniform will be further elaborated in the next section. Later parts will explore the heuristic potential of the spectacle for social analysis while looking at the body in uniform and emergent uniformities at the 2002 Football World Cup. My final remarks will reflect on the relationship between uniforms, the spectacle and everyday life in late modernity.

Reflections on uniforms and uniformity

Uniforms are a distinctive aspect of embodiment, shaping the self physically and psychologically and rendering the body presentable in specific social situations (Entwistle and Wilson, 2001). Like clothes in general, but with a particular function, they surface as a 'secondary skin' where the outer world interfaces with the body as an 'unfinished entity' (Bourdieu, 1981), as the 'intuitively grasped battlefield of one's identity' (Barley, 2004), and as the objectified self. What makes uniforms distinctive is that they are a material culture marker that identifies and places social actors in various hierarchies, units and categories. Furthermore, uniforms are socializing media which are used to demonstrate a sense of solidarity or identification with a particular unit. Uniformity hence is a structuring principle and the outcome of a rational endeavour, aiming at the containment of difference by means of standardization, predictability, controllability and related core notions of the modernity project.

146

At the sports spectacle, uniforms help to structure the chaotic mass of participants and construct a symbolic order within the space-time of the event. In this regard, both formal and less strictly formalized uniforms play a significant role in differentiating between actors and spectators, between opponent team players, back stage workers and volunteers, home supporters and away supporters, and so on. The presentation of uniform collectives is of main concern, if not to every single participant, then at least to its producers and organizers. Producers are intrigued by the aesthetic appeal of spectator masses dressed in uniforms as the sales value of the event rises with the apparently demonstrated mass interest. Organizers, who must secure the efficient operation of the event, clothe their personnel in uniforms which visually display roles and positions within hierarchies, units and categories. Japan's 16,500 2002 World Cup volunteers for example were provided with colour-coordinated uniforms by Adidas, one of the official FIFA World Cup sponsors. Uniform colours and bibs varied according to the assigned duties and positions among the volunteer stewards (cf Nogawa, 2004). Formal uniforms also clearly marked the differences between and among members of the regular police forces and the hardly visible, yet ever-present, riot police, not to mention the referees and players.

Formalized uniforms are symbolic reminders of the script of power in the public sphere. Uniformed police forces, the khaki of the colonial administration or referees in black thus visually emphasize the legitimacy of state power, bureaucratic authority, or football rules as a systemic principle unanimously accepted by all members of the social unit. My main concern here, however, is not with uniformity enforced by the strict obedience of explicit rules and order but with uniformity established by the deliberate submission or conscious adaptation to a non-institutionalized order. Since uniformity as a structuring concept has also appeared in new areas of consumption and everyday life, Nathan Joseph (1986) placed uniforms and their symbolism on a continuum of clothing ranging from highly ordered to the disordered end of the continuum. For an outfit to qualify as uniform, it is sufficient if many others are wearing the same thing, all more or less explicit about the correct look and all more or less conscious of a mysterious bonding by means of cloth (Fussell, 2002:3–4). Hence replica shirts, team colours, body painting and other forms of football 'fanwear' would appear closer to the disordered end of Joseph's continuum.

However, as Jennifer Craik (2005) noted, there is not much uniform about uniforms, as they are at the root of a complex set of messages, many of which are paradoxical, because they are imbued with symbols that reflect different meanings in different contexts (Calefato, 2004). This holds true for football replica shirts as well as for more formal uniforms because the dyadic relationship between the garment and its point of reference has no physical existence of its own but depends on the definition of the situation. Only when combined with other signs do uniforms acquire the potential for analogical reading. Precisely because nothing in the world can be taken for granted without being framed, watched, registered and controlled (Abercrombie and Longhurst, 1998: 78), the following sections attempt to demonstrate that the sports spectacle

establishes the frame of reference which attaches a particular meaning and function to uniformity while simultaneously suggesting quite a different reading of
meaning and function.

The 'unspectacular' of sports mega-events

Although many academic commentaries suggest that the world of sports has
long been a domain of the spectacle (eg, King and Springwood, 2001; Morton
and O'Brian, 1985; Mazer, 1998; Oriard, 2004), the nature of the spectacle, its
changing forms and comparative cultural, social and political meanings have
been surprisingly underexplored (Tomlinson, 2002:46). A basic problem of the
literature on sports spectacle is the confusion about the essentials of its topic.
As a term, 'spectacle' is more often used as part of a cultural critique or as a
descriptive term than as an analytical category. Tomlinson (2002:46) himself
concedes to having used the term in a 'simplistic fashion', as a 'descriptive category for large-scale, increasingly mediated sports events and their associated
symbolic and ceremonial dimensions', which is not much of a qualitative distinction from Maurice Roche's (2000:1) conceptualization of mega-events as
'large-scale cultural events, which have a dramatic character, mass popular
appeal and international significance'. Similarly, MacAloon (1984) conceptualized the Olympic spectacle as large-scale cultural performance in which cultures
or societies reflect upon and define themselves, dramatize their collective myths
and history, present themselves with alternatives, and eventually change in some
ways while remaining the same in others. Douglas Kellner (2001:40) then gave
to 'those phenomena of media culture that embody contemporary society's
basic values, serve to enculturate individuals into its way of life, and dramatize
its conflicts and modes of conflict resolution' the name of spectacle. But aside
from the, albeit very important, references to international scope, mass appeal
and media culture, a standard description of the functions of ritual would
equally fit or 'misfit' these definitions.

Kellner's introduction to his critical analysis of *Media Spectacles* conflates
sport spectacles with 'events like the Football World Cup, The Super Bowl and
NBA championships attracting massive audiences, while generating sky-high
advertising rates', and the next sentence equals spectacles with cultural rituals
that 'celebrate society's deepest values (ie, competition, winning, success, and
money)' (Kellner, 2003:6). The concatenation of spectacle, event and ritual in
one paragraph is quite indicative of the terminological distortion, though it may
also hint at the 'unspectacular' within contemporary events. Winfried Gebhardt's preliminaries to a sociology of the extraordinary (2001) specify a number
of characteristics of the event culture, but these features are far from being new
since they were evident in premodern festival culture, too. Hence if events were
basically the late modern form of the festival, or if spectacles are events, or cultural rituals, we could identify spectacles as being unspectacular in so far as
they use elements from ritual and festival for communal and social objections

including the renewal of social cohesion; the reaffirmation of the individuals' bonds with her or his social unit; the presentation or representation of social order; all for the purpose of social control. These characteristics comply with functionalist anthropological view of rituals as regulated symbolic expressions of sentiments and values that hold society together, or an instrumentalist reading of sports mega-events that extrudes from many sociological and historical inquiries into the relation between sports and nationalism.

From an anthropological perspective, Desmond Morris (1981) interpreted football fanwear as being subjected to dress codes and conventions in the same way that clothing habits of any other strata of society are. If 'soccer tribes' wear football replica shirts in order to show their loyalty to the team they support, the 50,000 visitors to the Japan matches, that were nearly all wearing the blue jersey of the national team, would have used garment and colour to express their sympathy for the team of players representing Japan at the Football World Cup. As will soon be clear, such a conclusion does not go beyond the surface of the textiles, neglecting both the diversity of football support and the plurality of meaning attached to clothes in general. But the Japanese media that focussed on the faceless blue body in the grandstands provided such a simplified reading of the World Cup as national event. Switching from close-ups of the action on the pitch to wide shots of the side-action beyond the pitch, broadcasters and print media alike produced the concomitant script for reading the progress of the match as a dialectical interaction between the team playing for Japan's glory and spectators cheering at 'their boys'. Such an image appealed of course to organizers that finally found their hosting ambitions legitimized through the emergent mass expression of football support. The airy equation of football support with nationalist pride pleased, to some extent, the conservative camp of politics and media, particularly since the hegemonic notion of the Japanese nation as a cultural monolith had come under immense pressure to accommodate with the growing heterogeneity of the Japanese people and the closer integration of the Japanese state within the East-Asian region. Yet because of the sense of ambiguity about what the nation is, and how it should be in the future, the conventional assertion of the media joining hands with the ruling elites in actively steering the image of the nation cannot pass unchallenged.

Doubts about the state-controlled account of nationalist uniformity at the football spectacle are all the more legitimate as the Japanese state clearly renounced the opportunity of promoting a new national self-image, either for inward presentation or for outward representation. Prospects for the successful re-imaging of Japan were to a certain extent hampered by the regional spread of host cities: since regional development politics had heavily impacted upon the choice of host cities in Japan, media representations of the World Cup in Japan emphasized rather regional diversity and local particularities than national uniformity (Arimoto, 2004; Sugimoto, 2004). Similarly, imaging strategies were complicated by the unwanted co-hosting situation – although Korea succeeded in rebranding itself as a country of highly sophisticated communication technology (Horne and Manzenreiter, 2004) from the first day of the tournament and the spectacular opening ceremony in Seoul. By contrast, the no less spectacular closing ceremony in Yokohama International Stadium utilized the well-known rich cultural heritage of presenting a 'Baedeker' tourist guide image of Japan. The show, in front of an estimated 1.5 billion television viewers worldwide, featured Japanese *taiko*-drummers, *kimono* clad geisha performers, *mikoshi*-shrines decorated with the national flag of the 32 participating countries, and a giant replica of Mount Fuji. The dramatic climax following Brazil's victory in the final against Germany featured 2.7 million 'dream origami cranes' pouring down into the arena from the roof of the Yokohama stadium. According to the local organizing committee, the 'Wings of a dream project' was selected because it enabled many Japanese 'to participate in an event unique to Japan that would remain in the memories of people throughout the world. At the same time, it embodied a message of hope for humankind and an image of Japan as a peaceful nation' (JAWOC, 2003). The Ministry of Education coordinated the paper crane folding project, in which 50 elementary and junior high schools participated together with boys and girls scouting organizations, the youth hostel association as well as members of the general public. It is unclear whether the same authority was aware that the Shinto Association of Japan was going to provide all the seats in the stadia staging Japan's matches with patriotic hand-drawn *hinomaru* flags. This organization was joined by many school principals, who were in charge of supplying the required amount of painted sheets for this mass display of the, still contested, state symbol.

The peace motif was the only occasion in which international politics appeared on the agenda. But in the background, quite diametrically opposed to the public message of the sports event, the state that soon was going to join the US invasion of Iraq used the World Cup to communicate its image as a strong and capable partner in security issues. Emphasizing stadium security and venue security concerns allowed the Japanese police openly to introduce strict security acts under the pretext of 'hooligan control' at airports, public venues and amusement quarters in metropolitan Tokyo. Authorities not only extended the Immigration Control And Refugee Recognition Act (Shutsunyukoku Kanri oyobi Nanmin Nintei Ho) to enable the deportation of 'hooligans' (*Asahi Shinbun*, 13 September 2001), but also considered exercising control over 'violent foreign NGOs' (*Asahi Shinbun*, 14 September 2001) in the name of anti-terrorism.

The media also produced alternating scripts to the dominant reading of the national spectacle that surfaced once the camera zoomed in on individual spectators. Not everybody was actually wearing the blue Adidas jersey of the national team, even though most were dressed in some kind of blue garment. Wearing colours is the simplest way of showing team loyalty and perhaps the most important. Marketing researchers found out that supporters attached higher meaning to colours than to tradition, iconic players or their team's home ground. As the positive evaluation of colours decreases with rising age, the result emphasizes the success of recent marketing strategies among the younger generation and the high importance this generation attaches to the communicative function of logos and other symbols that are easily visualized. As the Japanese

150

national team had changed its outfit a number of times since 1992, basically in line with the rhythm of the World Cup tournament calendar, new and former replica shirts mingled in the stands and therefore exhibited different layers of the team's history. Ownership of a former design can be interpreted as an act of resistance against the hyper-commercialization of the game in recent years, though in the Japanese context the older shirt is better understood as a status marker signifying the reputation of a 'real' supporter with a history as opposed to any 'fashion-following' supporter that jumped on the bandwagon only recently.

Buying and wearing fake replica shirts is another way of either evading or defying the sports industry. The joint occurrence of originals and copies in the stands alludes to the political economy of the global sports apparel industry and its Asian heavyweights in manufacturing and procurement. Asia has turned into the world's major sports wear factory where licensed manufacturers produce the original brand and sweat shops around the corner its copycat 'fake' design. Authenticity had its price as the original shirt was sold for 13,000 Yen. Street vendors in front of the stadia offered the copies for prices starting from 8,000 Yen, unhampered by the police or the yakuza (Japanese mafia) that together with the Israeli mafia controls that part of the Japanese underground economy.

The spectacular of the sports mega-event

The World Cup spectacle, as described so far, included football games, framing ceremonies that defined the time span of the event, stage acting and ritual behaviour for the purpose of delivering messages to the spectators about society at large. Hence sports spectacles simultaneously can provide grand theatre and secular ritual, popular entertainment and communal festival. An inclusive conceptualization as multi-dimensional and multifunctional cultural performances which may include, among others, play, ritual, stage acting, and ceremonial behaviour (Bormann, 2001) is seductive in as far as it opens an emergency exit leading out of the terminological debate. But it lacks any qualitative or essential information about the 'spectacular' of the spectacle.

The spectacular of sports mega-events has first of all been related to the impact of the modern mass media since Leni Riefenstahl's movie *Olympia* in the 1930s provided the adequate visual correlate to the Nazi Olympics by using the imagery of fascist aesthetics. Throughout the latter half of the 20th century, the sports media chiefly contributed to the establishment of the 'sports industrial complex' (Manzenreiter, 2005:2), while sports mega-events usually heralded a new round of broadcasting and transmission technologies or ever more sophisticated receiver gadgets entering the high-end user market. In 2002, mobile Internet technology, HDTV, digital TV, cable networks and multi-channel broadcasts provided some of the revolutionary trends on the Japanese media front. Sales of JVC digital satellite TV sets jumped by 70 per cent as the World Cup began, while the shipment value of TVs and videocassette recorders nearly doubled. Subscriptions to J.Phone, Vodafone's representative in Japan, and SkyPerfecTV!, a private digital TV broadcaster that acquired the Japanese rights for all the World Cup Final games for the highest price ever paid for a single sport event, rapidly increased just prior to the kick off. In line with technological development and rising market value, the number of media workers in charge of reporting the World Cup has increased.

Even though it was staged in their country, most Japanese experienced the spectacle only in mediated form. Some of the highest audience rates in Japanese television history, reaching nearly 70 per cent of all households, were measured during the tournament (Horne, 2005:426). Since sports bars and public viewing often provided a more appealing forum for watching the games, many Japanese experienced even mediated events as live. When Japan faced Russia at the Yokohama International Stadium, the National Stadium in Tokyo was densely packed with paying visitors who watched the match on a giant screen in the company of 50,000 others, most of them dressed in blue. Hence it was at least partly due to the media that the time-space of the spectacle exceeded the rather neatly drawn limits of the stadium and the standard playtime. The World Cup dominated reporting and commenting in many television formats beyond sport broadcasting. So-called 'wide shows', a Japanese 'info-tainment' format, and variety shows gave considerably more attention to David Beckham's haircut or the designer suits of the Italian national team than to the actual tournament progress. The *Asahi Shinbun*, one of Japan's leading national daily newspapers, acquired Official Supplier status with the local organizing committee and later clinched a long-term partnership programme with the Japan Football Association, arguably for more clearly differentiating its profile from its main rival, the *Yomiuri Group* that is strongly associated with professional baseball. MasterCard, having hired Brazil's living football legend Pele, managed to get a foothold in the credit-card market. Kirin Beer, official sponsor of the Japanese national team, found such high demand for its special low-malt World Cup beer that soon after the World Cup the Kirin Group renewed its JPY 6 billion sponsoring contract with the national team. Adidas, too, that reportedly sold over 600,000 replica shirts of the national team during the first two weeks of June, extended its sponsorship contract with the Japan Football Association for another four years.

Echoing the meta-social critique of Guy Debord's *La société du spectacle*, Kellner (2001) declared the 'sports entertainment colossus' to be responsible for the transformation of sports into a forum that sells the values, celebrities, and institutions of the media and consumer society. For Debord, who used the notion of the spectacle as a metaphorical key towards understanding consumer society, the spectacle exceeds the cultural form of the mediated event by a long way. While the mass media provide its most glaring superficial manifestations (1978:24), the spectacle is not just a mere visual deception produced by mass-media technologies: it is a view of a world that has become objective (1978:5), a social relation, mediated by images (1978:4), and thus the ultimate commodity. In marked contrast to orthodox Marxism, power relations in the society of the spectacle are not reproduced in the world of labour but in the cultural sphere of consumption. Yet the fetishism of the commodity prevents the subject from satisfying her/his actual human needs; it destroys any collective form of society by individualizing the subjects who are nonetheless forced into uniformities of action and thought for the purpose of stabilising the structures of domination.

The spectacle and performances of the self

Debord's tract is a major reference point for any sociological analysis of the spectacle but it has been criticized for being too compact to be analytically useful (Roberts, 2003). The reduction of social relations to representation, the trivialization of consumption as a passive activity and the denial of human agency provoked opposition as easily as the underlying ideas evoked imitators. While the spectacle as a cultural critique is sociologically incomplete 'because it conflates the spectacle into the central dynamic of capitalist social relations, eliding it with the commodity form' (Tomlinson, 2002:57), Debord at least deserves acclamation for placing a kind of cultural analysis at the centre of political economy, a programme that has been further elaborated by microsociological and cultural studies approaches towards popular culture. Similarly to the French situationist, Abercrombie and Longhurst claimed that 'the world is constituted as an event' (1998:78), since everyday life has been deeply saturated by the media. But their notion of the event is based on its constitutional performative quality: 'the objects, events and people which constitute the world are made to perform for those watching or gazing' (Abercrombie and Longhurst, 1998:78). Seen as a performative genre, spectacles premise agency by dissolving the strict separation of actors/performers from audiences/spectators. Under the gaze of the watchful surroundings, spectators themselves turn into performers of their own script which is organized in relation to the core action of the protagonists but does not necessarily comply with it. Again it is the mediated character of the spectacle and the chance of sudden stardom that amplifies the urge for rewards through performativity. Camera crews scrutinize the seating rows and insert particular eye-catching shots into the main action on the large stadium screen or the broadcasting feed.

The performative quality of the spectacle is crucial for adequately understanding the uniformities exhibited at the spectacle. Compared with the festival, the spectacle is more open since it does not discriminate between natives and strangers and encourages active participation and even shares. Foreign observers noted with surprise the seeming ease with which football supporters in Japan were ready to shift the focus of their support from one country to the other. Such a plasticity of loyalty is unusual among committed fans, though it resembles the postmodern spectator identity of the 'football flaneur' (Giulianotti, 2002), which is acquired by a depersonalized set of market-dominated virtual relationships. Hence Japanese football fans were ready to ally with those teams that either appealed to them because of major achievements in the past or super-star celebrities in their teams. The Japanese's enthusiastic support for England was partly caused by a widespread cultural inferiority complex towards the motherland, the *honba* of football, and partly it was elicited by the mediated hype about Beckham. Since donning a jersey with a St. George Cross had basi-cally the same function as dressing in Brazil's yellow shirt or the blue of Japan, there is no reason to believe that the mass performance of blue-dressed Japan-ese supporters at the World Cup in 2002 did in any way constitute a positive affirmation of the Japanese state.

Sugimoto's (2004) informants, mostly students and young adults, pointed out that the act of supporting had been their major reason for going to see the matches, not the game itself, a particular player, or a team. To appreciate the experience fully, they strived to get 'the right shirt', 'the right colours' or 'the right dress'. In this regard, vernacular clothing traditions were adopted for the particular purpose of performing the self. *Kimono, yukata, happi* or *fundoshi* have been largely superseded by Western clothes for everyday usage in public although they are commonly encountered at formal ceremonies and communal festivals. When worn in the football arena, these clothes assumed a metonymic function of expressing national identity or identification with the national team. Similarly, *chonmage* hairstyle or donning a samurai costume expressed a metaphorical reading of national identity which is associated with a specific segment of Japanese history and tradition. While uniforms ask to be taken deadly-seriously, such costumes explicitly demand *not* to be taken at face value.

Like uniforms, costumes and masquerades provide a transitional identity, albeit for a different purpose. As Bakhtin's theory of the carnival explained, rit-ualized masquerades enabled all members of a social community to experience the inversion of everyday hierarchies, the transgression of social boundaries and the subversion of established orientation guides for a predetermined time-space (Bakhtin, 1968). Both carnival and rural football historically emerged as festi-vals of status inversion, serving the double purposes of strengthening commu-nal bonds and re-legitimising power relations. For a certain period of time, when a state of exceptional circumstances framed the local community, everyday power relations were inverted and the austerity of the normal course of life was replaced by excess and immoderateness of the festival. In a similar fashion, the modern sports spectacle offers itself as a time-space of merry-making, mas-querade and deferral from the constraints of everyday life.

This anarchic element of the spectacle is difficult to contain, as the Japanese police discovered. Massive squads of riot police, who had been well prepared for the eventualities of foreign hooligans going on a rampage, had to deal instead with the young Japanese that hilariously acted out the transnational rituals of victorious football fans: pouring into the streets, ignoring (and some-times climbing on top of) traffic signals, waving flags, fraternizing with complete strangers, chanting '*Nippon! Nippon! Nippon!*' all through the night. In the streets of Tokyo, dozens of young men stripped to the waist, some even went further. In Osaka, hundreds dived into the Dotonburi River even though the local police had installed a temporary indictment against this particular style of celebration. In the end, criminal statistics showed that, rather than the foreigners, it was Japanese youth that had made headlines as offenders of public order and decency during the 2002 World Cup.

Debord ignored this unruly element of the spectacular because he related the spectacle solely to the festival, which made him blind towards the influence of the baroque theatre and the market fair that equally inform the modern spectacle. The theatre of the spectacle was the dominant propaganda art of the counter-reformation, which attempted to replace medieval chaos by mannered and passive spectator crowds attending public ceremonies within zoned spaces and under police surveillance. Forging collective identity by means of spectacle did not work on the premise of conviction but of overpowering, and since such demonstrations of state power were extremely expensive, the making of spectacles required the close collaboration of organizers and authorities. Market fairs enacted a different mode of social contract based on a particular conditionality of belief – the double spectacle of commodities and amusement, of merchandize and magic tricks, invites spectators not only to suspend but also to sharpen their disbelief – and the secular social bond of exchange and commerce, as Roberts (2003:65) noted. This implies, first, that spectacles have been associated with commercial purposes from early times on and second, that this relation was commonly accepted as long as merchants/artists and consumers/visitors were equally aware of the double nature of the spectacle. As the aura of the 'spectacle as-if' is sustained by an economy of knowledge that enables all sides to behave as if the pretensions of the spectacle can be taken at face value, organizers of spectacles utilize a sophisticated machinery of information and disinformation in order to hold up the illusion of the spectacular event by promoting an official image of the spectacle for public consumption. Hence the spectator at the World Cup usually believes to see a game, a play of two teams trying to excel at ball skills and technique, team play and/or fighting stamina. Yet s/he can equally well watch a number of well-paid specialists at work, or the proxy competition for market leadership between rivalling sports wear brands.

Establishing a coherent image is quite an impossible task in late-modern democracies. While traditional community unanimously agreed on the meaning of public rituals, communal festivals and spectacles, modern society hardly can. As complex social formations replaced traditional units, functional differentiation distinguished participants from spectators, actors from audiences and regular attendants from casual by-passers, whose insights, involvement and interests largely differ. Spectacles therefore are multi-vocal, and they have to be so because otherwise they would fail in communicating to multiple audiences, bridging the gap between frontstage and backstage, and in demarcating a time-space for performances of the self.

In closing this discussion, I suggest grasping spectacles as a particular mood, a tinge, and a state of the multi-dimensional and multifunctional cultural performances usually referred to as an 'event'. This disposition is obtained by the overpowering element of make-believe which mediates between frontstage (eg, hospitable/peaceful Japan) and backstage programmes (fortified/forceful Japan). Spectacles in general aspire after grandeur, and acknowledgement as unique, exclusive and extraordinary. Ritual symbolism, various staging techniques and the distributional channels of national and international media networks are used to achieve these goals. As the whole spectacle adapts itself around its own sensual, audiovisual potentials, it is the sensually stimulating, dynamic and exciting form that attracts mass participation and gives the spectacle its distinctive visual appearance. Success or failure is measured according to the extent to which mass participation and public acclamation for being a great event can be obtained.

Conclusion

The discussion above points out the multi-vocal nature of the World Cup mega-event as spectacle. I have shown that the spectacle is a particular occasion, or a time-space, for a certain sartorial practice. Hence uniforms are worn at the sports spectacle because of its carnivalesque character. People dress up, whether in uniform or as masquerade, because they want to be part of the party, and because they want to express themselves via the watchful surroundings. The uniforms or the uniformity of the spectators can represent the nation, if that is what we want to see or what the producers of the spectacle want us to believe. As I have shown, the image distorts when the viewed distance gets too close. Then it becomes apparent that the sport spectacle assembles not a uniform mass of spectators but a multitude of people, both as an audience for the sport performance and as actors in a variety of activities loosely connected with the performance on the pitch.

Football support and the donning of various uniform styles are not only linked with the nation as a statist project and transnational capitalism, but equally with the challenges of maintaining a consistent sense of self and personal identity in late modern society. To many Japanese people in the stadia, the World Cup offered a rare occasion for collectivist immersion, not in the nation but in the imagined community of world football which was achieved by the largely undisputed display of national symbols, colours and attitudes. Football support framed the 'nation in uniform', which in turn framed the narrative of the World Cup as an international experience. Hence, saying that the football spectacle offered to the Japanese the opportunity to overcome internal divisions and, at least during the games, see themselves as integrated and whole, as one people united under the same flag, the same wish, in the same blue shirt and temporarily even under the same shirt (when the Japanese national team faced its first opponent at Saitama Stadium, a giant blue replica shirt unfolded behind Japan's goal during the playing of the national anthem), is only one, rather obvious, narrative among many more possible about the 2002 World Cup experience.

For three reasons I take issue with the conventional claim that uniforms suppress a person's actual identity. Firstly, uniforms are neither in meaning nor in usage predetermined, but they serve as proxies to unburden the demand of constantly reproducing the outer appearance of the inner self. As Jack Fawbert has noted about replica football shirts, uniforms lack any intrinsic meaning but they may be understood as a '*metalanguage*, a system of symbols and codes used to discuss another language or system' (Fawbert, 2004:145). Because uniforms can be used for highly non-uniform purposes and non-uniform clothes can assume the quality of uniformity, context is of utmost importance for acknowledging both the unitizing quality of a garment and the actual meaning of the uniform. Secondly, the idea of clothing as wrapper or as a borderline between self and others seems to be based on the false premises of identity as being firm and unmodifying. If the Eurocentric notion of a stable core identity is traded for a more fluid, polymorphic patchwork identity, dress and uniform can be reconsidered as an ambiguous combination of boundary and non-boundary that frame the body and serve both to distinguish and connect self and 'Other' (Warwick and Cavallaro, 1998). Thirdly uniforms, rather than suppressing, are actually quite liberating. A fluid and osmotic self cannot be concealed by a uniform which is solely authorized to speak for a partial self. For this reason, uniforms may unburden the individual from the psychologically demanding task of defining itself against 'the other'. As Fussell noted (2002), the ultimate task of uniforms is intimately and symbolically to connect the individual to a specific community with a common purpose – thus repeating the experience of home.

Hence football replica shirts can be read as nodes that connect the social experience of living in late modernity with global capitalism. On the one hand uniform football support offers the opportunity for the experience of community, which is hard to find in compartmentalised and anonymous urban society. On the other hand, donning fan uniforms is a performative act of the self, embedded in the larger functional ritual of the sports spectacle. Thus the playful representation of partial identities and the public display of one's particularity neatly correspond with the neoliberal ideology of disorganized capitalism and its requirements for flexibility and self-marketing in the workplace.

Note

1 A number of persons have knowingly and unknowingly helped to organize my observations and thoughts. I want to express my thankfulness for invaluable assists to John Horne, my former colleagues and students at the Heinrich-Heine University in Düsseldorf, and the creative genius of the members of Gendai Sakka Yoshiki Gakkai (An Academy of Modern Football Style).

References

Abercrombie, N. and Longhurst, B. (1998) *Audiences. A Sociological Theory of Performance and Imagination.* London: Sage.

Arimoto T. (2003) 'Rokaru na mono no kaifuku to kosumoporitan na keiken. 2002nen Whai to Oita [The restoration of the local and the experience of the cosmopolitan. The 2002 World Cup and Oita], in Whang S. (ed.) *Whai sakka no nekkyu to isan. 2002nen Nikkan Warudokappu o megutte.* Kyoto: Sekai Shiso Sha, 22–42.

Bakhtin, M. (1968) *Rabelais and his World* Cambridge, Ma: The MIT Press.

Barley, N. (2002) 'Schlachtfeld der Identitäten' [Battlefield of identities], *Zeitschrift für Kulturaustausch* 4/2002, Available online at http://www.ifa.de/zfk/themen/02_4_mode/eindex.htm

Bormann, R. (2001) 'Eventmaschinerie Erlebnispark: Systemintegration durch performative Institutionen' [The theme park as event machinery. Systemic integration through performative institutions], W. Gebhardt, R. Hitzler and M. Pfadenhauer (eds) *Events. Soziologie des Außergewöhnlichen.* Opladen: Leske und Budrich, 137–160

Bourdieu, P. (1981) 'Men and machines', in K. Knorr-Cetina and A.V. Cicourel (eds.) *Advances in Social Theory and Methodology: Toward an Integration of Micro- and Macro-Sociologies.* Boston/London: Routledge and Kegan Paul, 304–317.

Calefato, P. (2004) *The Clothed Body.* Oxford: Berg.

Craik, J. (2005) *Uniforms Exposed. From Conformity to Transgression.* Oxford: Berg.

Da Matta, R. (1987) 'Hierarchy and equality in anthropology and world sport: a perspective from Brazil', Kang S., J. MacAloon and R. da Matta (eds) *The Olympics and Cultural Exchange.* Seoul: Hanyang University, Institute for Ethnological Studies, 43–66.

Debord, G. (1978) *Die Gesellschaft des Spektakels* [The society of the spectacle]. Hamburg: Ed. Nautilus.

Entwistle, J. and Wilson, E. (2001) *Body Dressing.* Oxford: Berg.

Fawbert, J. (2004) 'Is this shirt loud? Semiotics and the "language" of replica football shirts', in LSA (ed.) *Leisure, Media and Visual Culture: Representations and Contestations.* Eastbourne: LSA, 131–149.

Fussell, P. (2002) *Why we Are What we Wear.* Boston: Houghton Mifflin.

Gebhardt, W. (2001) 'Feste, Feiern und Events: Zur Soziologie des Außergewöhnlichen' [Festivals, celebrations and events: on the sociology of the extraordinary], W. Gebhardt, R. Hitzler and M. Pfadenhauer (eds) *Events. Soziologie des Außergewöhnlichen.* Opladen: Leske und Budrich, 17–31.

Giulianotti, R. (2002) 'Supporters, followers, fans and *flaneurs*. A taxonomy of spectator identities in football', *Journal of Sport and Social Issues* 26 (1): 25–46.

Hirose, I. (2002) 'Dare ga Wārudokappu no "higaisha" datta no ka?' [Who was the victim of the World Cup?], in: Asano T. and Hara H. (eds) *Shushi kessan Warudokappu. Kaisai shitehajimete wakatta kane, seiji, fukumaden,* Tokyo: Takarajima Sha (= Takarajima bessatsu REAL 039), S.185–187.

Hong, S. (2004) 'The World Cup, the Red Devils, and related arguments in Korea', *Inter-Asia Cultural Studies* 5 (1): 89–105.

Horne, J. (2005) 'Sport and the media in Japan', *Sociology of Sport Journal* 22 (4): 415–432.

Horne, J. and Manzenreiter, W. (2004) 'Accounting for mega-events: forecast and actual impacts of the 2002 Football World Cup Finals on the host countries Japan and Korea', *International Review for the Sociology of Sport* 39 (2): 187–203.

JAWOC (2003) *2002 FIFA World Cup KoreaJapan.* Tokyo: JAWOC.

Jeon, G. and Yoon, T. (2004) 'Cultural politics of the Red Devils: the desiring multitude versus the state, capital and media', *Inter-Asia Cultural Studies* 5 (1): 77–88.

Joseph, N. (1986) *Uniforms and Nonuniforms: Communication Through Clothing.* New York: Greenwood Press.

Kellner, D. (2001) 'The sports spectacle, Michael Jordan and Nike: unholy alliance?' in D. Andrews (ed.) *Michael Jordan, Inc. Corporate Sport, Media Culture, and Late Modern America.* Albany, NY: SUNY Press, 37–64.

Kellner, D. (2003) *Media Spectacle.* London and New York: Routledge.

King, C.R. and Springwood, C.F. (2001) *Beyond the Cheers: Race As Spectacle in College Sport.* Albany, NY: SUNY Press.

Kutcher, L. (1983) 'The American sport event as carnival: An emergent norm approach to crowd behaviour', *Journal of Popular Culture* 16: 34–41.

MacAloon, J. (1984) 'Olympic Games and the theory of the spectacle in modern society', in J. MacAloon (ed.) *Rite, Drama, Festival, Spectacle: Rehearsals Toward a Theory of Cultural Performance*. Philadelphia: Institute for the Study of Human Issues, 241–280.

Manning, F. (1983) 'Cosmos and chaos: celebration in the modern world', in F. Manning (ed.) *The Celebration of Society: Perspectives on Contemporary Cultural Performance*. Bowling Green, OH: Bowling Green University Popular Press, 3–30.

Manzenreiter, W. (2005) 'The business of sports in a globalising world'. Paper presented at the United Nations University Global Seminar, Sport and Physical Education – Peace, Exchange and Development, Gonowan, Okinawa, December 16–19, 2005. Online soon available at www.unu.org.

Mazer, S. (1998) *Professional Wrestling: Sport and Spectacle*. Jackson: University Press of Mississippi.

Moritsu Chihiro (2003) 'Media ibento to shite no gaitō ōen' [Street cheering as media event], in Ushiki S. and Kuroda I. (eds) *Wārudokappu no media gaku* [World Cup media studies]. Tokyo: Taishūkan Shoten, 124–147.

Morris, D. (1981) *The Soccer Tribe*. London: Jonathan Cape.

Morton, G.W. and O'Brien, G.M. (1985) *Wrestling to Rasslin: ancient Sport to American Spectacle*. Bowling Green, Ohio: Bowling Green State University Popular Press.

Nogawa, H. (2004) 'An international comparison of the motivations and experiences of volunteers at the 2002 World Cup', in W. Manzenreiter and J. Horne (eds) *Football Goes East. Business, Culture and the People's Game in China, Japan and South Korea*. London/New York: Routledge 2004, pp. 222–242.

Oriard, M. (2004) *King Football: Sport and Spectacle in the Golden Age of Radio and Newsreels, Movies and Magazine, the Weekly and the Daily Press*. University of North Carolina Press.

Roberts, D. (2003) 'Towards a genealogy and typology of spectacle. Some comments on Debord', *Thesis Eleven* 75: 54–68.

Roche, M. (2000) *Mega-Events and Modernity*. London: Routledge.

Sugimoto, A. (2003) 'Hyohaku sareta nashonarizumu. Japaniizu furigan no tanjo [The bleached nationalism. The birth of Japanese hooligans], in Whang S. (ed.) *Whai sakka no nekkyu to isan. 2002nen Nikkan Warudokappu o megutte*. Kyoto: Sekai Shiso Sha, 66–82.

Tomlinson, A. (2002) 'Theorising spectacle: beyond Debord', in J. Sugden and A. Tomlinson (eds) *Power Games. A Critical Sociology of Sport*. London: Routledge, 44–60

Ueno, T. (2004) 'Toward a trans-local comparative analysis of the 2002 World Cup', *Inter-Asia Cultural Studies* 5 (1): 115–123.

Whang, S. (2004) 'Football, fashion and fandom. Sociological reflections on the 2002 World Cup and collective memories in Korea', in W. Manzenreiter and J. Horne (eds.) *Football Goes East. Business, Culture and the People's Game in China, Japan and South Korea*. London/New York: Routledge 2004, 148–164.

Warwick, A. and Cavallaio, D. (1998) *Fashioning the Frame. Boundaries, Dress and the Body*. Oxford: Berg.

Deep play: sports mega-events and urban social conditions in the USA

Kimberly S. Schimmel

Introduction

Consider briefly how urban reputation is projected into the world. A city's image competes with other cities' images for recognition, prestige, and status. In the simplest of terms, we tend to think of a city as a 'good place' or a 'bad place' and position it somewhere on the global urban status hierarchy. Even a city's name can evoke a feeling, memory, or image that may range from terrible to terrific. When coupled with sport mega-events, these reputations are especially enduring. We might, for example, think of Sydney as clean and friendly, Atlanta as traffic-congested, and Montreal as financially burdened, and images connected to the 2001 terrorist attacks in the US might long spring to mind when someone mentions Salt Lake City. Sometimes, especially in the case of tragedy or disaster, connection with place may be so powerful that the city's name itself becomes shorthand for the event that occurred there, stigmatizing the city for years to come. Interestingly, other than naming a Treaty or an Accord after the city in which it was signed, rarely is this place/occurrence shorthand done in the case of 'good' events. But we need only say 'Chernobyl' to refer to nuclear disaster and to an entire era of nuclear regulatory failure. And events and images of the 1972 Olympic Summer Games have saturated our consciousness so thoroughly that a recent Hollywood depiction needs only one word in the title: 'Munich'.

The 'deep play' concept was originally coined in the 18th century by the philosophical radical Jeremy Bentham (1789) who used it to refer to a form of gambling in which the stakes are so high it is irrational to engage in it at all. Bentham argued that deep play should be outlawed because, in part, what might be won does not come close to offsetting the price of what might be lost. Clifford Geertz (1973) morphed the concept to suggest that deep play may be 'irrational' according to Bentham's utilitarian standpoint, but that there are more than purely economic considerations at stake. To paraphrase Geertz, it is not the money itself, though the more of it involved, the deeper the play, but what the money causes to happen: the migration of status hierarchies into the body of the event. Thus, the graduated correlation of 'status gambling' with deeper play is, for Geertz, more about making meaning than making money.

In this chapter I utilize deep play as a theme for discussing major sport development and social conditions in the US. Framed by theoretical perspectives in urban political economy, the chapter focuses on the development of infrastructures necessary to host large sporting events, set against broader economic trends and geopolitical transformations, whereby contemporary cities have become 'the battlegrounds on which global powers and stubbornly local meanings and identities meet' (Graham, 2004b: 8). I address both the escalating economic expenditures devoted to major sport infrastructure and also the intensifying militarization of urban space where 'security' has become the justification for measures that contribute to downgrading the quality of life for urban residents. Sport and sport-related infrastructure development is powerfully bonded to the material, cultural, and discursive representations of urban space. 'Themed' cultural landscapes and aggressive marketing and promotion of a city's image have been the hallmarks of urban design in the USA since the late 1980s. In the post '9/11' era, however, the physical planning of cities, the control of urban space, and management of urban residents and visitors is being reshaped by a far-reaching 'homeland security' agenda. At the intersection of all of these trends stands sport: reconstituting large areas of urban space for stadium and area construction; connecting city image creation to professional sport franchise location and hosting championship games; and, the increasing normalization of military doctrine and tactics in an attempt to control urban populations and 'secure' sporting events. My purpose is not to convince the reader that constructing sport mega-projects and/or hosting major sport *is* deep play, as either Bentham or Geertz would have it; admittedly there are limits to this application. Rather, I use deep play merely to provoke thought about the place and practice of major sport in contemporary US society.

Urban transformation, sport-related investment, and economic irrationality

Transformations in the US urban landscape in the post World War II period are well known. Decreasing traditional private capital investment in inner cities combined with white middle class population out-migration from inner cities resulted in weakened tax and commercial retail bases. A period of capitalist economic restructuring and social adjustment, which began in the 1980s and continues today, resulted in a shift away from mass production industries. This shift, combined with the failure of available ideologies (both welfare statism and neoliberalism) to come up with effective policy solutions, generated a series of crises and conflicts, including (among others) rising unemployment, increasing polarisation between socially excluded groups and the middle class, and deleterious environmental conditions (Jewson & MacGreggor, 1997). The decline of the central city was met with a simultaneous reduction in federal funding for redevelopment.

US cities are heavily dependent upon locally generated taxes to provide social services (such as fire and police protection, education, infrastructure maintenance, library construction, etc.). This differs from many European contexts (see, Jessop, Peck & Tickell, 1999; Smith, 1988) where there exists a more unitary and centralized urban finance structure. Some social critics have concluded that this local dependency means that the US has no national urban policy. But in fact it does. As urban studies theorist Harvey Molotch notes, 'The US urban policy is to create structures and ideologies that intensify competition among cities in what they will provide to urban investors' (Molotch, 1993: 25). This system of finance compels localities to maintain the revenue base by enticing mobile capital and supporting investment that increases the market value of real property, a point made quite explicitly by the federal government. After eliminating all policies designed to aid distressed cities, the Reagan Administration's first *National Urban Policy Report of 1982* (US Department of Housing and Urban Development 1982: 14) stated that it is the state and local governments that have primary responsibility for urban health, hence, they would 'find it is in their best interest to concentrate on increasing their attractiveness to potential investors, residents, and visitors' (see also Judd, 2002; Leitner, 1990). This US 'Doctrine of Home Rule' means that cities must handle 'their own' problems (Molotch, 1993: 24) and establishes a social dependency on private investment. Hence, local level politicians are held accountable for myriad of social problems even if those problems are induced by broad (regional, national, and global) structural transformations associated with late capitalism. Local politicians who do not appear to be 'getting something done' about declining urban conditions risk losing re-election. A generation of 'Messiah Mayors' (Teaford, 1990) thus began their careers in the 1980s and threw themselves into competitive struggle to reverse urban decline and construct a narrative of urban renaissance (Judd, 2003: 7). The result can now be seen in the hegemony of 'growth politics,' the use of public subsidies to entice private investment (including sport), and the manipulation and regulation of urban land, one of the few autonomous realms of local-level governance (Molotch, 1993; Schimmel, 2002; Zukin, 1991).

Since the 1980s, cities have been involved in a competition with each other so fierce that Haider (1992) refers to it as 'place war.' A shorter cycle of investment, more flexible forms of production, and changes in the production and circulation of commodities has aided the mobility of capital. City governments, shifting away from managerial functions and into entrepreneurial roles (see Harvey, 1989; Hill, 1983) provide a wide array of public subsidies including tax abatements, low-interest loans, direct grants, revenue bonds and land allocation in attempt to stimulate development. In addition, cities engage in various strategies designed to represent themselves positively in the new geographies of late capitalism or post-Fordism (Short, 1999). The more decentralized governmental system of the US, in comparison to much of Europe, allows for more local level urban boosterism. There are no limits on the amount US cities can spend on place advertising, in contrast to Britain, for example, where local officials operate within severe restrictions. Part of this place promotion advertises a city's 'good business climate' in an attempt to obtain or retain fixed investment. 'Reimagining', however, is especially intensified through competition for circulating capital, which can be thought of as 'footloose consumption' not bound to a specific locale such as retirees, tourists, and conventions (Short, 1999: 39, 42).

It is here that we turn our attention to sport. Sport has been linked to the dominant discourse of urban growth and regeneration in ways that are as powerful as they are problematic. These linkages are both material and symbolic and involve both fixed and circulating capital. The material dimension includes the reconstitution of urban space and the use of public funds for the purpose of sport-related infrastructure development and mega-projects such as stadia. Stadium construction is necessary both to retain existing major professional sport franchises (amidst franchise owners' threats of relocation) and to obtain expansion franchises or entice existing ones to move in. It is also necessary in order to host tourist related sport mega-events, including the National Football League's (NFL) Super Bowl Championship game (discussed below). The public's return on investment in major sport development is touted to include numerous material benefits, including employment growth and revenue creation, that solve urban problems and thereby benefit all residents. In addition, the symbolic benefits of hosting professional teams or sports mega-events are said to include enhanced city status and an increased 'quality of life' for the 'community as a whole'.

Almost two decades of social science research refutes the claims made by local-level growth advocates about the supposed benefits to the 'city as a whole' of sport mega-project development. Nevertheless, public investment in major sport facility construction continues apace. A recent national survey reported by Judd *et al.* (2003) revealed that two thirds of the central cities that responded to the survey had built or were undertaking to build sports stadia. Expressed in 2003 dollars, the aggregate cost of sport facilities in which US major level football, baseball, basketball, and hockey franchises play was $23.8 billion. The public sector's share of that amount was approximately $15.2 billion, which represented 64 per cent of the total (Crompton, 2004).

Funding mechanisms for major sport facility construction have changed over time. Crompton (2004: 41) identifies four eras, the most recent of which began in 1995 and 'has been characterized by an extraordinary proliferation of these facilities, a marked escalation in their costs, and a substantial increase in the proportion of the funding contributed by the franchise for facility construction'. As Crompton points out, however, even though the proportion of the cost contributed by the public is lower, because of the enormous price tags of new facilities, the total dollar amount of that lower percentage remains relatively unchanged. Furthermore, he concludes that public sector entities often receive less income from stadia now than in earlier eras. Speaking on the role that stadium construction plays in cities' attempts to capture tourism-related revenues, Perry (2003: 27) states that cities are often willing to 'sacrifice material logic for [the] symbolic identity' that comes from hosting major sport. Perry's position is shared by numerous of his colleagues in tourism studies, reinforced by sport economists, and echoed by sport studies and urban studies scholars. Current levels of public finance investment in sport mega-projects in the US are fundamentally economically irrational.

Urban hierarchies and status gambling

By the mid-1990s, US downtowns were transformed into 'packaged landscapes' (Boyer, 1993) designed to represent themselves as exciting, clean, and safe places to work and play. New corporate towers and luxury apartments alongside bars, restaurants, festival marketplaces, and shopping malls aimed to develop urban cores into sites that would serve both business professionals and middle-class residents and attract visitors. Fuelled by a culture of consumption, the post-industrial city was symbolically projected at 'spectacularized urban space' (Harvey, 1989) competing for tourism revenues and fixed capital investment from corporate, government, and retail sectors. The corporate/entertainment mix was copied by cities all over the US and resulted in a remarkably standardized 'template for economic revitalization,' right down to nearly obligatory components, which Friedan and Sagalyn (1990: 34) referred to as every Mayor's 'trophy case.'

In recent years, the commodification and marketing of culture (arts, theatre, fashion, music, and history or 'heritage') has moved to the forefront of the urban regeneration industry (Zukin, 1995). This usually involves (re)development and (re)use of a warehouse, historic, or waterfront district 'imagineered' (see Salmon, 2001; Short, 1999) in ways that create simulated tradition in attempt to attract capital investment. But as Salmon (2001) points out, while projects developed according to this strategy emphasize local distinction and the virtues of 'localism' (see also Grossn, 1996), they also advance some localities over others. The result is paradoxical in that 'cities across the nation are pursuing virtually identical strategies that are premised on the notion that each locality is culturally unique' (Salmon, 2001: 111). These strategies are ultimately destructive in that they heighten the competition between local areas for capital investment and place local tax bases under further strain. Thus, an urban status hierarchical structure emerges, and as Judd (2002: 296) cautions, 'just as some cities failed to become successful sites of production in the industrial age, in the next few years as some will fail to succeed as sites of consumption . . . abject total failure is possible'. US inner-urban competition, however, dictates that cities must compete and they must provide subsidies or risk the loss of status and degeneration that capital disinvestment assures. The imperatives of US urban policy leave the 'public entrepreneurs' of 'failure' cities feeling as if they have little choice but to invest more deeply in the competition.

It is within this context of 'creeping urban homogeneity' (Friedman, Andrews & Silk, 2004) that local governments and urban residents in the US have spent, since 1990, more that $10 billion to subsidize major sport facilities (see also Kaplan, 2003). As anchors of broader redevelopment schemes, massive sport stadia are the featured set-pieces (replacing the ubiquitous festival malls of the 1980s) cities use in an attempt to differentiate themselves from one another (Austrian & Rosentraub, 2002; Bale, 1994; Hannigan, 1998; Turner & Rosentraub, 2002). In the late 1990s there were approximately 113 major sport franchises in the US (Perry, 2003), each requiring a stadium or area – in some cases franchises of different sports share a 'home' facility in a city. With so many stadia dotting the urban landscape across the US, it is logical to ask how stadia 'differentiate' one city from another. First, there are more cities that desire to host a major league sport franchise than there are franchises available. Thus, hosting a major league team means a city can represent itself as a 'major league city' *vis-à-vis* other cities of lesser status. Second, because of these conditions of artificial scarcity in major league sport, franchise owners can move to more desirable locations. Therefore, cities engage in a veritable 'arms race' to build more massive and modern (and profitable to owners) stadia, thereby holding (or attracting) franchises in an increasingly high stakes gamble in which fewer cities can compete. Third, at the very top of the hierarchy are the super structures located in 'favourable' urban locations that meet the requirements for successful bids to host sports mega-events.

The most prestigious domestic, major sports event in the US is the National Football League's (NFL) championship game, called 'Super Bowl,' which rotates around US cities. The Super Bowl is unlike the championship series' in major league basketball, baseball, and hockey, in which games are located in the cities of the teams that qualify. Rather, Super Bowl sites are 'awarded' to cities after a competitive bidding process. Football stadia are now developed based not only on franchise owners' demands regarding profit and control, but also on the NFL's requirements for hosting a Super Bowl. These requirements reach beyond the confines of the stadium itself and onto the urban places the NFL considers to be Super Bowl worthy. For example, according to the bid specifications from 2000 made public by the city of San Diego the NFL requires that:

- the stadium must seat at least 70,000;
- the city must have at least 24,500 'quality' hotel rooms within a 20-mile radius;
- the city must provide free utilities and give up control of stadium-owned parking to the NFL;
- the city must provide staffing at 300 per cent above the normal levels for sell-out events at the stadium;
- the city must be able to provide 600,000 square feet of space for the 'NFL Experience,' a temporary interactive theme park (Alesia, 2004).

Occupying a position on the top of the urban status hierarchy of major sport cities requires massive infrastructure development, massive funding, and massive ideological support, especially if the public is called upon to foot the bill, which it almost always is. In addition to the 'economic impact studies' and supposed material benefits that are promised, major sport development schemes almost always appeal to a sense of solidarity based on territory and a sense of community. Hosting major sport provides a focus point for 'us all to rally around,' generates a sense of pride, and symbolizes 'us' as a 'major league' or 'world class' city. According to this mantra, sport stadia and major sport teams are 'community assets' that enhance our quality of life. For example, in a study commissioned by the Indianapolis Colts franchise of the NFL, titled *The Value of the Indianapolis Colts to Indiana Residents and Their Willingness to pay for a New Stadium*, the researchers concluded:

> The excitement generated by sports and the attention it attracts have been the factors that have made teams *valued community assets* [emphasis mine] inexorably associated with cities and their fans. . . . For more than 2000 years, this excitement and identity have made sports an important part of social life in virtually every society. . . . Further, [Indiana's major sports teams], . . . help to define Indiana's image and attract visitors and economic activity to the state (Rosentraub & Swindell, 2004: no pagination).

Such hyperbole and flawed historical perspective is common in reports commissioned by major sport teams. Indianapolis, it should be noted, is now building a $900 million stadium and convention centre, replacing the one it built in the 1980s to anchor downtown development and lure the Colts away from Baltimore (see Hudnut, 1995; Rosentraub, 2003; Schimmel, 2001).

When we consider the notion that major sport teams and events are 'community assets', we should be mindful of the hypermobility of capital and the fixed-placeness of the communities it exploits. In other words, capital is mobile; cities are not. In brutal contrast to the 'imagineering' accomplished by civic elites and city boosters regarding mega sport stadia, stand images of New Orleans residents crowding into the Superdome during hurricane Katrina evacuation. The Superdome was built with taxpayer money on the assertion it would 'be a benefit to the community as a whole; displacing no-one and providing such spin-off effects as more tourist money, [and] greater tax money generated by tourism' (Smith & Keller, 1983: 135). In 2005, ticket prices to attend an event in the Superdome averaged $90, season passes to watch the football team were $1300, and luxury box rental was $109,000 (www.neworleanssaints.com). Most of the 25,000 community residents who entered it as a so called 'Shelter of Last Resort' during the hurricane were probably first-time visitors. Media coverage of hurricane 'Katrina' showed us urban life in New Orleans outside the 'tourist bubble' (Judd, 1999) and reminded us that business and culture industry elites are 'most conspicuously beyond the reach of ordinary folks, of the 'natives' tied fast to the ground' (Bauman, 2001: 56; see also Smith & Ingham, 2003).

Part safe space – part spectacle (Perry, 2003), the new urban landscape had to be carved out of the remnants of the industrial past and tourists cordoned off from the harsh realities of existence for 'mobility frozen' (Ingham & McDonald, 2003) urban residents. 'Islands of affluence' (Judd, 1999) hide the overall decline of the post-industrial city, reducing it to a 'simulacrum' (Boyer, 1993), and a distorted representation of the real thing. Revitalized spaces with newly developed cultural attractions, walled off from the presumed dangerous places (and people), are created to solve urban image and social control problems. These spaces are defended by measures that solidify the relationships with capital, making them 'secure' for capital investment. Railroads, highways, and bridges are used to establish rigid zones of demarcation between the 'good' and the 'bad' parts of a city. Buildings and other barricading structures can serve the same purpose. Atrium malls, convention centres, and domed stadia were once thought to provide near perfect enclosures for protection against the sordid aspects of local urban life. But space can also be reclaimed through intensive policing and surveillance. Throughout the 1990s, as amenity infrastructure development and tourist zones became much larger, policing tactics extended into ever further reaches of US cities (Davis, 1992; Judd, 2003).

Sport and the militarization of urban society in the USA

As global violence telescopes within and through local places, so now physical, social, and psychological barriers are being constructed and enacted. In the wake of 9/11, and other catastrophic terrorist attacks in the last few years, the design of buildings, the management of traffic, the physical planning of cities, migration policy, or the design of social policies for ethnically diverse cities and neighbourhoods, are being brought within the widening umbrella of 'national security' (Graham, 2004b: 11).

At the present historical moment new relationships are emerging – and established ones are intensifying – between sport culture and the US geopolitical agenda and between sport events and the militarization of urban civil society. The link between major sports events and the ideological construction of support for the Bush administration's 'War on Terror' has very recently been taken up by a number of sport studies scholars. For example, extending what Giroux (2003: ix) has identified as the 'on-going militarization of visual culture,' King (2005) examines the ways in which major sport leagues incorporate Bush administration policy, both through marketing strategies and through spectacles and displays at sport events. King goes further to show how, simultaneously, the 'sportification' of political life is intensified through the Bush administration's association with major US sport. McDonald (2005) explores mediated contextualizing of major sport in the days immediately following 9/11. In addition, Atkinson & Young (2005) provide a broad analysis of political violence and the Olympic Games, which includes a detailed case study of the 2002 Salt Lake City Games and the relationship between terrorism, political ideology, and sport as presented via the mass media.

Less explored, however, are current relationships between major sport events and the transformed and transforming urban places in which they occur. This includes the ways in which US military doctrine and 'homeland security' concerns are shaping the urban landscape, including major sport infrastructure, and the lives and experiences of people who live, work, and visit urban areas. Confronting the rhetoric that attracting major sport will benefit the 'city as a whole' is the reality that the urban spaces in which they are held are being transformed from 'civil to militarized environments, in support of transnational hegemonic actors' (Warren, 2004: 216), and that major sport structures and events are being used to intensify and accelerate that transformation. It is important to stress, following Graham and his colleagues (2004a), that many 'changes' in the US urban milieu are a continuation of trends already underway before September 11 (some of which have been highlighted in this chapter) but reinforced and aggravated by concerns over terrorism.

The prognosis regarding the impact of the war on terrorism on urban life in US cities, and especially inner cities, is not an optimistic one. Peter Marcuse (2004) details a number of these predictions, and although he does not include a discussion regarding major sport/sport infrastructure, the implications are not difficult to conjecture. Among his predictions is the increasing decentralization of key economic activities to off-centre locations which, paradoxically, will be accompanied by property developers pressing local governments to assist them in maintaining earlier levels of centralisation. In addition, he says, more functions of daily life will occur within enclosed and protected spaces, through an increasing 'citadelization' of construction for major businesses and affluent residents. 'Barricading' strategies will intensify, further restricting movement and use of public space, and separating sections of the city from each other. Increasingly public funds will be diverted from social welfare programs into security and surveillance and control mechanisms. The results of the war on terror, summarizes Marcuse (2004: 264), will be a 'continual downgrading of the quality of life in US cities . . . particularly for members of darker-skinned groups'.

We await full systematic investigations into the connections between major sport/sport infrastructure development and these accelerating trends, but even brief excursions can be revealing. Stadium developments, as ever, symbolizing a city's urban status and late-capitalist regeneration 'success,' are now in addition positioned as 'terrorist targets'. The urban spaces in which major sport events occur are increasingly viewed as terrain on which military tactics and weaponry are necessary to protect capital investments, control crowds, and prevent and respond to terrorist attacks. Thus, many citizens accept the increasing militarization of sport facilities and events as a natural part of contemporary urban life. US military doctrine now serves as a guide to 'protect' an increasing array of sport events, both domestically and globally (Warren, 2004: 225).

As Warren (2004) explains, widely accepted and currently accelerating strategies for carrying out urban military missions were first detailed in the US Army's 1979 Field Manual titled *Military Operations on Urbanized Terrain* (MOUT). Until the 1990s it was assumed that MOUT doctrine would be primarily applied outside the US and other industrialized nations. A number of events in the 1990s, however, including racial violence in Los Angeles (1992), and bombings of the World Trade Center (1993), Murrah Federal Office Building in Oklahoma

City (1995), and the Olympic Summer Games in Atlanta (1996) resulted in 'Homeland Defense' becoming a recurrent theme in US military writing (Warren, 2004: 218). By 2000, the MOUT doctrine contained well established and broadly agreed upon strategies for carrying out both domestic and overseas operations. Drawing from information compiled by Glenn, Steeb & Matsumura (2001), Warren summarizes MOUT doctrinal strategies, some of which are as follows [emphasis in original]:

- *Intelligence, surveillance,* and *reconnaissance enhancement* include the development of technologies to prevent buildings, underground passageways, and other elements of the built environment from obscuring the location of adversaries . . . ;
- *Denial of access* strategies are designed to prevent entry into urban areas or limit penetration of both combatants and non-combatants . . . ;
- *Nodal operations* have the goal of selecting key spatial nodes within a city, rather than the whole metropolitan area to be directly controlled . . . ;
- *Non-combatant control* is intended to influence civilian 'attitudes and behaviours' to benefit the military . . . ;
- *Selective dominance* involves the ability to control areas without physically occupying them (Warren, 2004: 218).

The 2002 Salt Lake City Winter Olympic Games, the first Olympics to be designated as a 'National Special Security Event,' were the initial showcase for the Bush administration's war on terror was as well as an opportunity to display US military dominance to a global audience (see Atkinson & Young, 2005). The White House issued numerous press releases assuring US citizens that they and the Games would be protected through the investment of over $300 million in 'security' measures, which included: 4,500 military personnel; the resources of numerous federal, state, and local government agencies; a no fly zone over all Olympic venues and around a 45-mile radius of the city; portable x-ray equipment; biometric scanners; traffic barricades; surveillance cameras; armed soldiers at airport terminals; fighter jets; and Blackhawk helicopters. In addition, reported the President's Press Office, the Salt Lake City Games would also be the first Winter Olympics to 'subject all visitors at all venues to metal detectors (nearly 1000 of them).' Planning for the security of the 2002 Games began well before 9/11, but was enormously enhanced afterwards, even as the Bush administration declared, 'We will show the world we can safeguard the Olympic ideal without sacrificing our American ideals – openness, mobility, and economic opportunity in the process' (Office of the Press Secretary, January 10, 2002).

The Bush administration's 'war on terror' now extends to numerous US domestic sport events. In July 2004, the Department of Homeland Security hosted a 'Security Forum for Sports Executives,' including a full day seminar in which sport officials and security personnel were instructed about Homeland Security capabilities and responsibilities. In his address to the press regarding the seminar, (then) Secretary of Homeland Security, Tom Ridge, commented that, 'Working together with these representatives, we are sharing important information that will help sports facility owners and operators better prevent, detect, and respond to terrorist threats and ensure a safe and enjoyable experience for all' (Office of the Press Secretary, July 23, 2004). The 'best practices' that were encouraged by the Federal Government included installing surveillance cameras and other detection and monitoring equipment, increasing perimeter patrols, and establishing restricted areas of access.

By far the most intensive incursion of MOUT doctrine and related 'security' measures into US domestic sport occurs in the National Football League and especially the Super Bowl championship game. In 2006 the NFL ordered 'pat down' body searches of all fans entering all stadia where the teams play throughout the entire football season. Since the majority of NFL stadia are publicly owned and maintained, cost of extra security is often passed on to taxpayers. The Stadium Authority in Jacksonville, Florida is currently pursuing legal action against the NFL in an attempt to reclaim the cost of extra security since 9/11, including the cost of the pat downs that the Authority says costs $7,500 per game. In addition, a Jacksonville season ticket holder is suing the NFL claiming the pat downs violate his constitutional rights (NewsEdge Corporation, January 6, 2006).

These actions might be seen as relatively mild forms of resistance, however, against a league that controls the Super Bowl. They are especially mild when one considers the security measures put in place in 2005 when Jacksonville hosted Super Bowl XXXIX. Local government and police leveraged the extra security demands of hosting the game to 'expand their capabilities' of surveillance into Jacksonville's downtown. Their plan illustrates the trend in convergence between state and commercial surveillance described by Lyon (2004; 2001). For an initial cost of $1.7 million, the city contracted private security firm GTSI and its InteGuard Alliance partners, who had previously worked with the Pentagon, to install approximately 100 VPN encrypted video cameras throughout the stadium and the city. Initially deployed for the game, the system was designed to 'expand,' stay 'for decades' and go 'beyond the Super Bowl for other needs' (McEachern, January 24, 2005).

Super Bowl XL, between the Pittsburgh Steelers and Seattle Seahawks, was held at 'Ford Field' stadium in February 2006 in Detroit, Michigan. It was the first Super Bowl to be located close to an international border – half a mile from Canada. It also became one of the largest security operations in US history according to media accounts. The US asked Canadian officials to restrict private plane travel in Canadian air space near the stadium. A 30-nautical mile no-fly zone, barring planes from flying lower than 18,000 feet throughout the game, was in operation around the stadium. The FBI and Detroit police were assisted by 50 federal, state and local law enforcement agencies, following 18 months of preparation (*The Guardian* 'Sport' section, 3 February 2006, p. 12). An obsessive concern with 'security' permeated the usual pre-Super Bowl media hype and game preparation, as it was reported that, for example, 'SWAT teams – aided by digital map covering every inch of Ford Field' would 'be ready at a moment's notice' (NewsEdge Corporation, January 13, 2006).

Writing in 1983 Richard Hill described Detroit as a city that could no longer compete for development within the institutional rules of the game, absent of national and regional planning and coordination. More than two decades ago, Hill (1983: 116) asked, 'What is to be done to save Detroit?' Currently Detroit's image is an enduring symbol of post-Fordist urban decline. Less than a month prior to 2006 Super Bowl XL being played on Detroit's 'Ford Field,' the Ford Motor Company announced plans to eliminate 25,000–30,000 jobs, constituting 20 per cent of its workforce, and shut 14 factories in North America over the next six years. Nevertheless, city officials insisted that the Super Bowl would give the city a chance to 'polish its image' and 'showcase its improvements to visitors' (Haugh, January 3, 2006; Sarcaceno, January 29, 2006). Can there be any better example than Super Bowl XL in Detroit to observe the complex connections between major sport and contemporary urban trends and conditions in US society? Did any city have as much at stake? Or did Detroit have little else to lose?

Final thoughts

In this chapter I have used the concept of deep play to provoke thought about major sport in the USA. I have highlighted the connection between the development of infrastructures necessary to host large sporting events and broader economic trends and social conditions in US society. US urban change, and the role that major sport plays in it, is both a consequence and component of a complex political economic environment driven by inter-urban competition for capital investment and status enhancement. Here, in a society fixated on 'Being #1', winners emerge and losers are left to take a 'status bloodbath' (to borrow Geertz's use of Erving Goffman's term). I have asked that we ponder the 'economic irrationality' of contributing huge sums of public money to urban megaprojects that further erode the local state's (and the city's) ability to provide for urban social services.

Within this larger context of neoliberal finance-led, state-sponsored urban renewal, stadia often exist in close proximity to citizens who cannot afford the price of admission and upon whom the burden of increased taxation is disproportionately placed. Moreover, breakdowns in barriers to free trade and the free flow of capital are now accompanied by an increasing fortification of barriers between urban spaces and disruption of the flow of people throughout the city. Status-differentiated cultural power is reinforced and 'defended' by state-sponsored surveillance and control tactics and an escalated militarization of urban civil society. Nowhere are these trends more evident than in the case of major league sport and sports mega-events. Borrowing heavily from Geertz's discussion of deep play, hosting major sports events in the US might be seen to provide a 'meta-social commentary' upon the matter of sorting citizens and cities into fixed hierarchal ranks and organizing a collective experience around that arrangement. In the 'revitalized' postindustrial US city, professional sport

171

is high among the consumption-based strategies that distinguish 'prestige communities' (Ingham & McDonald, 2003) from all the rest. Although in reference to quite a different context, Geertz tells us that prestige – the necessity to affirm, define, celebrate, justify and 'just plain bask in it' – can be a driving force in a society. Might this indeed also be the story 'Americans' tell themselves about themselves?

References

Alesia, M. (2004, December 21) 'I believe we'll get one'. Available at www.Indystar.com. Accessed April 15, 2005.

Atkinson, M. & Young, K. (2005) 'Political violence, terrorism, and security at the Olympic Games', in K. Young & K. Wamsley (eds) *Global Olympics: Historical and Sociological Studies of the Modern Games.* London: Elsevier, 269–294.

Austrian, Z. & Rosentraub, M. (2002) 'Cities, sports and economic change: A Retrospective', *Journal of Urban Affairs* 24 (5): 549–563.

Bale, J. (1994) *Landscapes of Modern Sport.* London: Leicester.

Bauman, Z. (2001) *Community: Seeking Safety in an Insecure World.* Malden, MA: Blackwell.

Bentham, J. (1789) *Theory of Legislation.* Translate to English by Ogden, C. (1931). London: Paul, Trench & Truber.

Boyer, C. (1993) 'The city of illusion: New York's public places', in P. Knox (ed.) *The Restless Urban Landscape.* Englewood Cliffs, NJ: Prentice Hall, 111–126.

Crompton, J. (2004) 'Beyond economic impact: An alternative rationale for publicsubsidy of major league sport facilities', *Journal of Sport Management* 18: 40–58.

Davis, M. (1992) 'Fortress Los Angeles: The militarization of urban space', in M. Sorkin (ed.) *Variations on a Theme Park: The New American City and the End of Public Space.* New York: Hill and Wang, 154–180.

Department of the Army (1979) *Military Operations on Urbanized Terrain FM 90-10.* Washington, DC: US Government Printing Office.

Friedan, B. & Sagalyn, L. (1990). *Downtown, Inc.: How America Builds Cities.* Cambridge, MA; MIT.

Friedman, M., Andrews, D. & Silk, M. (2004) 'Sport and the façade of redevelopment in the postindustrial city', *Sociology of Sport Journal* 21 (2): 119–139.

Geertz, C. (1973) 'Deep play: Notes on the Balinese cockfight', *The Interpretation of Cultures.* New York: Basic Books, 412–453.

Giroux, H. (2003) *Public Spaces, Private Lives: Democracy Beyond 9/11.* Oxford: Rowan and Littlefield.

Glenn, R., Steeb, R. & Matsumura, J. (2001) *Corralling the Trojan Horse: A Proposal for Improving US Operations Preparedness in the Period 2000–2025.* Santa Monica, CA: RAND Arroyo Center.

Goss, J. (1996) 'Disquiet on the waterfront', *Urban Geography* 17: 221–247.

Graham, S. (ed.) (2004a) *Cities, War and Terrorism: Towards an Urban Geopolitics.* Oxford: Blackwell.

Graham, S. (ed.) (2004b) 'Introduction: Cities, warfare, and states of emergency' in S. Graham (ed.) *Cities, War and Terrorism: Towards an Urban Geopolitics.* Oxford: Blackwell, 1–26.

Haider, D. (1992) 'Place wars: New realities of the 1990s', *Economic Development Quarterly* 6: 588–601.

Hannigan, J. (1998) *Fantasy City: Pleasure and Profit in the Postmodern Metropolis.* London: Palgrave.

Harvey, D. (1989) *The Condition of Postmodernity: An Inquiry into the Origins of Cultural Change.* Oxford: Basil Blackwell.

Haugh, D. (January 3, 2006) 'Super Bowl hosts polishing image: Much-maligned Detroit hopes the game will showcase its improvements to visitors'. Available at www.chicagotribune.com. Accessed January 30, 2006.

Hill, R. (1983) 'Crisis in the motor city: The politics of economic development in Detroit', in S. Fainstein *et al.* (eds) *Restructuring the city: The Political Economy of Urban Development*. London: Longman, 80–125.

Hudnut, W. (1995) *The Hudnut Years in Indianapolis, 1976–1991*. Bloomington, IN: Indiana University.

Ingham, A. & McDonald, M. (2003) Sport and community/*communitas*', in R. Wilcox *et al.* (eds) *Sporting Dystopias: The Making and Meanings of Urban Sport Cultures*. Albany, NY: State University of New York: 17–33.

Jessop, B., Peck, J. & Tickell, A. (1999) 'Economic crisis, state restructuring, and urban Politics' in A. Jones & D. Wilson (eds) *The Urban Growth Machine: Critical Perspectives Two Decades Later*. Albany, NY: State University of New York, 141–162.

Jewson, N. & MacGregor, S. (eds) (1997) *Transforming Cities: Contested Governance and New Spatial Divisions*. New York: Routledge.

Judd, D. (1999) 'Constructing the tourist bubble', in S. Fainstein & D. Judd (eds) *The Tourist City*. New Haven, CT: Yale, 53–53.

Judd, D. (2002) 'Promoting tourism in US cities', in S. Fainstein & S. Campbell (eds) *Readings in Urban Theory*. Oxford: Blackwell, 278–299.

Judd, D. (2003) 'Building the tourist city: Editor's introduction', in D. Judd (ed.) *The Infrastructure of Play: Building the Tourist City*. Armonk, NY: M. E. Sharpe, 3–16.

Judd, D. *et al.* (2003) 'Tourism and entertainment as local economic development: A national survey', in D. Judd (ed.) *The Infrastructure of Play: Building the Tourist City*. Armonk, NY: M. E. Sharpe, 50–76.

Kaplan, D. (2003) 'Forecast: Venue financing tougher in '03', *Street and Smith's SportsBusiness Journal* 5 (37): 1, 25.

King, S. (2005) 'Sport culture and the emergence of jockocracy'. Unpublished paper presented at the annual conference of the North American Society for the Sociology of Sport, October 26–29, Winston-Salem, NC.

Leitner, H. (1990) 'Cities in pursuit of economic growth', *Political Economic Quarterly* 9 (2): 146–170.

Lyon, D. (2001) *Surveillance Society: Monitoring Everyday Life.* Buckingham: Open University Press.

Lyon, D. (2004) 'Technology vs. 'terrorism: Circuits of city surveillance since September 11, 2001', in S. Graham (ed.) *Cities, War and Terrorism: Towards an Urban Geopolitics*. Oxford: Blackwell, 297–311.

Marcuse, P. (2004) 'The "War on Terrorism" and life in cities after September 11, 2001', in S. Graham (ed.) *Cities, War and Terrorism: Towards an Urban Geopolitics* Oxford: Blackwell, 263–275.

McDonald, M. (2005) 'Imagining benevolence, masculinity and the nation: Tragedy, sport and the transnational marketplace', in M. Silk, D. Andrews & C. Cole (eds) *Sport and Corporate Nationalisms*. New York: Berg, 127–141.

McEachern, C. (2005, January 24) 'Security scores at Super Bowl'. Available at www.varbusiness.com. Accessed January 14, 2006.

Molotch, H. (1976) 'The city as growth machine: Toward a political economy of place', *American Journal of Sociology* 82, 309–330.

Molotch, H. (1993) 'The political economy of growth machines', *Journal of Urban Affairs* 15: 29–53.

NewsEdge Corporation (2006, January 2) 'Who pays for security' – Tampa sports authority sues Bucs for security costs', *St. Petersburg* Times. Available at www.securityinfowatch.com. Accessed January, 14, 2006.

NewsEdge Corporation (2006, January 13) 'Supersizing bowl security for Super Bowl XL', *The Detroit News*. Available at www.securityinfowatch.com. Accessed January, 14, 2006.

Office of the Press Secretary, U.S. Department of Homeland Security (July 23, 2004) 'Department of Homeland Security hosts security forum for sports executives'. Available at www.dhs.gov. Accessed January 14, 2006.

Office of the Press Secretary, U.S. Department of Homeland Security (January 10, 2002) 'Preparing for the world: Homeland security and the Winter Games'. Available at www.Whitehouse.gov. Accessed August 5, 2004.

Perry, D. (2003) 'Urban tourism and the privatizing discourses of public infrastructure', in D. Judd (ed.) *The Infrastructure of Play: Building the Tourist City*. Armonk, NY: M. E. Sharpe, 19–49.

Rosentraub, M. (2003) 'Indianapolis, a sports strategy, and the redefinition of downtown Redevelopment', in D. Judd (ed.) *The Infrastructure of Play: Building the Tourist City*. Armonk, NY: M. E. Sharpe, 77–103.

Rosentraub, M. & Swindell, D. (2005, March) 'The value of the Indianapolis Colts to Indiana residents and their willingness to pay for a new stadium'. Available at www.Indystar.com; PDF accessed April 15, 2005.

Saraceno, J. (January 29, 2006) 'To help its troubled image, Detroit puts on Sunday best. Available at www.usatoday.com. Accessed January 20, 2006.

Salmon, S. (2001) 'Imagineering the inner city? Landscapes of pleasure and the commodification of cultural spectacle in the postmodern city', in C. Harrington & D. Bielby (eds) *Popular Culture: Production and Consumption*. Oxford: Blackwell, 106–119.

Schimmel, K. (2001) Sport matters. Urban regime theory and urban regeneration in the late-capitalist era, In C. Gratton & I. Henry (eds) *Sport in the City: The Role of Sport in Economic and Social Regeneration* London: Routledge pp. 259–277.

Schimmel, K. (2002) 'The political economy of place: Urban and sport studies Perspectives', in J. Maguire & K. Young (eds.) *Theory, Sport & Society*. Oxford: Elsevier, 335–351.

Short, J. (1999) 'Urban imagineers: Boosterism and the representation of cities', in A. Jones & D. Wilson (eds) *The Urban Growth machine: Critical Perspectives Two Decades Later*. Albany, NY: State University of New York, 27–54.

Smith, M. (1988) *City, State, and Market: The Political Economy of Urban Society*. New York: Basil Blackwell.

Smith, M. & Keller, M. (1983) 'Managed growth and the politics of uneven development in New Orleans', in S. Fainstein *et al.* (eds) *Restructuring the city: The Political Economy of Urban Development*. London: Longman, 126–166.

Smith, J. & Ingham, A. (2003) 'On the waterfront: Retrospectives on the relations between sport and community', *Sociology of Sport Journal* 20(4): 252–275.

Teaford, J. (1990) *The Rough Road to Renaissance: Urban Revitalization in America, 1940–1985*. Baltimore, MD: Johns Hopkins.

Turner, R. & Rosentraub, M. (2002) 'Tourism, sports and the centrality of cities', *Journal of Urban Affairs* 24 (5): 487–492.

US Department of Housing and Urban Development (1982) *The President's National Urban Policy Report*. Washington, DC: US Government Printing Office.

Warren, R. (2004) 'City streets – The war zones of globalization: Democracy and military operations on urban terrain in the early twenty-first century', in S. Graham (eds.) *Cities, War and Terrorism: Towards an Urban Geopolitics*. Oxford: Blackwell, 214–230.

Zukin, S. (1991) *Landscapes of Power: From Detroit to Disney*. Berkeley: University of California.

Zukin, S. (1995) *The Cultures of Cities*. Cambridge, MA: Blackwell.

Olympic urbanism and Olympic Villages: planning strategies in Olympic host cities, London 1908 to London 2012[1]

Francesc Muñoz

A miniature city, replete with modern conveniences and facilities, had arisen magically atop the hills, within eyesight of the great Olympic Stadium – atop the modern Mount Olympus, below which lay the modern Plains of Elysium . . . A miniature world was here set up, rigidly protected from the world outside.

Official Report of the Organising Committee of the Los Angeles Olympic Games (1932)

Introduction

The central argument of this chapter is that the urbanization of the Western world during the 20th century cannot be understood fully without consideration of the contribution of major urban events. The Great Exhibitions and the Olympic Games are two clear examples of this type of urban mega-event. In Olympic urbanism, the villages – designed as a shelter for the athletes and occupied by residents after the Games – stand out as urban artefacts that enable us to explore the relations between architecture and urban planning to communicate a specific urban image. It is in the Olympic Village that architecture most clearly places itself in the service of creating the image that the host city aims to project internationally.[2] In this sense, building typologies, formal languages and urban design itself are part of an urban landscape specifically conceived to highlight given values of modernity and specific values of the place. At the same time, the architecture of the Olympic Villages manifests the ambition to reproduce, in controlled fashion in a small, limited space, the urban models and architectural proposals that, due to rigidity and difficulties, cannot be put into practice in the real space of the city. As the quotation that introduces this chapter shows, the architecture of Olympic Villages recreates a miniature world, a spectacular image of the city without the deformations, shortcomings and excesses of the real urban space where urbanism cannot completely control the forces that shape the city. Gradually, at the same time as architecture acquired an important role in urban planning and programme design in the course of the 20th century, the Olympic Villages ceased to be ephemeral constructions, such as military barracks or camps complemented by the city's hotel accommodation, and became completely novel constructions, conceived first as part of the process of city extension over the territory and then later as experiments in the transformation of the urban form. As some Olympic experiences show, the urban transformation that results from the organization of the Games can be used as a guideline for the future development of the city. Cities like Barcelona have succeeded in changing its urban profile dramatically when hosting the Games but have also taken advantage of this experience of urban regeneration to design strategic and future planning views for the future.

Olympic Villages: a brief history of developments in the 20th century

The Olympic Games just before and after the Great War (London, 1908; Stockholm, 1912; Antwerp, 1920; Paris, 1924; and Amsterdam, 1928) were characterized by answering the accommodation problem with an 'emergency residential menu' (Muñoz, 1997), comprising all manner of temporary dwellings – even the ships that had transported the athletes – in order to satisfy the accommodation needs that the Games involved. Although Paris saw the first experiment of a discreet Olympic Village (a cluster of wooden huts in an unoccupied area near the Colombes stadium with additions such as a mail and telegraph service), the first Olympic Village as such was built in Los Angeles for the 1932 Games. Along with the village built for the Berlin Games, in 1936, it represents what I call the 'inaugural villages', establishing the basic model of Olympic Village that was to be reproduced in the future: a multifunctional structure which, in addition to accommodating the athletes, included facilities such as places of entertainment, rest and bodily care, and leisure areas.

Following World War II, it was not until the 1960s that the Villages in Rome (1960) and Mexico (1968) introduced new elements of complexity into the morphology and functions of the basic model of Olympic Village built in Los Angeles and Berlin.[3] Indeed, the Rome Games were a breakaway from their forerunners in terms of Olympic urbanism. For the first time, there was a regional conception of the urban mass, and behind the location of the installations and constructions there was a project for the territorial expansion of the city. The Olympic Village was inserted into a programme of residential zoning that was much more than just a solution to the temporary accommodation of the athletes, a characteristic shared by all subsequent Olympic Villages. It was with Rome in 1960 that the architectural form of the Olympic Village became a lynchpin in the projection of the city's image. In fact the Olympic Games as a whole changed a great deal in the second half of the 20th century, as many of the contributions to this collection explore in more detail, with the increased internationalization and commercialization of their contents. Thus the globalization of sport in terms of visual mass-consumption went hand-in-hand with growing plans for entire sport districts as a new way of extending or transforming the city. Olympic urbanism begun to be considered as an important element in ambitious urban development programmes and architecture was to guarantee not just the functionality of the projects but also spectacle as an added value. Evidence of this evolution is seen in the Villages of the 1970s (Munich, 1972 and particularly Montreal, 1976) that, unlike those of the previous decade, were based not on urban growth but on enhancing and renewing the existing city.

The Olympic Villages of the last two decades of the 20th century show a heterogeneous group of projects: the experience of socialist urbanism in Moscow (1980) and the regeneration plans for Seoul (1988) and Barcelona (1992) contrast with the ephemeral nature of the Villages at the university campuses of Los Angeles (1984) and Atlanta (1996). In the case of Moscow, the Olympic Village was considered part of the city's 1971–1990 development plan, in the context of the 10th Five-year Economic and Social Development Plan. These plans divided the city into eight planning zones that were finally developed by the awarding of the Games. Though quite different in themselves, the Seoul and Barcelona operations shared an emphasis on urban renewal programmes that regenerated major urban areas such as Chansil, a floodable area on the banks of the river Han in Seoul, and Poblenou, the industrial centre of the 19th-century city in Barcelona.

The 1984 Games in Los Angeles represented an opposite model with minimal urban impact, since only four of the 21 Olympic facilities were new buildings. In this way, no Olympic Village was built and the athletes were accommodated on three university campuses. This minimalist format was reproduced in Atlanta (1996), where the installations of the Georgia Institute of Technology were used as an Olympic Village, with the addition of the newly built 'Village Festival Center', a big shopping mall, and the 'Olympic towers', two apartment blocks that completed the residential accommodation on offer.

Architecture and Olympic urbanism

The importance of architecture in the formal definition of Olympic Urbanism is clear when elements such as building typologies, formal languages or the city-planning model that lies behind the majority of the projects are considered.[4] In *Olympic Buildings* Martin Wimmer (1976) suggests a classification of 20th century Olympic Villages according to different building typologies.

Following Wimmer, there is a first stage, characterized by the use of bungalows and single-family dwellings in the case of the villages built up during the early decades of the 20th century. This is an urban form clearly inspired by the residential suburbs or the industrial colonies that characterized the former expansion of European cities – the German *Siedlungen* or the whole range of working-class dwelling typologies based on the 'garden city' ideal suggested and promoted by Ebenezer Howard. A second stage started with the incorporation of multi-family dwelling blocks in the Kápylá Village in Helsinki (1952), a model that was repeated in Rome (1960) and Tokyo (1964). A third stage corresponds to the construction of large dwelling complexes organized by means of the repetition of high-rise apartment blocks with different designs according to the case, as happened in Mexico (1968), Munich (1972), Montreal (1976) and Moscow (1980). We might also add the case of the Villages of the last two decades of the 20th century, characterized by a variety of building typologies (multi-family and single-family units of different heights) as in Seoul (1988) and Barcelona (1992); and by the ephemeral nature of operations in Los Angeles (1984) and Atlanta (1996), introducing the typology of the multifunctional container instead of housing blocks.

A more interesting analysis can be made by comparing the formal languages of these construction projects, paying attention to architecture and urban design as vehicles to communicate signs of modernity that are always combined with other elements belonging to the local arena.[5]

The first Olympic Villages: Taylorization, rationalism and localism

The two Olympic Villages of Los Angeles (1932) and Berlin (1936) show a clear link between modernity and locality. In the first case, the village incorporated and reflected many elements of the Taylorized and Fordist lifestyle that already characterized North American cities, such as mass-production and dependence on the automobile. The mass-produced roofs, doors and façades of the houses in the Olympic Village were actually transported by T-model Fords, also mass-produced, to be installed as fast as they were dismantled after the Games. At the same time, the village architecture was a direct reference to the 'Spanish' style of the USA's west coast, with a strong presence of local cliché, from the entrance to the village to the floral decoration of the gardens outside each housing unit.

In the case of the Doberitz Village in Berlin, the conception of the rationalization of the house are clearly present. The pursuit of the ideal of domestic 'efficiency' had been introduced into social housing projects in Germany since the beginning of the century. Those ideas were clearly inspiring the design of the Olympic Village, emphasizing 'comfort, simplicity and cleanness'.[6] The strong influence of rationalism is even clear when analysing the landscape design. This is to say, the urban landscape created by the Olympic Village was devoted to producing an integrated whole, shaping the little hills around the housing units or introducing suitable animal species for the environment. The ambition of controlling the visual environment was clearly to make the most of the scenic possibilities of the landscape, designing even the views from the living-rooms inside the different dwellings. At the same time, local features were integrated to an extreme. For example, each house in the Berlin Olympic Village was branded with the name of a German city and its rooms were decorated in keeping with elements alluding to the 'economic and cultural' life of the city to which the house was devoted.

178

From functionalism to radicalism: modern urban Olympic Villages

The three Olympic Villages of the 1960s represent mimetic interpretations of the Modern Movement's proposals. They have also in common the ambition for physically expanding the existing city. In the case of Rome (1960), the Village even reproduced the 'pilotis' on which the housing blocks stood and the spaces between the blocks, according to the well-known images of modern architectural projects. The Miguel Hidalgo and Villa Coapa Villages in Mexico (1968) represented a much more radical version of functionalist approaches. Both Villages were strongly influenced by the European experiences in the construction of high-rise prefab housing estates during the 1960s. The Mexican Olympic Villages shared the ambition for creating city-districts, meant to be self-sufficient urban areas and designed under strict rules of zoning. Finally, in this style, albeit over a decade after the Mexico Olympics, the Moscow Village in 1980 introduced an even more standardized vision of the vertical city ideal. In fact, the Russian Olympic urbanism clearly reflected the national policy regarding residential architecture that had developed since the postwar reconstruction period in the Soviet Union.

The Villages of the 1970s, conversely, present different approaches that can be related to other traditions in contemporary architectural design. This can be seen particularly with respect to the new radical perspectives in urban design regarding the spatial and physical organization of the city functions that were intensively developed during the 1960s. Firstly, there was the work of the Japanese metabolist architects, who imagined cities and urban structures growing and physically extending like live organisms on territory. Secondly, there was technological Pop Architecture characterized by the proposals of the architects in the Archigram group, influenced by Buckminster Fuller. These architects used to illustrate their projects located in hyper-specialized cities where new functions like consumption or tourism were the key words to understand the nature of the urban project. The Archigram group also served as an inspiration for works such as the Pompidou centre in Paris. Both radical perspectives orientated the architectural proposals during the 1960s towards the creation of 'megastructures' – tower buildings with different designs integrating both services and facilities in different layers or levels. The megastructure was suggested to be the future of the urban form by absorbing the functions of urban space and constituting a new basis not only for the design of housing but for the organization of modern urban life as a whole (Solà-Morales, 1994). These radical orientations were clearly present in the Olympic Villages developed in Munich (1972) and Montreal (1976). The former was set in an Olympic park clearly orientated towards urban leisure, where the buildings were constructed for the future purpose of shopping and where even the green areas were conceived in terms of recreation and leisure. In Montreal's Olympic Village, four huge pyramidal structures, megastructures intended as microcities, concentrated all the functions, from residential to catering, via leisure. The basements and first floors

179

were devoted to services, and the sixth floor and above contained dwellings for the athletes.

Postmodern views: the Villages of the last two decades of the 20th century

The role of architecture as a promoter of the new urban image that began in the Village of Rome acquired a structural role in the conception of Olympic urbanism after the Moscow Games in 1980. The Olympic Villages in Seoul (1988) and Barcelona (1992) show many of the common elements characterizing the urban renewal experiences in Western cities during the last decades of the 20th century. The list of landmarks in this new geography of urban renewal is quite long. The gallery of renovation sites since the 1980s goes from Battery Park in New York to London's Docklands, from La Défense in Paris to the never ending collection of waterfronts turned into leisure and entertainment areas: from Baltimore to Rotterdam, from Genoa to Antwerp. In all these experiences of urban regeneration, the use of architecture as a cultural symbolic support for the urban planning programme was a common feature (Crilley, 1993). This type of postmodern architecture and urban design combined homogenization, repetition and replication of the global branded landscapes of leisure and consumption with the manipulation of local and vernacular clichés.

In the Olympic Villages of the 1960s and 1970s, that I have called 'modern', localism was reduced by the overwhelming physical presence of the architectural proposals inspired by the functionalist narrative. It is in this light that we should understand the initiatives to recover some of Rome's historic buildings in the 1960 Games; or the Olympic cultural programmes strongly influenced by local traditions in Mexico (1968) or in Munich (1972). The Villages I refer to as 'postmodern', conversely, show how local elements were once again incorporated, as in the cases of the first Villages of the 1930s, with the image that architecture accords to Olympic Village urbanism. A good example is the 'Korean-ness' of the architecture in Seoul's Olympic Village, inspired by values such as 'the tranquillity and modest elegance [. . .] expressing a spirituality deeply rooted in the country's culture, observable in the spaces created, in the sculptures and the colours' (Brandizzi, 1988). This approach meant, for example, that the highest buildings in the village were on the outside to 'protect' the lower-rise construction located in the interior of the Olympic Village.

The 'Korean-ness' of Seoul's architecture became 'Mediterranean-ness' in the case of Barcelona, where references to the historic city were constant in the urbanism of the Olympic Village. The architectural project actually proposed an 'in vitro' architecture: that is to say, there was the ambition of creating a new neighbourhood organically linked to the existing city in the site where the Olympic Village was built. This was extremely difficult since the superimposition of different architectural forms and languages that produces history – and can be easily found in the existing historical city (of, say Barcelona) – is never present in a brand new built area. The solution was to use an architecture able to 'simulate history'. This meant using different materials and designs; the project tried to give the impression of being an historical area by superimposing different architectural textures. The built environment in Barcelona finally produced a kind of 'in vitro' formal controlled diversity based on the variation of formal elements like façades, arches and balconies.

Finally the Olympic Villages of Los Angeles (1984) and Atlanta (1996) were, apart from the essentially ephemeral nature of the operations, exercises in urban simulation that attempt to recreate urban landscape using decor elements. A good example was the use of 'Mediterranean' colours in urban design and signposting in the case of Los Angeles – conceived not just for visitors but also for global television viewers. In this way, the Mediterranean atmosphere was meant to create identification with all the Olympic installations, using the iconography and chromatic attributes of the backdrops to give this impression on the television screen.[7]

Understanding Olympic urbanism: urban regeneration and planning strategies in Barcelona

As previously discussed, Olympic urbanism has been able to extend cities historically, building new facilities and considering the Olympic Village as the main contributor to this process of urban expansion. The Olympic urban projects and plans have been included in master plans and planning schemes for the city as a whole. At the same time, Olympic urbanism has also been able to identify the new urban areas with some specific images linked to modernity or to some selected characteristics of the local environment and culture. In some cases, Olympic urbanism has even transformed the urban profile of a city, having a strong impact on the post-Olympic evolution of the whole urban space. The Barcelona experience is a useful case study to explain these processes and suggest some lessons for the strategic role of Olympic urbanism in cities during the 21st century. Firstly, because of the implementation of urban projects based on long-term planning strategies. Secondly, because of the post-Olympic management of the relationships between the new urban areas and the pre-existing city. Both perspectives are likely to be key issues in thinking about design issues for the next Olympic cities: Beijing 2008 and London 2012.

These two guidelines that can be observed in the Barcelona experience are clearly present in the former decision of locating the Olympic village on the city waterfront. At that time, the seafront was a very deprived and innaccessible area, despite the fact of being very close to the historic core of the city. Instead of encouraging any new physical extension of the urban fabric, the Olympic Village project was devoted to the urban regeneration and transformation of this neglected waterfront where the obsolete industrial plants and lack of centrality were the main features.

Regarding the first mentioned guideline, the planning strategy, the regeneration project was not only focusing on the Village area itself. From the very beginning, there was a clear perception of the opportunity for extending the renewed area, reaching the river Besos, a natural limit of the city, and even connecting the extended renovation area with other urban waterfronts of coastal metropolitan municipalities along the East and West coast. The whole idea of a 'metropolitan waterfront' was thus emphasizing the possibilities for converting a problematic urban area into an opportunity urban site.[8] The whole Olympic project on the waterfront was inspired by the idea of the mixture of uses – residences, infrastructures, public space, and new beaches – and the main goal of transforming the area into a new vibrant urban space. Looking at the situation fifteen years later, it is hard to explain the amazing success of the city as a 'cool', world-renowned, tourist destination, without considering the radical change in the landscape and the urban skyline that Olympic urbanism represented in the early 1990s. Furthermore, present day Barcelona can not be explained without considering the role that the Olympic waterfront plays in the city's urban infrastructure.

Regarding the second guideline, the management of the relationships between the new Olympic areas and the pre-existing city, the extension of renovation projects in the waterfront area has been reinforced with the location of new regeneration and strategic projects that currently play an important role linking the waterfront with the pre-existing neighbourhoods. In this sense, there are two main planning decisions to be remarked upon. Firstly, the intensive production of public spaces that are in fact used by different urban populations from all over the city. Secondly, the location of centrality projects surrounding the waterfront area. These projects represent new centrality conditions and cover different planning areas: a technological district (the so-called '22@ project'), a linear public park following the river Besos, a high-speed urban train station, and a new complex of buildings devoted to culture, exhibitions and symposia formerly created for the celebration of the cultural event 'Forum of Cultures Barcelona 2004'. All these new centrality projects have been located in different places along the waterfront. This proximity effect is reinforcing the final completion of the waterfront extension and generating an important centrality in a previously peripheral area that had remained relatively 'untouched' from the point of view of planning action.

In conclusion, it is clear that the main feature of the 1992 Olympic Village project, the location of a centrality space in a non central and deprived area, is still inspiring these other on-going initiatives in Barcelona. As the Barcelona experience clearly shows, regenerating deprived urban areas can be a very effective way to improve the city profile as a whole. Investing in urban areas traditionally fractured by changes in the economic market and neglected by the planning process has usually been done not to promote public social policies but to improve the attractiveness of city space. This is to say, the more diversified a city is – both in economic and social terms, the more complex and attractive it has to appear to global capital and other investments that can theoretically be located in a multiplicity of places. Despite the fact of improved accessibility that better transportation possibilities and telecommunication systems represent, activities and investments are not usually located indifferently but by taking advantage of local differences, peculiarities and characteristics. Places are much more important than ever before. This is the paradox that goes hand in hand with globalization. As has been suggested, in the case of Barcelona at least, the opportunities that can appear when organizing an Olympic Games go much further than the event itself and can be extended to reinforce the capability to transform surrounding urban space in subsequent years.

The lessons from Barcelona's Olympic experience, however, are not all positive ones. Firstly, the process of regeneration initiated in the waterfront has considerably increased housing prices during the last decade. This is a process that has been extended to the whole city, making housing accessibility quite difficult for the local population. This is, in fact, the main recognized problem in the city at the time of writing. An average family must dedicate more than 54 per cent of their annual income to pay their rent or mortgage. As a consequence, a very important number of families are currently leaving the city to live in other metropolitan municipalities where they can afford more accessible housing. Simultaneously, the renovation of so many areas and the touristic promotion of the city show a very intensive process of specialization of some neighbourhoods in activities directly and indirectly linked with the global economy of tourism. Success as a tourist destination is an obvious positive economic input but at the same time, the previously held goal of achieving a diversified and integrated city, both in urban and social terms, has not yet been fully accomplished. On-going processes like gentrification and the 'brandification' of urban space go hand in hand in reinforcing the lack of diversity of many urban areas in the city. The apparent multicultural scene in Barcelona has more to do with a transient population and tourist visitors than with an integrated and diversified urban living space. The relative lack of quality of the architectural projects on the new waterfront, redeveloped to host the Forum of Cultures in 2004, can also be understood as the logical result of these processes. The new landscape that has appeared in the redevelopment areas along the waterfront reminds one of a kind of second-hand Florida, highly disconnected from the local urban landscape and culture, reproduced in a very short-time, and generating strong disagreements between local inhabitants. These processes show how some of the former ambitions of Olympic urbanism have not been achieved and even seem to have been abandoned. Finding the equilibrium between success in the global arena and solutions for local social problems is today, just as it was in 1992, the main challenge for the city.

The Olympic Villages of the 21st century: between revival and branded images

The Olympic Villages built since 2000 and the projects proposed by the cities competing to host the 2012 Games reveal the main values and images that are currently used in architectural design and urban planning at the present moment. In this sense, the different bids submitted to the IOC by candidates for the 2012 Summer Olympics were organized around similar attributes and key-words such as 'sustainability', 'safety', 'compactness' and 'landscape'. With differences and nuances, all the Villages proposed for the 2012 Games shared the ambition of creating spaces meant to be environmentally friendly and sustainable, socially safe, inspired by the ideal of the 'compact city', and including a very simplified vision of landscape, specifically defined in terms of visual consumption.

In short, Olympic urbanism is currently associated with the most successful ideas coming from ideas about urban marketing and branding. As happens with urbanism in general, the visions that are predominant at the present moment have to do with an international context defined by a global market of places, cities and urban images. In a large majority of projects, submitted to international contests, the idealized image of the European 'compact city' coexists alongside the new icons of new technology and sustainability. The first Olympic Village showing how these new ideas were rising to prominence was the one in Sydney for the 2000 Summer Olympics, developed at the heart of a marshland area near the port, in Homebush Bay. The project transformed the area into a metropolitan nature park. The landscape projects integrated into the whole plan, the introduction of animal species in the area, and the general low density of the housing typologies were framed into the discourse of a new sustainable urbanism involving meticulous landscape management. This approach also had an influence on the design of the village for the Athens Olympic Games and the forthcoming Beijing Olympic Village (2008).

In the case of Athens, the idea of the ecological park in which the Village was set, the presence of eco-routes and other soft elements coming from the sustainable city narratives coexisted with the revival of the Modern Movement proposed by architects. To be precise, and quoting the text of the Olympic Village project, it was designed:

> Keeping with the principles of the Modern Movement, with its highlight ideas such as correct orientation of buildings, appropriate natural ventilation and good air circulation in housing.

As can be observed, this is a clear postmodern exercise of interpretation of modernity that reprises some features of the traditional image of Le Corbusier's *ville radieuse*. The final result even reminded one of the modern neighbourhood architecture that colonized the peripheries of European cities during the 1960s and 1970s.

In the case of Beijing 2008, the future Olympic Village picks up the sustainable and ecological discourse to address the Village as a 'green district' where the intensive presence of telecommunication technologies also links the project with the narratives of the informational city. The entire Village is in fact conceived as an 'e-community', with the existence of an 'on-line square' devoted to all activities related to digital interaction. This is a telematic urban environment that also guarantees safety with CCTV and sophisticated surveillance systems.

These two images, the sustainable city and the digital city, the green city and the techno-city, were both present in the various villages proposed in the bids for the 2012 Olympic Games by London, Madrid, Moscow, New York and Paris. With some differences, they all swung between the two scenarios. The cases of London and Paris are particularly interesting, since the Olympic Village was presented as a model for the development of future urban regeneration plans and projects. It must be said that some of these future programmes were presented as inspired by the 'compact city' idea. In London, the winner, the idealized model of the mixture of uses, the use of sustainable materials and renewable energies are understood as guidelines to be followed by future 'sustainable communities' to be developed in the East End of the city. In the case of Paris, the bid proposed a village in the 17th District, based on four key principles (clarity, serenity, safety and mobility) that shape both landscape management – including the implementation of parks and canals – and spatial configuration, with, for example, physical barriers that protect the Village from the outside.

The cases of New York and Moscow, conversely, were addressed far more on the basis of the renovation of a major centrality area: the Olympic Village proposed in New York's bid was characterized by new residential uses for an old industrial sector in Queens. In the case of Moscow, the project for the Olympic Village shaped a new residential area overlooking the river Moskva, a 'picturesque green space', as was presented in the project, framed by other Olympic facilities laid out along the river's course through the city. Finally, the area that included the Olympic Village in Madrid's bid was integrated into a whole new district, a future green ring leading the city's eastward expansion, inspired by:

> The urban organization of the Mediterranean city, guaranteeing an intense community life . . . compatible with . . . contemporary aspirations to a harmonious habitat in proximity to nature.

The scope of the different proposals was, then, very broad: the regeneration of non-central areas to be followed with further future developments in London and Paris; the renewal of central areas accounting easily exploitable landscape elements such as a river, in New York and Moscow; and the physical expansion of the city in the case of Madrid. Despite the diversity of situations, all the candidates for the 2012 Olympic Games proposed villages with urban programmes that, as pointed out earlier, located the space of the Olympic Village between the planning revival and the brand images of logo-architecture.

Olympic Urbanism: rethinking cities and places

Despite marked discontinuities, the trajectory I have outlined for the Olympic Village in the 20th and 21st centuries reveals a clear evolution in its urban role.

Francesc Muñoz

From the former Olympic meetings in London in 1908 or the first serious attempt at building an Olympic Village in the 1924 Paris Games, urban design has been performed to accomplish more and more functions. The Olympic Village in Doberitz, for the Berlin Games in 1936, included for the first time new facilities and services, such as saunas and gymnasiums. During the 20th century, other leisure facilities have been introduced making the Olympic Village more complex, not only because of its increasing dimension and scale but also because of the multiplicity of functions: accommodation, circulation and management of flows, the interaction with the pre-existing city, and more recent requirements such as new information and telecommunication technologies or the need for safe urban conditions. Contemporary Olympic Villages and the projects recently submitted to the IOC are reminders of how Olympic Urbanism can play an important role in the process of the transformation of urban spaces and sometimes regions.

The experience of urban transformation where this potentiality has been most clearly revealed remains that of Barcelona. The changing of the city's urban scale that took place during the 1990s, the global promotion of its image that located the city amongst the highest positions regarding global tourism rankings, and the development of on-going urban projects directly inspired by the former Olympic building strategies, make the case of Barcelona remarkable and specifically important. The Barcelona experience shows clearly how Olympic urbanism can represent new opportunities for the hosting city in dealing with both the reinforcement of urban centrality and higher social integration. These are goals that can be achieved simultaneously if Olympic urbanism is conceived from the outset as a catalyst for future urban growth and development, and as a generator of urban strategies, rather than of specific Olympic projects alone.

If lessons can be learned from the Barcelona experience about developing Olympic projects in the future, these would involve the idea of conceiving of a city as a totality and with the drawing of a long-term strategic vision devoted to general and ambitious goals such as territorial integration, economic diversification and the promotion of urban complexity. These are difficult objectives to be successful with, as Barcelona's evolution during the last decade shows. Methodologies and strategies used would also need to be different, depending on the local urban context, but the vision of Olympic urbanism as a way of rethinking the city and projecting it towards a better future should be the main ambitions for the next Olympic cities of Beijing and London.

Notes

1 Previous discussions of Olympic Urbanism by the author, upon which this chapter draws, can be found in Munoz (1997) and Munoz (2005).
2 Our argument thus complements discussions of the function, meaning and processes involved in the opening and closing ceremonies utilized by hosts of sports mega-events.

186

© The Editorial Board of the Sociological Review 2006

3 The Olympic Villages of London (1948), Helsinki (1952) and Melbourne (1956) were characterized by a return to ephemeral construction, the use of military camps or Olympic Villages that occupied part of the social housing already included in the city's urban design.
4 Due to limitations on space, only the projects for Olympic Villages that were subsequently built are discussed here.
5 This combination was proposed by the Baron Pierre de Coubertin, the figure behind the Olympic Games, when speaking of the requirements to be met by an 'Olympic Village': 'It is time for architects to turn dreams into reality, to apply themselves to bring forth a resplendent Olympia, original in its modernity and mindful of tradition . . .' (de Coubertin (1910) *Une Olympie Moderne*).
6 These three attributes had been perfectly summed up in what was perhaps the ultimate refinement of rationalist ideals applied to housing design, the 'Frankfurt kitchen' in 1926 (Organisations Komittee fur die XI Olympiade 1936, 1936).
7 See the Official Report of the Organising Committee of the 1984 Los Angeles Olympic Games (LAOOC, 1985).
8 A very good indicator of this heavy industrial past is the fact that Besos river was the second most polluted river in Europe in 1982, following the Dniepper river in the former USSR.

References

Brandizzi, G. (1988) 'Architecture and the Games', in *Spaziosport*, Volume 7, pp. 166–181.
Coubertin, de, Pierre (1910) 'Une Olympie Moderne' In M. Wimmer (ed.) *Olympic Building*. Leipzig: Editions Leipzig. Also available in English as 'A Modern Olympia' in P. de Coubertin (1966) *The Olympic Idea: Discourses and Essays*. Koln: Carl Diem Institute, Deutsche Sporthochschule Koln.
Crilley, David (1993) 'Architecture as Advertising. Constructing the Image of Redevelopment', in G. Kearns and C. Philo (eds) *Selling Places. The City as Cultural Capital, Past and Present*. Oxford: Pergamon Press, pp. 231–252.
LAOOC (1985) Official Report of the Games of the XXIIIrd Olympiad Los Angeles 1984. Los Angeles: Los Angeles Olympic Organizing Committee.
Muñoz, F. (1997) 'Historic Evolution and Urban Planning: A Typology of Olympic Villages' In M. Moragas Spa, M. Llines, and B. Kidd (eds) *Olympic Villages: a Hundred Years of Urban Planning and Shared Experiences*. Universitat Autònoma de Barcelona, Lausanne: International Olympic Committee, pp. 27–51.
Muñoz, F. (2005) 'El urbanismo de las Villas Olímpicas, 1908–2012' In *Quaderns d'Arquitectura i Urbanisme, 245*. Col·legi d'Arquitectes de Catalunya, Barcelona, pp. 110–132.
Organisations Komittee fur die XI Olympiade 1936 (1936) The Xth Olympic Games Official Report. Berlin: E.V. Wilhelm Limpert.
Solà-Morales, I. (1994) 'Fer la ciutat, fer l'arquitectura', in *Visions Urbanes. Europa 1870–1993. La ciutat de l'artista. La ciutat de l'arquitecte*. Barcelona: Centre de Cultura Contemporània de Barcelona/Electa, pp. 401–410.
Wimmer, Martin (1976) *Olympic Buildings*. Leipzig: Editions Leipzig.

Notes on contributors

Richard Coleman (r.j.coleman@shu.ac.uk) is a Principal Research Fellow in the Sport Industry Research Centre at Sheffield Hallam University. He is the Centre's fieldwork manager and specializes in the economic impact and media evaluation of major events. He has written numerous reports for commercial clients and has also authored journal articles on the Flora London Marathon and World Snooker as well as writing *Measuring Success 2* (which reviewed 16 impact studies) for UK Sport.

Scarlett Cornelissen (sc3@sun.ac.za) is a senior lecturer in political science at the University of Stellenbosch, South Africa. Her research interests include international urban development trends and their implications for foreign policy-making in South Africa; the political economy of the global tourism system; and the politics of major events. In addition to *The global tourism system: governance, development and lessons from South Africa* (Ashgate, 2005), she has published on a wide variety of topics in such journals as *Review of International Political Economy*, *Journal of Modern African Studies* and *Third World Quarterly*.

Chris Gratton (C.Gratton@shu.ac.uk) is Professor of Sport Economics and Director of the Sport Industry Research Centre (SIRC) at Sheffield Hallam University. He is a specialist in the economic analysis of the sport market. He is co-author (with Peter Taylor) of six books specifically on the sport and leisure industry (including *Sport and Recreation: An Economic Analysis* and *The Economics of Sport and Recreation*) and together they have published over 100 articles in academic and professional journals. SIRC has developed a specific expertise in the study and evaluation of the staging of major events. Although the focus of most of these studies has been the economic impact of the events, the most recent have included a broadening of the evaluation criteria to incorporate value for money indicators and public profile indicators (through analysis of media coverage).

C. Michael Hall (cmhall@business.otago.ac.nz) is Professor in Marketing, at The University of Canterbury, Christchurch, New Zealand. He was formerly with the Department of Tourism, University of Otago; Visiting Professor,

School of Service Management, Lund University Helsingborg, Sweden, and a Docent in the Department of Geography, University of Oulu, Finland. He has published widely on various dimensions of tourism, contemporary mobility and regional development particularly with an emphasis on peripheral locations.

John Horne (John.Horne@ed.ac.uk) is Senior Lecturer in the Sociology of Sport and Leisure at the University of Edinburgh. He has published many articles and book chapters on sport, leisure and popular culture and is the author of *Sport in Consumer Culture* (2006, Palgrave) and co-author of *Understanding Sport* (1999, Spon, with Alan Tomlinson and Garry Whannel). He is the co-editor of *Sport, Leisure and Social Relations* (1987, *Sociological Review Monograph* No. 33, Routledge & Kegan Paul, with David Jary and Alan Tomlinson), *Japan, Korea and the 2002 World Cup* (2002, Routledge, with Wolfram Manzenreiter) and *Football Goes East: Business, Culture and the People's Game in China, Japan and Korea* (2004, Routledge, with Wolfram Manzenreiter). He has also edited two Leisure Studies Association publications: *Leisure Cultures, Consumption and Commodification* (2001) and *Masculinities: Leisure Cultures, Identities and Consumption* (2000, with Scott Fleming).

Wolfram Manzenreiter (wolfram.manzenreiter@univie.ac.at) is Assistant Professor at the Institute of East Asian Studies, University of Vienna, where he lectures on modern Japanese society. His major research interests are concerned with the social and economic implications of sport and popular culture in contemporary Japan. He is author of several books and articles on popular culture, leisure and sport in Japan. Currently he is working on a new book entitled *Sport and Nation in Japan*. In addition to the co-edited volumes with John Horne, *Football Goes East* (2004) and *Japan, Korea and the 2002 World Cup* (2002), his recent works include the monographs *The Social Construction of Japanese Mountaineering* (2000), and *Pachinko Monogatari: Japan's Gambling Industry* (1998), both published in German.

Salomé Marivoet (smarivoet@sapo.pt and smarivoet@fcdef.uc.pt) is a researcher with the Centro de Investigação de Estudos de Sociologia do ISCTE (Instituto Superior de Ciências do Trabalho e Empresa) and has lectured at the Faculdade de Ciências do Desporto e Educação Física of the Universidade de Coimbra and the Faculdade de Motricidade Humana da Universidade Técnica de Lisboa. She is the author of two studies on Portuguese sports habits, coordinated the Portuguese investigation in a European Council research project on the profile of the violence in sport, and has been an expert adviser to the European project *Eurofan*. She has also been a member of the Extended Board of the International Sociology of Sport Association (ISSA). She is the author and co-author of many books and articles on the sociology of sport, violence and hooliganism, including *Aspectos Sociológicos do Desporto* (1998 and 2002); 'Portugal' in J. Coakley and E. Dunning (eds) (2000) *Handbook of Sports Studies*; 'Violent disturbances in Portuguese football' in E. Dunning *et al.* (eds) (2002) *Fighting Fans*; and 'The Public at Football Stadiums' in Comeron, M.

and Vanbellingen, P. (eds) (2002) *Prevention of violence in football stadiums in Europe*.

Francesc Muñoz Ramírez (Franc.Munoz@uab.es) is professor of urban geography at the Autonomous University of Barcelona. He has also taught on the Architecture and Urbanism European programs at the Universitat Politecnica de Catalunya, in Barcelona, and the Erasmus Universiteit in Rotterdam. His professional experience includes both research and consulting work in fields such as urban demography, strategic planning and specific assessment in urban and cultural projects – working for institutions like the International Olympic Committee. He has participated as a Fellow in prestigious research meetings such as the Salzburg Seminar and as an expert of the Council of Europe. He has published numerous articles on Urban Studies and Architecture and has participated in several collective books in Spain, Portugal, Italy, Slovenia and the USA. His most recent work includes a contribution to the *Urban Studies Review* entitled 'Cities, International Journal of Urban Policy and Planning' and a first book *urBANALización: Paisajes comunes, lugares globales* ('urBANALization: Common Landscapes, Global Places') G. Gili, Barcelona.

Maurice Roche (m.roche@sheffield.ac.uk) is Reader in Sociology at the University of Sheffield. His research interests include modern social theory and the sociology of popular culture. His main publications include *Mega-Events and Modernity: Olympics, Expos and the Construction of Global Culture* (Routledge, 2000), *European Citizenship and the Cultural Exclusion* (Sage, 2000), and *Rethinking Citizenship: Welfare, Ideology and Change in Modern Society* (Polity, 1992). He is also the editor of *Sport, Popular Culture and Identity* (Meyer & Meyer Verlag, 1998).

Kimberly S. Schimmel (kschimme@kent.edu) is an Associate Professor of the Sociology of Sport in the School of Exercise, Leisure, and Sport at Kent State University in the USA. She has published many articles and book chapters on the political economy of sport, sport and local/global urban development, and sport and urban politics. She is co-editor of *The Political Economy of Sport* (2005, with John Nauright) in Palgrave's International Political Economy series. She currently serves on the Extended Board of the International Sociology of Sport Association (ISSA) and is co-editor (with Steven J. Jackson) of book and media reviews for the *International Review for the Sociology of Sport*.

Simon Shibli (s.shibli@shu.ac.uk) is a Co-Director of the Sport Industry Research Centre at Sheffield Hallam University and is a CIMA qualified management accountant. His specialist interest areas are the finance and economics of the sport and leisure industries. Simon has worked on the economic impact and wider evaluation of major sports events since 1997 for both national agencies and private sector clients. He was the principal author of UK Sport's guide to conducting economic impact studies of major sports events, *Measuring Success: The Economics – A Guide*.

Index

Kamilla Swart (SwartK@cput.ac.za) is Senior Lecturer in Tourism Management and acting head of department of the Centre for Tourism Research in Africa, Faculty of Management, Cape Peninsula University of Technology, Cape Town. She is a co-author of *Sport Tourism* (Fitness Information Technology, 2002) and worked at the Cape Town 2004 Olympic Bid Company. She has published on varied topics relating to the bidding of sport tourism events and the impacts of sport tourism events in South Africa (*Journal of Sport Tourism* and *Third World Quarterly*). She has recently initiated a 2010 FIFA World Cup research project focusing on developing a strategic framework for maximizing community benefits associated with this event.

Dave Whitson (Dave.Whitson@ualberta.ca) is Professor of Political Science, University of Alberta in Canada. He is co-author (with Donald Macintosh) of *The Game Planners*, (with Trevor Slack, Ann Hall and Gary Smith) of *Sport in Canadian Society* and (with Richard Gruneau) of *Hockey Night in Canada*. He has written numerous articles on the use of sports and other hallmark events in urban regeneration strategies, sport and the mass media and sport and masculinity. His latest edited book (with Richard Gruneau) is a collection of articles about hockey in Canada, *Artificial Ice: Hockey, Commerce, Culture*.

Xin Xu (xx12@apu.ac.jp or xinx@princeton.edu) is an Associate Professor of International Relations at Ritsumeikan Asia Pacific University, Japan, and a Visiting Fellow in the Princeton-Harvard China and the World Program at Princeton University's Woodrow Wilson School of Public and International Affairs. His research specialism is international relations and Chinese foreign policy.